THE LOST EMPIRE OF EMANUEL NOBEL

Romanovs, Revolutionaries, and the Forgotten Titan Who Fueled the World

DOUGLAS BRUNT

ATRIA BOOKS

NEW YORK ■ AMSTERDAM/ANTWERP ■ LONDON
TORONTO ■ SYDNEY/MELBOURNE ■ NEW DELHI

An Imprint of Simon & Schuster, LLC
1230 Avenue of the Americas
New York, NY 10020

First Atria Books hardcover edition May 2026

ATRIA BOOKS and colophon are trademarks of Simon & Schuster, LLC

Manufactured in the United States of America

1 3 5 7 9 10 8 6 4 2

Library of Congress Control Number: 2025946011

ISBN 978-1-6680-7474-9
ISBN 978-1-6680-7476-3 (ebook)

For *The Core 5*

There is no present or future—
only the past, happening over and over.
—Eugene O'Neill

When everyone is dead
the Great Game is finished.
Not before.
—Rudyard Kipling

CONTENTS

PROLOGUE

DECEMBER 1918

EMANUEL NOBEL CLOSED the door to his suite of rooms at the Grand Hotel and walked outside to the cold air of early winter as he weighed the most important decision of his life.

He strolled the cobblestone streets of Kislovodsk, a resort town in southern Russia where for seven months he'd taken refuge from the slaughter of civil war that had engulfed his country. Armies opposed to the Communist takeover buffered the quiet town from the frenetic and fast-shifting battle lines.

In the street he passed others who, like him, had left their homes but stopped short of abandoning Russia entirely. By his estimation the town now contained the aristocracy of "half of Petrograd" (today Saint Petersburg), assorted government ministers, and several relatives of the murdered Tsar Nicholas II. Only a few months earlier Communist guards had dragged Nicholas, his wife Alexandra, and their five young children to the basement of the house where they'd been imprisoned and shot the huddled family point-blank. Then, fueled by a mix of vengeance, hate, and alcohol, the guards stood over the bodies and repeatedly stabbed them with the bayonets of rifles. They threw the corpses into a hastily dug pit, poured acid over top, and buried the remains.

In the wake of this terror, Emanuel received word that Joseph Stalin's secret police had arrested Emanuel's two younger half brothers and were holding them in a dank cell in the Peter and Paul Fortress in Petrograd, only a stone's throw from the headquarters of Nobel's family business. Stalin had emerged as one of the most powerful and ruthless leaders of the revolutionary communist government. Now the party leaders of the new regime—the Moscow Soviet—had summoned Emanuel to the capital, wanting to press him into their service in order to stabilize the war-torn Russian economy.

His advisors urged him to refuse the Soviet and remain in the region of Russia not under communist control until he could safely escape the country altogether. These loyal colleagues had prepared forged travel documents, designed a costume of a peasant to fit him, and coordinated an escape route to reach the Finnish border traveling by covered wagon. They begged Emanuel to flee Russia immediately, afraid that it might already be too late. The Communists were consolidating their control beyond the capital, and Stalin's armies were closing in fast.

It was now December 1918 and winter was here. As Emanuel passed through the town market, the blue-eyed and gray-bearded bachelor politely greeted the proprietor of one of the shops. He selected his provisions and approached to pay. The resort-town community had long since run out of roubles, yet it was not practical for this set of unlikely refugees to pay for bread with diamonds the size of teeth. So, shortly after Nobel had arrived, he devised a new currency in cooperation with the local bank, which printed new notes. He established a system to guarantee the currency using the residents' deposits of jewels, stocks, and other hard assets.

Emanuel opened his billfold and smiled as he removed a few of the notes. The proprietor had often remarked on Emanuel's broad and friendly face, his self-possession. Nobel exchanged notes for the purchase and left with his goods. The proprietor, as did all the royals and aristocracy encamped in the town, appreciatively called these bills "Nobel Notes."

Emanuel returned to his suite at the Grand Hotel, where his colleagues awaited him. If he could survive the Soviet's attempt to seize his businesses, he would remain one of the wealthiest men in the world.

His executives stood before him in the comfortable suite while he removed his heavy coat. Then Emanuel Nobel quietly informed them of his decision as to whether he would remain in Russia and face down Stalin or if it was time to run.

PART I

OIL KINGS

1837–1903

CHAPTER 1

Prison or Russia

DECEMBER 1837

Eighty-one years earlier . . .

IMMANUEL NOBEL WAS desperate. He sat close to his wife in his family's small rented home in the port city of Stockholm, Sweden, to discuss the dire news. The cramped room was heated by a fire, the doors closed against the harsh winter winds that whipped across the Baltic Sea.

The brash and energetic inventor was unusually solemn; even the playful clattering of the couple's three young boys could not brighten his spirits. His dream had been to keep his boys close, to give them an education of earned wisdom by his side in his laboratory and workshop, an experience he believed to be more valuable than any classroom could offer. He and his wife, Andriette, had been loyal partners through many trials in pursuing this dream for the Nobel boys. But it was not to be. Not for now. His workshop was gone. The bankruptcy court had ruled against him, and an angry creditor had threatened to have him imprisoned.

Immanuel had reached the heartbreaking conclusion that he needed to get out of Sweden. To stay would mean debtors' prison, where he could be of no help to his family. Yet to flee the Swedish authorities and strike out on foreign soil with three young children in tow seemed an impossible burden. Immanuel and Andriette decided that he should set out on his own, carrying little money but with his plans for many useful inventions that, with a fresh start in the greener pastures of the expanding Russian Empire, could bring him fortune. His absence would be brutal on those left behind. Of the children, perhaps their oldest, Robert, would be the hardest hit. At eight years old, Robert was the most prepared to learn by his father's side and would feel Immanuel's absence most keenly. But his parents believed that Immanuel's absence would be brief and that he would soon be able to send for his family to join him.

Over the years, he had made several small fortunes in Stockholm from his innovations but had lost even more, always gambling that his next idea would be the truly big one. If not a genius, Immanuel certainly had a knack for ingenious designs to make a range of useful items. He had developed this talent despite having essentially no formal training. He had poor handwriting, atrocious spelling (he was possibly dyslexic), and had completed only a few years of school before he was sent to sea in 1815 at age fourteen to serve as a cabin boy in the Mediterranean service of the Swedish fleet for three years.

His time at sea was marked by several hardships, including the death of the ship's captain and several of the crew, which ended any interest he might have had in a naval career. When he returned to Stockholm in 1818, he sought to make a living pursuing his natural talent for mechanical design and architecture. Immanuel was a mostly self-taught engineer and chemist, an Edison-type tinkerer rather than a product of the hallowed halls of the universities of Europe.

He had begun experimenting with explosives as early as 1832 but often faced setbacks. His most significant early achievement with gunpowder was to blow to bits his rented home and workshop in Sweden, which created a mountain of debt and growing concerns among his customers. Separately, he worked as an architect and engineer and successfully completed a floating bridge in Stockholm using his custom design for airtight flotation pontoons made of metal and wood. He tried but failed to earn a patent in Sweden for the design.

The stakes got higher for Immanuel as a growing family came to depend on his success. In 1827 he had married Andriette Ahlsell, whose father made a modest living as a shop clerk in town. The couple rented an apartment in the Stockholm suburbs and soon had three sons: Robert (b. 1829), Ludvig (b. 1831), and Alfred (b. 1833).

In these years of the early and mid-1830s, Immanuel started a rubber factory to make "elastic materials and bands" from the newly popular substance. (Charles Macintosh had founded the world's first rubber factory in England in 1820.) Immanuel earned acclaim for his rubber products, including a request from Crown Prince Oscar, admiral of the Swedish fleet, to experiment with a waterproof overcoat for sailors, though nothing commercially viable came of the effort.

The industrious, self-taught inventor continued taking one step forward and two steps back until finally, on November 30, 1837, in response to a creditor's complaint, the Office of the Governor of Stockholm issued the verdict that Immanuel had fourteen days to pay all his debts or face incarceration in debtors' prison.

Once the decision was made that Immanuel would flee, his wife and children faced the grim consequences. Andriette had no funds, no job, minimal education. She had three dependent children, ages four, six, and eight. There was no time frame for her husband's return, no certainty that he would be able to send money home, no guarantee that he would fare any better in Russia than he had in Sweden. It was a gamble for the fate of the family, but Immanuel believed it was the only path available to them. By December 15, 1837, Immanuel had evaded the authorities and left his family behind.

He traveled first to Finland, which had recently become a duchy* of the Russian Empire. In Finland he had several business contacts who he hoped might help him, and from there he could get to Saint

* In order of ascending authority: a duke (or duchess) rules a duchy, a prince rules a principality, a king rules a kingdom, and an emperor (or tsar or kaiser) rules an empire. Any of the higher orders can include multiple of any order below. For example, an empire can include multiple kingdoms and principalities. Kaiser Wilhelm II ruled Germany, within which was the Kingdom of Bavaria.

THE NOBEL FAMILY: THREE GENERATIONS

Immanuel Nobel, 1801–1872
The Pioneer

Robert Nobel, 1829–1896
The Adventurer

Ludvig Nobel, 1831–1888
The Engineer

Alfred Nobel, 1833–1896
The Chemist

Emanuel Nobel, 1859–1932
The Financier

Petersburg. Immanuel was confident that the growing economy of Russia would be more receptive to his inventions than his native Sweden.

As the harsh winter arrived in Stockholm, Andriette started working odd jobs for well-to-do families in town, then opened a small booth at a local market, selling milk and vegetables, all while doing her best to look after her three young boys. Ludvig, her middle son, would humbly write as an adult, "The small amount of moral and intellectual value I may happen to possess is the result of the setbacks and sufferings I saw our beloved mother exposed to in my earliest childhood."

Immanuel spent a year in Finland, where he built a network of connections among industrialists and military officers who were impressed by his experiments with explosives. These connections opened doors for him with government officials in Saint Petersburg. Immanuel moved to the Russian capital, where praise of his work preceded him, and he received invitations to present his innovations to high-ranking ministers of the Tsar's government and leading members of the aristocracy. Though the range of his inventive efforts still had the spread of a shotgun blast—including improvements for the loading and firing of rifles, adjustments to steam engine design, and the making of propellers for ships—Immanuel had made one particular breakthrough that brought him early renown and a reward from the Tsar's military. Through a combination of experiments with explosives and his work to build watertight containers made of metal, wood, and rubber, Immanuel invented a rudimentary but very effective undersea mine.

Immanuel was adept at navigating his connections, and in the summer of 1840 he received a dinner invitation from the Swedish-born shipbuilder Johan Eberhard von Schantz,* an officer in the Russian Imperial Navy. Joining Schantz and Nobel at the fancy dinner were Alexander Menshikov (minister of the navy), General Karl Schil-

* Schantz had circumnavigated the globe from 1834 to 1836 as commander of the Russian ship *America* and later served in Russia's Baltic Fleet during the Crimean War.

der (adjutant general to Tsar Nicholas I), and Moritz Hermann (civilian chairman of the Tsar's Committee for Undersea Mines). The dinner conversation turned to undersea mines.

General Schilder discussed his recent bungled and discouraging experiments with gunpowder mines floating just beneath the surface of the water. Schilder described the scene with exasperation. Russian engineers had attempted to detonate the floating bomb by electric pulse through an underwater cable that connected the mine with a technician on land. He described a raft of problems, including frequent unintended detonations and the near-impossible task of dragging a cable through hundreds of yards of deep water from the placement of the mine to the technician without snapping or ruining the cable.

Immanuel boldly chimed in, pointing out the additional challenge that the technician would face in order to detonate the mine from such a great distance at the right time. Immanuel declared that remote detonation by cable was a clumsy and altogether failing approach. Schilder challenged whether Immanuel had a design that might work any better. Immanuel affirmed that he could deliver an undersea mine that would meet the requirements of the Tsar's committee and recorded in a letter home that Schilder replied, "If the thing succeeded I could demand whatever I wished."

Immanuel knew that a contact mine was the winning approach. Rather than using a cable, the mine should detonate upon impact with a vessel. Weeks after the dinner, on October 12, 1840, Immanuel demonstrated his mine to several of the Tsar's generals and Grand Duke Mikhail Pavlovich, youngest brother of the Tsar. Nobel arranged for a wooden barge to float down the Neva River toward a mine he'd laid. He and a crowd of onlookers stood on the riverbank to observe. The expectations of the Grand Duke and the generals were quite low. For years they'd struggled to develop underwater mine technology that was effective yet stable enough to be more lethal to the enemy than to themselves. They'd suffered through disheartening displays of prototype mines in which explosions tended to come at the wrong time or not at all.

They shuffled their feet and murmured from the hilltop overlooking the river, waiting for Immanuel's orchestration of events to unfold. There was perhaps a glimmer of optimism from General Schilder, who had supported the spirited Swedish inventor.

The old barge approached, pulled by a towline attached to a boat whose oarsmen slipped their vessel safely around the mine, then pulled the trailing barge toward the explosive device. Impact was only moments away. Nobel held his breath, as did Schilder, who felt that by this point his standing with the Tsar was also on the line. The barge made impact with the mine and set off a great explosion.

To the amazement of all, the demonstration was a monumental success. Even as shards of wood were still falling back to the earth, Schilder leapt toward Immanuel and grasped him in a bear hug, kissed him, then danced around the hilltop. The Grand Duke also felt the euphoria of the successful test. He congratulated Immanuel and decided on the spot to acquire the rights to Nobel's mines.

The following day the mine committee delivered the official report to the Grand Duke that Nobel's mine was "thoroughly satisfactory and completely in agreement with the intended goal," and that detonation "simply through contact with a floating body" was "a discovery of major importance."

The demonstration was a historic occasion, and Immanuel later memorialized the scene in an oil painting. But despite the Grand Duke's enthusiasm on the day of the test, to Immanuel's frustration, the resulting business negotiation was drawn out for two years. There was a preference in Russia to develop entrepreneurship domestically, and a faction of the Tsar's mine committee felt that a Russian engineer might be able to duplicate Immanuel's success. In general, during the reign of Tsar Nicholas I, there was a wariness about the encroachment of Western political and cultural values that carried over to doing business with Western companies. As further evidence of this ideological bent, the approach of foreign business from the East, from Asian countries with autocratic forms of government similar to the absolute monarchy of the tsars, was less strictly regulated. This aversion to the West would be an obstacle with which all three generations of Nobels would contend.*

But trying to rival the thriving economic systems of the West while also repelling its democratic and free-market systems were incongruous ambitions. Unsurprisingly, the Tsar's generals could find no successful homegrown alternative to Immanuel's mines, and upon a repeat of the demonstration in September 1842 during which his mine made an impressive blast in front of Crown Prince Alexander (the future Tsar Alexander II), the Russian inspector general awarded "the Foreigner Nobel" twenty-five thousand roubles (more than $4 million today) to supply the Russian navy with mines. By this time, Immanuel had been apart from his family for nearly five years. With this windfall in hand, he immediately sent for Andriette and the three boys to join him in Saint Petersburg.

The family's gamble on Immanuel and Andriette's sacrifice had paid off. With joy and optimism, the second generation of Nobels arrived on Russian soil to join their father, and the family soon welcomed a fourth son, Emil, in 1843.

The Nobels moved to a Russian Empire that was geographically massive. The tsars had been annexing enormous stretches of land for the empire for so long and with such success that the empire's vastness became a defining characteristic. Though the elite nations of Western Europe still considered Russia a second-rate power, at its peak in the nineteenth century the Russian Empire had a landmass of 8,800,000 square miles—four times larger than the Roman Empire, and larger than the United States, China, and India combined (and almost thirty percent larger than present-day Russia).

The broad lateral expanse that encompasses so many varied

* Despite ideological differences with much of Western Europe, among the Russian aristocracy there was a desire culturally to be more European than Asian, and the official language of the Russian court was French.

cultures makes Russia a Eurasian land, acting as a sort of hinge between the East and West. The empire had the logistical headache of ruling over peoples of 104 nationalities speaking 146 different languages. With so many border touchpoints, Russia was (and remains) surrounded by several traditional and ancient adversaries. To the east is Japan. To the south, the Turks of the Ottoman Empire. To the north, the fierce border of the Arctic and the White Sea. To the west is Sweden, the military rival of Peter the Great, along with the rest of Europe, which has alternately been friend and foe.

Despite this encirclement of threats, throughout the centuries Russia's greatest defense has been distance. Moving people and gear across Russia has historically been difficult. The river systems mainly travel north and south, not east and west. Only with the advent of railroads did moving people and goods across the breadth of Russia become more feasible.

At the time Immanuel established himself in Saint Petersburg, most Western Europeans considered Russia to be a semi-Asiatic, backward nation that was incapable of mounting a serious offensive threat. Lord Durham, the British ambassador in Saint Petersburg during the reign of Nicholas I, wrote, "Her power is solely of the defensive kind. Covered by the impregnable fortress with which nature has endowed her—her climate and her deserts—she is invincible, as Napoleon discovered to his cost."

Durham's assessment of Russia's defensive orientation was the prevailing wisdom of Parliament, yet in the hundred and fifty years preceding the Nobels' arrival, Russia had expanded its borders more than any country of Europe. And within Russia, the reign of Nicholas I brought a sense that the country's military power was on the upswing and that its economy was set to boom. There was national pride in the empire, and it was a fertile environment for a bold entrepreneur like Nobel. Nicholas seemed interested in modernizing all aspects of Russia except for his divine right of absolute rule.

Immanuel and his family joined the small but close-knit community of Swedes in Saint Petersburg. This respected group of immigrant tradesmen and business owners buttressed Immanuel's connections to ministers of the Russian government.

With a stable home in Saint Petersburg and some money he'd earned from his government contract for mines, the Nobels were able to provide their boys with a more formal education than they themselves had received. Immanuel employed private tutors for his sons, in part because Russian schools offered few options for foreign students, but also because he wanted his sons to have the additional learning opportunities he had had—to gain knowledge through direct experience rather than only to receive it in a classroom. Immanuel insisted that his boys spend much of their time alongside him in the Saint Petersburg factory that he had leased for the manufacture of munitions, carriage wheels, and boilers for steam engines.

Robert and Ludvig, the older sons, later offered opposing perspectives on this aspect of their childhood. Robert, who throughout his life was known to be an irascible and difficult partner in business, recalled his "perverse upbringing," saying that his father's unfocused approach to life and work revealed "the desire to be everything and at the same time nothing." Ludvig, a natural leader and problem solver, recalled his childhood very differently, writing, "We never cease to be aware of the lack of knowledge that is inherent in us and we find a constant source of pleasure in studies . . . that experience of life and the world around us has enabled us to achieve."

The three oldest boys—Robert, Ludvig, and Alfred—would each live long enough to make a significant mark on the world, and from an early age the three demonstrated very different dispositions and gifts that would become more pronounced with time. In 1848, Immanuel wrote a letter to his wife's brother in Sweden that included an assessment of the talents of each of his three oldest boys, and these early judgments proved to be remarkably accurate. (Emil was only five years old at this time, ten years younger than Alfred, and presumably too young to be included in the list of appraisals.) "That which Providence has dealt out less to one of them another seems to have received in greater measure. In my opinion, Ludvig has the greatest genius,

Alfred the greatest capacity for industry, and Robert the greatest courage for speculation."

Perhaps Immanuel mentioned his son Ludvig first, though he was the middle son by age, because he was by far the most likable. Ludvig was handsome, with a bright, broad face and wide-set blue eyes. Not tall, but athletically built, he seemed to engage and lift up any room with his presence. Robert, the oldest, was quite severe looking, to match his ornery disposition. He was quarrelsome and short-tempered, and his relationship with his brothers would wax and wane over the years as he contended with personal insecurities and envy. Alfred was extremely industrious, as his father noted, and also, like his father, had a natural talent for chemistry. Socially Alfred was a bit withdrawn, somewhat awkward around men and painfully so around women. Far less handsome than his brother Ludvig, Alfred had complicated relationships with women (he would never marry) that later created high drama in the family.

Through the balance of the 1840s, the Nobel family unit was intact. Immanuel and his three oldest boys worked side by side at the Nobel & Sons Foundry and Workshop on Malaya Wulfova Street and expanded the business to the design and manufacture of steam engines, scaffolding, lathes, and window frames. The factory earned an excellent reputation throughout Saint Petersburg, and the Nobel-designed windows installed in the grand Kazan Cathedral, one of the most spectacular structures along the Nevsky Prospekt, the main boulevard through the heart of the capital, were their best free advertising.

Immanuel also designed a central heating system for residential and commercial use. He connected a boiler that forced hot water through a network of pipes. The first installation was in his own home. He then repeated the success in a hospital, a hotel, and several other homes. These were the first central heating systems in Russia.

The Nobel foundry had also improved upon the design of their undersea mines since Immanuel's early demonstrations for the Grand Duke. The updated chemical-contact mines (meaning that contact with the mine triggered a chemical reaction that detonated the gunpowder) were cone-shaped, two feet long and fifteen inches wide at the breadth of the cone. Each held eight pounds of gunpowder. A lead-glass tube about the size of a pencil, filled with sulfuric acid, protruded from the mine and was suspended over a mixture of potassium chlorate and sugar. These chemicals were covered with a thin lead casing. When impact with a ship bent the lead and broke the glass tube, the mixture of chemicals created an instant flame that detonated the main charge.

As the expansionist foreign policy of Tsar Nicholas I brought Europe closer to war in the early 1850s, Russian military spending surged. The Tsar sent a purchase order to the Nobel foundry for three five-hundred-horsepower engines to be installed in the warships *Volya*, *Ganud*, and *Retvizan*. Only twenty years old, Ludvig was closely involved in the design and manufacture of these marine engines, which would prove valuable experience for the young engineer.

With Russia on a war footing over contested lands in the Crimea, where Nicholas hoped to acquire a warm-water port on the Black Sea, there was increased demand for Immanuel's undersea mines. During these years, Immanuel sent Alfred to America to study chemistry. In New York he met with, among others, Swedish-born John Ericsson (who designed the first ironclad warship, the USS *Monitor*, which saw action in the American Civil War). Despite Alfred's absence, the Nobel foundry delivered a dozen more marine steam engines and more than a thousand mines to the Tsar's navy.

By October 1853, Russia was officially at war against the alliance of France, Great Britain, and the Ottoman Empire in what became known as the Crimean War. Tsar Nicholas I had sought to acquire valuable coastal lands from the weakening Ottomans. France and Great Britain joined the Ottomans to counter Russia's southward expansion.

In these decades, Britain exerted military force mainly through the Royal Navy, and British admirals would jest that the army was merely another projectile to be fired upon land by the mighty ships of its navy. In 1853, Russia's fear was that the British fleet would sail to the eastern edge of the Baltic Sea and shell Saint Petersburg into oblivion. The city needed better defenses from a naval attack. The Tsar put the Nobel family to work.

In the summer of 1854, the Nobel factory, which now boasted a thousand employees, delivered 245 mines for the defense of the home waters. The logical place for deployment was around Kronstadt, an island fortress in the Baltic only twenty-five miles from the coast of Saint Petersburg that afforded some protection against a naval assault.

Ludvig Nobel, now twenty-two, stayed onshore. He climbed over the rooftops of Kronstadt's waterfront buildings and perched himself on chimneys with a view over the Baltic, where the Royal Navy would make its approach. Scanning the water, he could see his older brother Robert commanding a convoy of small boats that carried anchors, lines, and the Nobel-built mines, each of which contained almost ten pounds of gunpowder.*

From his boat, Robert looked up at his brother on the rooftops to interpret his signals that directed the placement of the mines. Robert attached each mine to a line and anchor so that it held steady a few feet below the surface. Russian citizens observed with fascination the handiwork of these industrious Swedes. The Nobel boys worked quickly, and they needed to. The British fleet had set sail on March 11 to begin the Baltic campaign and would soon be upon them.

Sir Charles Napier, Britain's most accomplished admiral of the time, had departed from England on the *Duke of Wellington* as Queen Victoria herself looked on. The indomitable Royal Navy seemed assured of quick victory. The Russian navy was feeble by comparison. Napier would simply sail into the Baltic and from an unopposed position would blast Saint Petersburg into submission.

---

* The mines were a successful deterrent, though later analysis of the mines indicated that each required a greater amount of gunpowder to disable the largest ships of the British fleet. The following year Nobel deployed hundreds of similar mines in the Gulf of Finland that caused extensive damage to a combined British and French fleet, disabling the *Merlin*, *Firefly*, *Otter*, *Exmouth*, and *Vulture*.

Napier considered the Kronstadt fortress to be the strongest in the world. He planned to navigate the shallow coastal waters and bring the *Duke of Wellington* and his other massive ships of the line into firing range so that he could reduce the fortress to rubble. But he knew Russia had mined the waters. He sent the small steamer *Arrogant* forward for reconnaissance, and British sailors managed safely to collect one of the mines. They returned with Nobel's mine so that the officers could conduct an evaluation. In a controlled detonation, the British found the performance of the mine to be disturbingly successful.*

Napier was no fool. Between the gunners on Kronstadt and what he described as those "infernal machines" that had been designed and deployed by the family Nobel, Napier reported back to the First Lord of the Admiralty that "any attack on Kronstadt by ships is entirely impracticable." Wary and frustrated, Napier turned his fleet around. The admiral may have saved many of his queen's ships, but the result of his Baltic campaign was a disgrace for the most powerful navy in the world. This reversal for the British fleet was so unexpected that upon Napier's return to England, his previously high-flying career crumbled.

With the Royal Navy repelled, Russia's leadership viewed the Nobels as saviors. In a war that was otherwise going very badly for Russia, it was a rare bright spot and it occurred in close proximity to the capital and the Tsar's palace. Immanuel reached a new pinnacle of success, and with a rash of new orders arriving at the Nobel foundry for engines and munitions to supply Russia's military, it seemed certain that he would become a very wealthy man. In response to these favorable winds, Immanuel borrowed capital to invest in a massive expansion of his factory to fill the influx of orders.

---

* Proving that some of Immanuel's ideas were wildly impractical, around this time he drafted a treatise on the deployment of mines that contemplated a muzzle and towline attached to trained seals that would follow verbal instructions for laying the mines. Immanuel wrote the treatise for Sweden's King Charles XV, though there is no evidence he actually sent it to the King.

Though Nobel's undersea mines had proved successful in repelling the British fleet from the Baltic, the outlook of the war for Russia did not improve.

Historians consider the Crimean War to be the first modern war for its prevalent and effective use of artillery. Armies took to the field and deployed long-range weapons using innovative tactics and with an amount of firepower that far surpassed any prior war.

At issue in the Crimean War was of course the Crimean Peninsula, critical coastal real estate on the north edge of the Black Sea that has been contested for thousands of years by the armies of the Greeks, Romans, Byzantines, Mongols, Ottomans, Russians, and Ukrainians. From the time of Peter the Great to Vladimir Putin, Russia has wanted this land. Nicholas I won several key battles in Crimea, including the slaughter of the British cavalry in a battle that Alfred Tennyson described in his poem "The Charge of the Light Brigade" as the British rode headlong into fortified Russian artillery. The brutal result signaled the beginning of the end of the horse as a means of attack.

Aside from the hapless cavalry charge, the British and French had superior military training and weaponry and soon turned the tide. Russia suffered decisive losses. Amid the failures of the Russian campaign, the early success of Nobel's harbor defense was quickly washed from public awareness. Far more resoundingly, the war proved how woefully out-of-date the Russian military had become. The brave and costly Russian victories over Napoleon decades earlier were now a distant memory as the ill-prepared armies of the Tsar were humiliated by the combined Ottoman, French, and British forces.

The paranoid and aggressive posture of Nicholas I that had led Russia to war had been, in part, a reaction to the brutal fate of his predecessors. His grandfather Tsar Peter III was betrayed and murdered. His father, Tsar Paul I, was betrayed and murdered. The Russian throne was not a safe place to be. On the very day of Nicholas I's ascension in 1825, he faced a mutiny of three thousand soldiers that nearly killed him in what became known as the Decembrist Revolt. The reign of Nicholas I was baptized in blood and violence.

In 1826, during the first year of his rule, Nicholas I created a unit of secret police called the Third Order. This was the forerunner to all future Russian intelligence organizations, and their deployment began a reactionary period during which communication was tightly controlled, and even literature was placed under the purview of the secret police. Both criticism and praise of the Tsar in literature were forbidden. He simply was not to be discussed.

Nicholas I never pardoned any of the mutineers of the Decembrist Revolt, though several of his advisors had suggested he do so. Nicholas had developed his own view of the Russian people and what they needed in a leader. He imparted his mindset to his son, Alexander, telling him: "In Europe the ruler must have the art of being sometimes fox, sometimes lion. That is what General Bonaparte taught politicians. In Russia, he must be only the lion."

To underscore his point, Nicholas I forced his young heir to witness the corporal punishment of an army deserter. Russia treated her soldiers viciously, and the standard punishment for attempted desertion was a flogging of fifteen hundred blows. Alexander stood close to the ghastly scene, flanked by royal guards who towered over their young charge. Fifty feet away, dozens of soldiers formed two lines to make a gauntlet. At one end, the wretched deserter was stripped to the waist, with his wrists bound. Two soldiers yanked him through the gauntlet while the blows rained down on his back. A drummer standing to the side of the courtyard kept the rhythm while Alexander watched with watery eyes. The blows continued and the anguished screams grew louder. The deserter begged for mercy. Strips of skin hung from his back.

Before the prisoner could complete the gauntlet, he collapsed and became silent. Soldiers came close to inspect. The man had no skin left on his back, only exposed bone and blood. He no longer begged, no longer breathed. Even so, the blows continued until reaching the prescribed number, thudding against the lifeless form that had once been a soldier. Haunted, Alexander remembered another phrase of Napoleon's that ran counter to his father's philosophy. "A whipped soldier loses the most important thing—his honor!"

Nicholas I's nationalist and expansionist impulses continued the legacy of his grandmother, Catherine the Great, who had died when he was almost five months old. Catherine's ambition had been to expand the empire's borders to the south, to control the Crimean Peninsula, which juts into the northern side of the Black Sea, then to conquer the ancient city of Constantinople on the southern shore of the Black Sea. Perhaps the clearest evidence that the monarchs of the Romanov dynasty, established by Michael Romanov in 1613, believed they were the true inheritors of the Eastern Roman Empire and rightful occupiers of Constantinople was the frequent use of the name Konstantin for their male heirs.

Nicholas coveted these warm-water ports in the south because they afforded easy access to markets in both the East and West. The fortress city of Constantinople had been a religious, political, and economic hub for centuries. Strategically located at the mouth of the Bosporus—the narrow passage leading from the Black Sea eventually to the Mediterranean—Constantinople has been fought over from the ancient Persian wars to modern times.

Not only would Nicholas I fall short of these objectives, he would not live to see the end of the war. A fatal case of pneumonia would end his rule at the age of fifty-eight, and in March 1855 his son took the throne as Alexander II. The son he'd hoped to prepare with harsh lessons and stern advice would have to pick up the pieces.

Yet Alexander, thirty-six years old when he inherited the throne, had already shown signs that he did not share his father's brutal disposition. As Nicholas I's character had been forged by assassination plots and attempted coups that led to his reactionary and harsh regime, Alexander II had a more stable childhood. He was surrounded by violence but was never the intended target, and he enjoyed a smooth transition to power.

The new Tsar quickly sued for peace to end the war, and within his government he favored a much less aggressive foreign policy. He was inclined to test whether being something other than the lion could work in Russia.

Alexander II intended to usher in both political and economic reforms that would lead to drastic changes to the empire's business environment. In some ways, the free-market and entrepreneurial approach signaled by Alexander II seemed to benefit a man like Immanuel. But there were other policies of the new Tsar that would prove catastrophic to the Nobel business.

Nicholas I
Reigned 1825–1855
Died of pneumonia, age 58

Alexander II
Reigned 1855–1881
Assassinated, age 62

Alexander III
Reigned 1881–1894
Died of kidney disease, age 49

Nicholas II
Reigned 1894–1917
Abdicated
Assassinated in 1918, age 50

CHAPTER 2

Reform, Repress, Repeat

As a small firm whose largest customer was the Russian military, the success of the Nobels was correlated to that of the Russian Empire. When Nicholas I's son Alexander II took the throne in 1855, he moved quickly to negotiate for peace with the combined enemy forces of the British, French, and Turks. He concluded negotiations in March of 1856 with the Treaty of Paris, ending the Crimean War. Russia agreed to demilitarize its southern border along the Black Sea and to return seized lands to the Ottomans, but otherwise Russia got off easy. As a result of the war Russian ministers came to see that the empire desperately needed to modernize to keep up with the great powers of Europe.

Alexander II aimed to meet the challenge. But his plans did not include the Nobels. His treasury was already overextended, and in the immediate term, Alexander's modernization meant the redirection of funds away from mines and warships to other efforts. Never mind the purchase orders already sent to the Nobel foundry, and never mind that Nobel had already invested in the expansion of his factory and purchased raw materials to fill the now-deceased Tsar's orders. The new regime felt no obligation to honor the commitments of the old. Alexander II left Immanuel and his sons holding the bag.

As a result, Immanuel needed money. He filed a claim to enforce the government contract, but the courts ruled against him. He sought investment, but in the postwar Russian climate it was nearly impossible to raise capital. The Nobel factory tried to cobble together small pieces of new business while under the burden of massive debt and a factory far larger than required, all as creditors were clamoring for repayment. After three uphill years, Immanuel recognized the futility of his effort. Bankruptcy was upon him yet again.

He had long since settled his legal entanglements in Stockholm, and in 1859 Immanuel, furious and defeated, returned to Sweden with Andriette and their youngest son, Emil. Ludvig seethed that such a massive effort by his family could be so poorly rewarded by the Tsar. It was a bitter lesson that he would not forget.

The three older brothers remained in Saint Petersburg in part to clean up the mess and in part because they had come to consider Russia their home. They had been living in Russia for more than sixteen years by this point—their entire adult lives. Ludvig, the middle son, now twenty-eight and the most capable of the three, was also the first of his generation to become a father.

Meeting a wife in Tsarist Russia was not so easy for a Swede. Opportunities for courtship were extremely limited. Russians were generally wary of foreigners, and there were only a few thousand Swedes in the insular community within Saint Petersburg. The differing social norms expected of men and women would be an outrage today. Unmarried women rarely went out in public without a chaperone, while unmarried men, even from the well-to-do families (perhaps especially), were encouraged to gain sexual experience and sow wild oats with prostitutes prior to getting married.

When the time came for marriage, the Lutheran church often facilitated the matches within the Swedish community. But in Ludvig's case he became enamored with a cousin on his mother's side living in Sweden: Mina Ahlsell, the daughter of his mother's brother. Ludvig and Mina had come to know each other during Ludvig's occasional trips to visit with family back in Stockholm, and Mina had also made visits to Saint Petersburg. It was common at the time for cousins to wed, and Immanuel supported the match, even writing letters to his brother-in-law expressing hope of an engagement. Ludvig and Mina became engaged in September 1855. Then came a scandal.

Ludvig and Mina were engaged but living apart. Ludvig became smitten with an older married woman, twenty-nine-year-old Anna Lindal, and began an affair. Anna was the daughter of a close friend of Ludvig's mother, and Anna traveled in the social circles of Saint Petersburg's Swedish community. She had married a much older man, a doctor from Finland, two years before and had a one-year-old son. Letters suggest that Anna's husband had begun to suffer severe effects from syphilis that compromised even his sanity. In any event, Ludvig's fiancée was in Sweden and Anna's husband was sick in bed, giving Ludvig and Anna ample time to become intimate. Anna gave birth to Ludvig's son Hjalmar Crusell on September 4, 1856.*

This of course got the engagement with Mina off to a rough start. Family letters suggest that outside of the two participants in the affair, only Immanuel and Mina came to know the truth. Anna's dying husband and Ludvig's mother were spared the full story. Ludvig and Mina made amends, however, and after what became a multi-year engagement, they finally married on October 7, 1858.

The reconciliation between Ludvig and Mina in the aftermath of the affair seems to have been sincere. Letters written between them and letters written by family members about them indicate a loving and faithful marriage. The couple had a son, Emanuel, born in Saint Petersburg on June 10, 1859. Emanuel's birth came less than eight

---

* Anna Lindal's husband, Gustaf Crusell, died not long after the affair in 1858 of complications due to syphilis. Hjalmar was only two. Ludvig and his first wife, Mina (and later Ludvig's second wife, Edla, after Mina died in 1869), raised the child in the Nobel family, where he was treated with respect. Hjalmar went on to hold executive positions in Ludvig's businesses, though his status as a son was not publicly acknowledged, and family letters indicate that even Edla was not aware that Hjalmar was her husband's son.

months after the wedding, which makes one wonder about the timing of conception, though there is no record that discusses the issue.

The backdrop for this tumultuous period in Ludvig's personal life was a professional life in utter chaos. Now with a family of his own and facing financial insecurity reminiscent of his own childhood, Ludvig worked hard to overcome the bankruptcy of the family business.

He took the lead role in managing what remained of the Nobel factory during his father's absence and continued (unsuccessfully) to litigate in the courts for compensation from the Tsar while also managing his father's creditors, even earning their praise. With Ludvig's help, the creditors eventually sold Immanuel's remaining Russian assets. Ludvig was thus relieved of the failed business and with his modest savings rented a small industrial building on the banks of the Neva, hoping to start afresh. In 1862 he founded the Ludvig Nobel Machine Factory. He mainly built engines and munitions—things for which he'd already demonstrated great skill.

His timing was good. Now some years after the Crimean War, the 1860s brought military spending back to the fore. Prussia (the most powerful of the Germanic states prior to the unification of modern Germany) was on the march, presenting Europe with a new expansionist threat. Otto von Bismarck, Prussia's Iron Chancellor, led Prussia to military victories over Denmark and Austria as a part of his plan to combine all Germanic states to create the German Empire. All of Europe was rearming, including Russia, and Ludvig's new munitions business was thriving.

He was a constant presence on the machine shop floor, overseeing minor adjustments to the fabrication process. When not at the side of his employees, he was sketching design improvements for rifles, grenades, and steam engines. He hired a few Russians, but mostly he hired immigrants from Sweden and Finland who already possessed the skill set for factory work. And Ludvig was the unquestioned chief. The only other Nobel working with him was his son Emanuel, who occasionally toddled into the factory to visit his father.

1862 was also a good year for Ludvig's younger brother Alfred.

While still living in Saint Petersburg near his older brothers, Alfred managed his first-ever detonation with nitroglycerin, having advanced the work he'd begun with undersea mines alongside his father.

Robert, the eldest brother, was having somewhat less professional success. With the matter of their father's bankrupt assets concluded, Robert had left the machine shop. Ludvig was quite easygoing, so there was no particular bad blood between them, but the relationship between Alfred and Robert had become fractured. Their falling-out was not due to business but rather their love of the same woman. In the limited pool of available romantic partners, they had both fallen for a young woman named Pauline Lenngren. The Lenngren family was close with the Nobels, and Pauline's parents became Emanuel's godparents at his christening in 1859.

Pauline was only nineteen at this time, several years younger than Robert and Alfred, and only three years older than the youngest Nobel brother, Emil. Through a combination of some charm and the benefit of scarce competition, Pauline attracted the affections of all three available Nobels.

Robert proposed in 1859 and the two quickly married. Emil, by then living in Stockholm, was still infatuated and continued to write love letters to Pauline, which Robert encouraged her to ignore. Robert told her that any letter in response to Emil would have "the same result as pouring oil on the fire."

Alfred also remained lovesick for Pauline, which was made worse by his proximity to the married couple in Saint Petersburg. Robert became furious and encouraged Pauline to treat Alfred with "coldness" to "bring him to his senses," which fueled a rivalry between the brothers.

Within a few years, Robert and Pauline left Saint Petersburg and lived alternately in Finland and Sweden. He worked for a time in Sweden as a brewer of Bavarian beer (he earned his certification as a master brewer in 1863, the same year Adolphus Busch got his start in America), living frugally in his parents' home while Pauline returned to her parents' home in Finland. He later worked as an importer/exporter of kerosene and illumination lamps, then founded a factory making bricks for construction. None of these efforts brought him the success he craved and that he witnessed his younger brothers achieving.

Robert had won the girl, but married life did not settle him professionally and his career continued with fits and starts. Letters from Robert to his wife and brothers are riddled with grievances and a knack for placing the blame for his unhappy circumstances on anyone but himself. He wrote to Pauline of his time working in Finland, "I shall never again make my home in Helsinki, everything has been so hateful for me there and I would rather die than be there." Ensuing letters between Ludvig and Alfred are marked by a degree of sympathy for their older brother and a sense of obligation to help him achieve success.

By 1863, Alfred had also left Russia and was back in Sweden, where he rejoined his father, mother, and Emil. He continued to experiment with nitroglycerin in a newly leased workshop that he shared with his father. Immanuel, true to form, had been tinkering with a range of inventions, including a machine gun similar to the American version developed by Richard Gatling that could fire three hundred rounds per minute.

Alfred had remained a bachelor and was dedicated to his work. A letter from Alfred to Robert in December 1864 suggests a reason for Alfred's decision not to marry. In the letter he wrote of an abscess that was causing him pain: "The worst of all is that the doctor assures me that it is the old Venus that has popped up and he thought it necessary to acquaint her with Mercury." Mercury was another name for quicksilver, which was the common treatment at the time for syphilis. Additionally, Alfred's use of the word *Venus* mirrors the well-known contemporary expression "A night with Venus, a lifetime with Mercury." The letter is a strong indicator that both Alfred and his doctor believed that Alfred had syphilis.*

---

* Data from 1869 reveals that forty-five percent of Russian prostitutes had syphilis at that time. The Russian Empire had legalized brothels in 1843, and Alfred had likely strayed beyond the companionship that was available to him at the Lutheran church.

In any event, Alfred was a near workaholic who was also far more focused than his father. He was committed to the goal of developing practical explosives. Amid Alfred's progress, the Nobels suffered a tragedy in 1864 when a massive accidental blast occurred in Alfred's lab in Heleneborg, Sweden. The explosion reduced the wooden structure to a scattering of blackened splinters. The windowpanes of homes more than a hundred yards away shattered. The Swedish newspaper *Post-och Inrikes Tidningar* reported:

> *Most horrible of all was the sight of mutilated corpses thrown here and there. Not only were their clothes torn off, but for some of them the head was missing, the flesh of the legs sliced off . . . [O]ne saw shapeless masses of meat and bone which bore little resemblance to a human body.*

Emil was among the several dead who had worked in the lab. The twenty-year-old had been experimenting with different mixtures of gunpowder and nitroglycerin. He had prepared a refinement to his research while both his father and Alfred were outside the lab. When the mixture detonated, Immanuel and Alfred were near enough to be thrown off their feet, and Alfred was peppered with shards of glass and wood. Emil was blown apart.

Immanuel was despondent over the death of his youngest son, and four months later suffered a stroke from which he never fully recovered. Alfred persevered through the tragedy and continued to experiment with combinations of gunpowder and nitroglycerin to create a more stable explosive. He earned the patent for the blasting cap (the "Initial Ignition Principle") in July 1864, which began a new epoch in explosives. He founded the Nitroglycerin Company Ltd in October of that year. Immanuel became a shareholder in the company, more in recognition of prior work than for his ongoing involvement.

Alfred was not only an inventor but showed remarkable business savvy, quickly establishing factories in Norway and Finland to supply the rapidly increasing demand for dynamite in the construction of canals and railroads, as well as for use in mining. Alfred hired Robert as the managing director of the Finland plant in 1866. It was no doubt humbling for Robert to accept employment from his younger brother. For Alfred's part, romantic rivalries aside, he loved his brother and recognized in Robert the pioneering spirit that their father had also seen, and Alfred believed that Robert would succeed in the role.

Back in Saint Petersburg, Ludvig and Mina's family was growing. Carl (b. 1862) and Anna (b. 1866) joined the eldest child, Emanuel. Ludvig prioritized the same kind of on-the-job training for his sons that his father had, and as opposed to Ludvig's childhood, for this generation of Nobels that education came without the family suffering through a bankruptcy and the long absence of a father.

Ludvig's munitions and engine factory was thriving. In 1864 the Russian Ministry of War decreed that all munitions must be manufactured domestically, and in 1866 Alexander II had decreed the same for all railway and other related industrial equipment. Ludvig was still a citizen of Sweden, but his firm was incorporated in Russia, which made him eligible for the Tsar's business. Ludvig rapidly developed a new technique for the manufacture of grenades superior to that of the imported German model, and he managed to do it more cheaply. In March 1864 he wrote, "I have a great deal to do and am working every day like a manual laborer, for I have bombs to mould." By 1867, his factory had delivered more than fifty thousand grenades to the Tsar.

Ludvig also published a series of articles that outlined an economic policy to spur industrial development in Russia. He argued for higher import duties on foreign machinery, combined with the elimination of import duties on raw materials. He recommended that there should not be any state-owned businesses but rather that all factories be in private hands, and that the role of the government be limited to making loans for start-up capital. He also identified Russia's most glaring problem: a largely illiterate and untrained workforce—perhaps the least educated in all Europe. Noting a hallmark of the literacy gap, Sir Robert Bruce Lockhart, a British diplomat and spy in Russia, was at first puzzled by the peculiar signs he saw above shops even on the main streets of Moscow and Saint Petersburg. These painted signs had not only the name of the shop and the owner but also pictures of "a loaf of bread, a cube of sugar, or a ham." He soon realized the pictures were necessary because so few of the city's residents could read.

Ludvig managed to find sufficient talent. He built his workforce from a combination of Russian and many Swedish and Finnish employees. Through the 1860s he continued to fill large orders for the Russian military, including an order in 1867 to convert 270,000 muzzleloading rifles to breech-loading. A muzzleloader is the style of rifle that was commonly used in the American Civil War and is loaded from the front end of the barrel, whereas the more modern breechloader (which loads rounds at the breech end, close to the trigger) is faster and easier to operate. France, Sweden, and other European nations were similarly modernizing equipment in response to the aggression of Prussia's military. Ludvig developed the turning lathe, a method of boring the interior of a rifle barrel that was superior to methods used elsewhere in Europe.

Despite the family's reversal in fortune at the start of Tsar Alexander II's reign, Immanuel's sons soon proved that they were capable of taking the family businesses far beyond what their father had managed to do.

The surge in demand for armaments throughout Europe during the 1860s was a boost to Ludvig's success, and there were legislative changes that benefited him as well. Tsar Alexander II enacted social and economic reforms designed to modernize Romanov Russia and bolster the empire's industrial complex. Many of these policies mirrored the ideas Ludvig had earlier proposed in his writings.

Alexander promoted a form of local self-government called *zemstvo*, he improved the legal status of Jewish people, and he expanded Russia's universities, secondary schools, and elementary schools.* He

* In 1854 Russia had only 3,600 university students, far fewer than any of the major European powers.

banned corporal punishment, perhaps in reaction to his childhood trauma resulting from the brutal flogging his father had forced him to watch. He lessened the censorship of the press, which had been absurdly aggressive during his father's regime. And in Alexander's most memorable act, with the stroke of his pen on February 19, 1861 (Old Style; March 3 by the Gregorian calendar), he freed more slaves than anyone else in history, before or since.

The emancipation reform of 1861 freed twenty-three million serfs, more than thirty-four percent of Russia's total population, and earned him the nickname "Alexander the Liberator." The following day, March 4, President Abraham Lincoln began his first administration.*

These contemporary leaders of nations, one an autocratic tsar, the other an elected American president, were surprisingly like-minded reformers and indeed demonstrated mutual sympathies. During the American Civil War, Alexander II ordered warships to harbors in New York and San Francisco to support the Union, at a time when Lincoln worried that Great Britain might intervene on the side of the Confederacy.†

In Russia, the primary issue regarding the freedom of the serfs was that their new status was not accompanied by new skills, nor much of a plan for their future. By the proclamation of 1861, the serfs could now purchase land from their former lords, but in practice it was not so easy or affordable. Nor was there much infrastructure in Russia to teach the labor force useful skills that would allow them to participate in the industrial movement. Alexander handed them freedom but not any economic or political power.

As a result, millions of serfs moved to urban centers and simply traded one grueling existence for another—long hours, low pay, brutal

* On January 1, 1863, Lincoln issued the Emancipation Proclamation, freeing the slaves, nearly two full years after Alexander II's reform.

† Amid Alexander's benevolent reforms, there is evidence of the cruelty of the times, and certainly of Russia's past. For example, his reign permitted the near-genocidal behavior of the Russian military in the Russo-Circassian War. Such a checkered past as Alexander's reflects the long and difficult road to bring an ancient empire from its dark and barbaric history into an enlightened future.

working conditions with equally bad living conditions in overwhelmed cities. These millions of low-skilled laborers created a new and disgruntled working class.

In the midst of this unprecedented shift in the social order, the ideas of Karl Marx, a German-born political theorist and economist, developed a following. Marx first published *The Communist Manifesto* in 1848 and later published the first volume of *Das Kapital* in 1867 (volumes two and three were published posthumously by his colleague Friedrich Engels in 1885 and 1894). Marx and Engels called for the workers of the world to unite. According to their theory of scientific socialism, class warfare was inevitable, and the proletariat—the working class—would in violent revolution overthrow capitalism. The means of production would end up belonging to the society, not to the exploitative capitalists and private owners. Class struggles were inevitable. The Manifesto was truly a call for revolution, Marx and Engels declared, "the workers have nothing to lose but their chains." The twenty-three pages of the Manifesto would have enormous and lasting impact on the world. Communism is the name for the political system based on Marx's social and economic ideas.

Communism, socialism, and anarchism were the three main ideologies that attempted to subvert the monarchies and democratic parliamentary systems of the nineteenth century. These ideologies preached different treatments for private property (see Appendix). Regarding private property in general, the political theorists behind these systems made a distinction between the ownership of personal possessions and the ownership of productive property (meaning businesses and infrastructure). For example, under communism, it was okay to own jewelry or a painting but not okay to own a copper mine or oil well (and to set the wages of the people who worked there).

Socialists permitted private ownership of businesses but believed in a high degree of government intervention to distribute wealth among the people, resulting in a near-equitable outcome. Communists, however, did not believe in private ownership of businesses at all. Marx and his disciples believed that the state should own all productive property and that a central government authority would plan and operate the nation's industry.

The critical difference between communism and socialism lay in whom the state permitted to own businesses, yet Marx believed that communism was compatible with socialism in the sense that he viewed socialism as a necessary step toward his goals. Marx believed communism was the final stage of socialism. He envisioned a phased revolution that would change capitalist systems first to socialist systems, then finally to a communist system, which was the highest order of political evolution.

The contest of ideas among these ideologies was held throughout the nineteenth century at the congresses of the International Workingmen's Association* (referred to as the First International). Two men dominated these debates: Karl Marx and his ideological rival, the Russian anarchist Mikhail Bakunin.

Bakunin was a massive man, thickly bearded, and four years older than Marx. While Marx fought mainly with his pen from behind a desk, Bakunin was frequently on the barricade walls with a rifle and a knife. He was arrested many times for leading uprisings throughout Europe, including in Dresden, Austria, and Russia. In the 1840s Tsar Nicholas I threw him into a cell of the Peter and Paul Fortress in Saint Petersburg, where he was chained to a wall and interrogated by the Tsar. Nicholas I was so impressed by Bakunin's bravado that he commuted the sentence from death to exile.

As an anarchist, Bakunin shared Marx's desire for equality for the people, but Bakunin favored equality of opportunity rather than equality of outcome. Bakunin was closer to a modern-day libertarian. The fundamental difference between Marx and Bakunin was that while Marx believed that the state should be a powerful central authority that controlled the economy, Bakunin did not believe in having any state authority. Anarchists believed the authority of the state should be shattered into millions of pieces of equal size, each then picked up by an individual. Economic and social order would come by the free association of the people, and the productive property of the state would

---

* The First International dissolved in 1872. Subsequent Internationals that formed in Europe were primarily socialist.

be held in common. The core question of the debate was whether the existence of the state is beneficial or harmful. Marx wanted a strong communist state that would own and control industrial assets and that would make wealth equal for the people. Bakunin believed that such state control was merely a recipe for a new kind of autocracy. He wanted no state authority at all.

Monarchies, parliaments, and the world's industrialists like Nobel kept a wary eye on the progress of these subversive ideologues that had so far kept largely to the shadows. Throughout the nineteenth century, there was not a single socialist, communist, or anarchist system of government in the world. But more citizens of Europe were beginning to listen to their messaging. Marx's primary idea—that the motivation of capitalism was the exploitation of the labor force—reached a large and ready audience in Russia by virtue of an educated few who could give voice to the printed word. Because almost all the freed serfs and others who made up Russia's proletariat (Marx's preferred term for the working class) were illiterate, it fell to a small group of exceptional speakers to bring Marx's concepts to the masses.

Alexander II's business-friendly policies were undeniably leading to burgeoning industrial growth. As measured by one important metric, in 1855 Russia ranked dead last in all of Europe in the number of miles of railroad lines but over the next fifteen years went soaring up the list. But rapid progress is often vulnerable to exploitation, and the blossoming of capitalism in Russia was so rife with corruption that many business owners as well as members of the working class became deeply opposed to the capitalist system.

Ironically, Alexander's grant of legal freedom to over twenty million serfs and the concurrent removal of restrictions to organize and publish led to the formation of a powerful anti-tsarist movement that was a fusion of Marxist disciples among university academics with the disgruntled and undereducated working class. Marx's doctrine, which was defined by class struggle and the eventual revolution of the working class, called for an end to private ownership of industry and for a new system of collective ownership by the people. Under the Tsar's new laws, the writings of Marx and his disciples could be published and republished, read by activists on street corners or in pubs and outside factories.

Even Russian literature began to turn against the Tsar. Russian novelists and poets like Ivan Turgenev became famous for ideological literature that criticized the autocracy and offered endearing portrayals of the peasantry.

At the same time, a watershed moment in the world of science issued a new challenge to the divine right of tsars. The Russian Orthodox Church and absolute autocracy have always gone hand in hand. The Tsar was anointed by God. The people thought of the Tsar himself as no ordinary human but as a sort of demigod. In November 1859 Charles Darwin published *On the Origin of Species*, the Russian translation arriving at almost the precise time that the first freed serfs were leaving the empire's remote farms to enter the cities. Darwin's theories infuriated the clergy but were quickly adopted and popularized by the intelligentsia (the intellectuals and those in higher education who exerted social and political influence to oppose the autocracy). His popular theory of evolution challenged the teachings of the Church and undermined the Tsar's "divine right" to rule. In more secular parts of the world, Darwin's theories were less unsettling, but for a monarchy whose vested political power was conjoined with the authority of the Church, Darwin's theory was especially threatening.

Though the throne had never been the safest place to be, the danger to its occupant had traditionally come in the form of a palace coup. Historically, the assassins of a tsar had always been the tsar's own son, brother, or some other family relation seeking to usurp power. The Tsar had never been vulnerable to threats from the general population, but suddenly, due largely to his own reformist policy changes, Alexander II was exposed.

In April 1866, the unthinkable happened. As Alexander II was walking through the gates of the Summer Garden in Saint Petersburg, an armed man named Dmitry Karakozov rushed forward and shot at him. A nearby peasant-born tradesman had seen the assassin's charge and managed to knock Karakozov's arm, causing the bullet to miss. The tradesman was later ennobled for having saved the Tsar.

Karakozov had come from a family of minor nobility and studied at Moscow State University, where Nikolai Ishutin, founder of the revolutionary Ishutin Society, was a university lecturer. These men were a part of the intelligentsia that was coalescing in urban centers that were home to both the universities and the working class. Karakozov joined the Ishutin Society and soon wrote his own manifesto that declared Alexander to be the enemy of the people who was sucking the blood of the peasants. He was the first revolutionary to make an attempt on the life of a tsar. Guards captured him immediately and five months later he was hanged.

In response to the attempt on his life, Alexander cracked down on Saint Petersburg University and Moscow State University by conducting surveillance, making periodic searches, and forbidding student organizations of any kind.

Although Karakozov's bullet had missed the Tsar, it did penetrate the mystique of a protective veneer around the Tsar that had previously made him untouchable. Right away, the most astute recognized that the assassin's bullet had indeed hit an important target. Among these was the great Russian novelist Fyodor Dostoevsky.

During the repressive reign of Alexander's father, when Dostoevsky was only twenty-seven, he had been arrested for having read banned political works and was sentenced to death by firing squad. On the day of execution, Dostoevsky stood waiting with the second group to be put to death. The first group stepped forward, and as Dostoevsky watched the riflemen do their work, he released his bladder. As he stood with pants soaked by his own urine, a horseman arrived carrying a letter with a stay of execution that saved his life. Instead of killing Dostoevsky, Nicholas I exiled him to four years' hard labor in Omsk, Siberia. Dostoevsky later borrowed from the experience of what he believed to be the last moments of his life for use in his novel *The Idiot.*

Remarkably, in the years after exile, Dostoevsky became a supporter of the Russian monarchy, albeit with hopes for some reform.

The steps Alexander II had been taking appealed to Dostoevsky, who not only began to write more favorably of the government but even joined the peripheral social circles of the Russian court. When the great novelist heard of the assassin's attempt on Alexander in 1866, he ran to the apartment of his friend the Russian poet Apollon Maykov and shouted, "They shot at the tsar!"

Maykov asked if the Tsar was dead. Dostoevsky responded no, then with full understanding that the aura of invulnerability surrounding the Tsar had been pierced, he repeated again and again, "But they shot, they shot, they shot . . ."

There would be five more unsuccessful attempts on Alexander II's life. Though Alexander had resisted his father's assertion that in Russia one must rule as a lion, he began to see the truth in it. Alexander started to listen to his advisors, who advocated more draconian social and economic policies. His regime took on a repressive tone and enacted greater restrictions on the press. But Alexander would come to learn that the only thing more dangerous than to begin reform is to stop it.

The composition of the Tsar's enemy was an urban mob of uneducated and illiterate workers loosely led by a small and uncoordinated faction of intellectuals. The Tsar did not face the conflict with anything that resembled a conventional army. In fact, those who opposed the government had hardly any guns at all.

As a result, the revolutionaries resorted to terror. And in a strange twist, the preferred weapon of Russian terror was dynamite, an unintended gift from the Nobel family.

CHAPTER 3

"Everyone Rushed for Everything at Once"

IN MAY 1869 Ludvig's home life faced calamity. His wife, Mina, only thirty-seven years old, died in childbirth. Like Ludvig's mother, Mina had been a supportive wife and loving mother, which allowed Ludvig to be so fiercely committed to meeting the challenges of Russia's tumultuous business environment.

Moreover, the couple had enjoyed a happy marriage. A few years before her death, Ludvig had written to his older brother, "Today is our fifth anniversary and happier can no mortal be than I have been in my marriage." But now Mina was gone and Ludvig's newborn child, Charlotta, died twelve days later. Two of his other children had died in infancy, leaving Ludvig with three young children to raise. The oldest, Emanuel, was ten.

Ludvig had already come to believe in Emanuel's aptitude for the family business and was making plans for his future leadership role. The two had the benefit of living in the same home during these formative years—something Ludvig and his father had not. Ludvig hired private tutors for Emanuel and for his high school years enrolled him in a technical school in Barmen, Germany, to ensure that his son acquired the traditional elements of an education. Emanuel also spent many hours in the factory with his father. The boy was a quick and eager study, and the bond between father and son was a source of happiness for both during the dark time after Mina's death.

But between the grief and stress of coping with newly motherless children and his extremely busy factory, Ludvig needed rest and assistance. Men of Ludvig's station at the time often had a pragmatic approach to marriage. His circle of friends introduced the widower to Edla Collin, who had just arrived in Saint Petersburg from Stockholm to take a teaching position at a parish school for Swedish students. She was only twenty-two when she met the thirty-nine-year-old Ludvig, but the two formed a quick understanding and married in October 1870.*

By 1872, Robert had tired of working for Alfred in the glycerin business and was looking for new adventures. Ludvig offered his older brother a job back in Russia. Ludvig's business was operating in the black, and he was flush with enough cash to offer Robert loans to pay down the debts he'd incurred from prior failed businesses. Robert accepted the proposal and, given how overburdened Ludvig was, became a welcome addition to Ludvig's business despite his difficult nature.

Around the time of Robert's decision to return to Russia, the Nobel patriarch died. Though Immanuel had been infirm in the years since the explosion that killed Emil and his own subsequent stroke, newspapers in cities around Europe remarked upon his passing. Immanuel's obituary, which covered the majority of the front page of the September 20, 1872, edition of the Swedish newspaper *Svalan*, gently recognized his bold pursuit of fantastic ideas yet his failure to convert his innovations into financial success: "He was fortunate to live in our times, when the inventor is not in a hurry to make gold and the magician need not fear an inquisition." The admiring article was a sign of remarkable progress for a man who had fled the Swedish bankruptcy

* The new couple named their first child Mina (b. 1873), after Ludvig's first wife.

courts a few decades earlier. The Nobel name commanded international respect. With the death of Immanuel, leadership of the family passed to the next generation.

When Robert arrived in Russia, the first task of his new employment was to oversee the manufacture of shoulder stocks for 100,000 rifles to be delivered to the Tsar. To accomplish this the firm needed a large amount of quality hardwood. Robert took meetings across Europe with experts in the cultivation of walnut trees and the fabrication of rifle stocks and by 1873 began a trip more than fifteen hundred miles south from Saint Petersburg to the Caucasus* of southern Russia, famous for walnut trees that grew eighty feet tall. He carried a bag of Ludwig's money for the purchase of trees—twenty-five thousand silver roubles. Up to this point Robert had proved to be an unreliable business partner for each of his younger brothers. Ludvig hoped that his brother could complete the task at hand. It never occurred to him that Robert's impulsiveness might lead to unforeseen good fortune.

Most people living in the Western Hemisphere have only a vague notion of the Caucasus. The region is 170,000 square miles, slightly larger than California, more than three times the size of England. From antiquity to the present it has been the scene of some of the bloodiest clashes between armies. The region, strategic for its natural resources and warm-water ports with quick access to global trade on the Mediterranean, has long been the obsession of Russian leaders from Peter the Great and Catherine the Great to Stalin and Putin. The Caucasus occupies the blurred line between Europe and Asia and contains a volatile mix of the peoples of each. There are large populations of Eastern Orthodox Christians and Shia and Sunni Muslims—more than fifty ethnic groups in total, speaking a multitude of languages.

The North Caucasus consists of the mountainous regions of southern Russia won during the nineteenth-century conquests of the tsars, territory that includes modern-day Chechnya and Dagestan. The South Caucasus consists of Georgia, Armenia, and Azerbaijan, which

* New York City to Miami is almost thirteen hundred miles.

are the critical land path between the Caspian Sea (landlocked, except by the Volga River, which reaches north to Saint Petersburg) and the Black Sea (which connects south to the Mediterranean and beyond). In Azerbaijan, on the western shore of the Caspian Sea, is the city of Baku.

In January 1873, just before Robert set out for the Caucasus, Ludvig wrote him an encouraging letter: "Here a major undertaking awaits you and I wish from the bottom of my heart that it may lead to your independence and future gratification . . . [Y]our remarkable ability to, with force and fervor, engage with a new undertaking are for me a solid guarantee."

Rather than traveling south on the Volga, Robert went south by land, mostly by horse and carriage, to Tiflis, the capital of Georgia. He then turned east, passing through Baku, where he boarded a steamship. While in Baku, he saw the hallmarks of a large opportunity in its infancy.

The name "Baku" is derived from the Persian *bad kube*, meaning City of the Winds or Cradle of the Winds. The summers are hot and humid, the winters cold. A European executive wrote in his published memoirs of Baku, "When the wind blows from the north across the mountains which are eternally covered with ice and snow, it is biting cold. The wind changes direction often. Most nights it blows with half hurricane force." The climate is semi-arid; some years there is no rain at all in the summers, and the landscape surrounding Baku is a blend of desert, shrub desert, and steppe.

The mountainous stretch of land between the Caspian and Black Seas can be, depending on one's viewpoint, the eastern edge of Europe or the western edge of Asia or a place unto itself. It has been conquered, liberated, and reconquered so many times throughout the ages that it's no longer possible to distinguish aggressor from defender. The region contains an ethnic mix of inhabitants who are the product of recurrent ancient wars. The ethnic animosities never rest, creating a persistent tension in the region.

The city of Baku, then recently annexed by the Russian Empire by victory over the Ottomans, is situated on a protected bay along the Caspian Sea. Ancient fortifications dating back to Alexander the Great rest along the coastline like defeated gods. It is the setting of the mythological story of Jason and the Argonauts and the Golden Fleece. And long before the Greek settlements, there were the fire-worshiping followers of Zoroaster, whose faithful priests of the Magi performed their communion at the temple of perpetual flame (which was the result of the constant flow of flammable natural gas through fissures in the limestone).*

Looking for the storied walnut trees, Robert toured the lands surrounding Baku and witnessed bubbling pools of viscous crude. The ground could not contain the abundant petroleum and gas within. These natural resources, which had only recently become of great value in the modern world, burst into plain view and made spontaneous sparkles of flame. Robert visited the religious temples and grasped that while the oil had inspired worship in the region, it had not attracted any commerce of note. He saw very few derricks† for drilling, and these were rudimentary and cheaply constructed. Primarily the locals skimmed the oil from the surface and transported it by wooden cask for use as a lubricant or salve. American advances in the drilling and distribution of oil—much less the modern techniques for refining oil to produce kerosene for illumination—had not reached Baku by 1873.

Amid his startling observations of the abundant petroleum, Robert did make attempts to survey the walnut forests and even wrote to Ludvig that he intended to establish the manufacturing site for the rifle stocks in Baku. But after three months in the Caucasus, he

---

* The last priest of the Magi died in 1880, after which the Tsar forbade the entry of pilgrims to the sacred site. Today tourists light cigarettes from the open and "eternal" flame.

† A nineteenth- and early twentieth-century derrick was a wood-framed tower that supported the equipment for drilling the well, then for inserting the well casing or pipe used to extract the crude oil from the well. The earliest wooden derricks were as short as fifteen feet high. As drilling depths grew deeper, larger wooden derricks were more than one hundred feet high.

determined that the twenty-five thousand roubles of his brother's money that he carried would be better invested in petroleum.

Two recent events convinced Robert to abandon trees for oil. First, in 1872, only months before his arrival, Baku experienced its first gusher. A Russian businessman named Ivan Mirzoev drilled a well that brought oil spurting 122 feet high. Yet, when Robert arrived, there were still only seventeen wells.

The second event, which helps explain the relative scarcity of wells, was that the political climate had only recently changed to encourage investment and development in the Caucasus. Prior to 1873, the Tsar granted parcels of land in the petroleum regions under a contract system, which gave a person the right to work up to two and a half acres of land for a period of four years. At the end of that period there was no guarantee that the lease would renew, which stymied any incentive to invest in the land. The lease holder might have to hand it all back. But on January 1, 1873, only weeks before Robert's arrival in Baku, the Tsar revoked this law and set more than three thousand acres of prime oil lands for auction to private speculators.*

Robert was in Baku at the perfect time to exploit these developments, and the Nobel family was uniquely capable of succeeding with the opportunity. In the government circles of Saint Petersburg, Ludvig's manufacturing plant was acclaimed as an industry leader. He was an expert at building engines and munitions. Baku, on the other hand, was still technologically backward. This was in part due to the generally unskilled Russian labor force and in part due to the Romanovs' prior policy that had discouraged investment.

Most inhabitants of the Caucasus weren't thinking about oil at all. Working farms were scattered across beautiful and diverse landscapes, arid stretches next to shrub-covered plains that led to a range of mountains. Goats with bells around their necks played a melody. When

* In tsarist Russia the nobility owned the land, the Tsar (and the church, of which the Tsar was head) being the largest landowner of all. The first exception to this was the reform of Alexander II that allowed peasants to purchase land from the nobility.

there wasn't a war between any combination of Russians, Turks, Armenians, or others, the countryside could appear peaceful.

In the mid-1870s, as prospectors began to dig hundreds of wells in Baku, the vast majority were dug by hand with a spade. And as Robert observed, the petroleum was captured in leather sacks and wooden casks. He recognized the opportunity for the Nobels, with their superior technical know-how, to capture and transform the market.

Robert had been a passenger on a Caspian steamship with a Dutch captain named Bruno De Boer. The Dutchman and his brother owned a petroleum refinery* in nearby Tiflis, as well as some oil-rich parcels of land in Baku that he was willing to sell. The two settled on the full amount of the walnut money for the deal. Robert was suddenly in two new businesses: prospecting for crude oil and refining crude oil into a finished product.

The redirection of the capital happened without Ludvig even knowing about it. Robert was forced to act quickly and alone or risk losing the opportunity. To send a letter by post from Baku to Saint Petersburg took between two and six weeks each way, so that the complete exchange of an idea could happen about eight times per year. Robert decided there simply wasn't enough time to consult Ludvig. Like Jack returning to his mother with magic beans, Robert had happened upon a different transaction.

Robert made a trip back to Saint Peterburg to explain why investing in oil made more sense than investing in rifle stocks. He needed Ludvig's support because he knew he'd require far more capital to make his plan work.

---

* The terms *crude oil* and *petroleum* refer to naturally formed underground reserves of liquid hydrocarbons. This is the oil we see in old photos that blasts into the air during a gusher. This crude oil can be refined to make products for a range of uses that include lubricants, fuels for illumination, and fuels for the combustion engine. The Nobels made several of these refined products, and various terms were used in written accounts of these products, such as *paraffin*, *naphtha*, and *kerosene*. Accounts written by people not working in the petroleum industry (journalists, for example) often used these terms interchangeably and incorrectly. For readability, in this book I use only the general phase *petroleum products* except when a distinction makes a material difference to the story.

At first, Ludvig met the news with resignation. His unpredictable older brother had cemented his reputation for capriciousness by hatching his most wild idea to date and disregarding the task he'd been sent to carry out. But Ludvig did not throw these magic beans out the window. He thought that perhaps there could be a beanstalk, and he imagined this change in course would cost him only a modest amount. Robert's need for additional capital would come to an end once he tired of the scheme, as he had with all his others. Over the following days, however, as Ludvig examined the evidence Robert presented, he began to share in the excitement.

Robert and Ludvig devised a plan to develop a comprehensive system that encompassed each phase of oil production, from drilling to refining to distribution. But this plan required significantly more capital.

In Baku, there were many small companies that focused only on prospecting and drilling for petroleum. When these companies struck oil, they would sell the crude to a company whose focus was to refine it into a usable fuel or lubricant. The refineries would then contract with one of the many distribution companies that shipped all manner of goods, including leaky wooden barrels of petroleum products, on barges across the Caspian Sea and the river systems of Russia.

Robert and Ludvig now owned oil wells as well as a refinery. The brothers believed that the key to success was to achieve large scale in each phase of the business. The road map for this strategy, later termed vertical integration, had been tried and tested in America by John D. Rockefeller, founder of Standard Oil.

Rockefeller, Henry Flagler, and four other partners founded Standard Oil in Ohio in 1870 when Flagler used a single page to write the articles of incorporation for what would become one of the largest industrial concerns of the nineteenth century. With plenty of investment capital and strong sales, Standard Oil rapidly expanded. The firm prospected for new oil, acquired competing refineries, and negotiated extremely advantageous pricing with the major railroad companies for distribution that effectively throttled Standard's competition. Rockefeller reinvested company profits to build an extensive network of pipelines to move the oil as well as to acquire ownership stakes in railroad and shipping companies. In just over a decade of business, Rockefeller achieved control of more than ninety percent of American refined oil and supplied not only America with the fuel for illumination but increasingly the rest of the world too.

The Nobel brothers quickly set out to put a version of the American methodology into practice in Baku. The Nobels' efforts represented exactly the type of capitalist-driven growth the Tsar had hoped his policies would engender—talented businesspeople putting capital at risk to develop a surge of industry that would make Russia an economic equal of the elite powers of Europe.

Robert returned to Baku in November 1873, staked by Ludvig, determined to modernize the drilling, refining, and transportation of oil in the region. Though Ludvig was Robert's investor, he was no longer Robert's boss. The petroleum business was separate from the foundry. Now an independent businessman, Robert met the challenges in Baku with energy and enthusiasm. He sent excited letters back to Ludvig in Saint Petersburg describing the enterprising and industrious nature of people from all walks of life, working shoulder to shoulder with the absence of any class distinction. "The society is truly American! Long live equality! Only the authorities with their bureaucracy and slowness are reminiscent of the old world." In the streets of Baku one could overhear conversations spoken in Azerbaijani, Russian, Arabic, Persian, Turkish, French, German, English, Swedish—all within a stone's throw. On the same brief stroll, one would pass neighboring mosques, synagogues, churches, and pagan temples—those who attended the different houses of worship all mixing in the same outdoor markets and working the same jobs.

Robert was a talented chemist, a fact acknowledged by the already famous Alfred, the two brothers having worked alongside each other and their father for many years. Robert made his initial focus to improve the chemistry of refining crude oil. Among other experiments, he tried using caustic soda to purify the crude, a method pioneered by a German chemist. Getting better and better results refining the crude from the Nobel wells, he persuaded Ludvig to send more money so that he could build a new refinery. In 1875 he began business as the Robert Nobel Refinery and hired an all-Swedish crew that included chemists, engineers, and a machine shop foreman. Robert quickly earned a reputation as the most competent refiner in Baku.

For several years, Russia had imported up to forty thousand tons of kerosene annually to Moscow and Saint Petersburg all the way from firms in the United States (almost exclusively from Standard Oil) that could deliver the product more cheaply and efficiently than Russia's small domestic firms in Baku. In October 1876, the Nobel refinery shipped its first three hundred barrels of kerosene (just over forty tons) to Moscow, and the gauntlet was down. The Nobels were just getting started.

By this time, the total capitalization of the petroleum company was 185,000 roubles ($2,800,000 today),* of which Ludvig had invested 150,000 roubles. Robert recognized that success required immediate scale, which required far more investment. In 1876 he wrote to Ludvig, "The required capital is too large for you alone to be the sleeping partner. In this business large profits can come only with large investment."

Ludvig knew he had an industry-defining play before him. Rockefeller and the Americans had been fueling the world for a decade, and Russia was now the next frontier for supply. Ludvig had a foothold in the region, had the technical expertise to run circles around the less sophisticated local competition, and since the time of the Crimean War the family name had commanded the respect to attract investment. In 1876, Ludvig decided to make his first trip to Baku so that he could kick the tires on Robert's operation. Ludvig brought along his sixteen-year-old son, Emanuel.

Photographs and contemporaneous accounts reveal that there was a resemblance between the men in the Nobel family but that the fea-

---

* Assuming 18g of silver per rouble, and the price of silver approximately $1.30/ounce in the 1870s.

tures combined to different effect. Robert's countenance betrayed his disagreeability, and Alfred's awkward appearance betrayed, or contributed to, his social anxiety. Emanuel was much like Ludvig in that his face revealed his good nature. They had the same broad and pleasant features. The only difference now being that Emanuel's sparkling blue eyes made an arresting contrast with his youthful, jet-black hair, which he combed back, while Ludvig's hair had already begun to turn quite gray.

The father and son had researched the petroleum opportunity before arriving. They read and discussed the 650-page book *Petrolia: A Brief History of the Pennsylvania Petroleum Region*, which reviewed in detail how the Americans had solved questions of drilling, transportation, and storage. That the Nobels' land in the Caucasus held abundant oil reserves was not in question. How to extract, refine, and transport it was the challenge.

Ludvig and Emanuel stood on the deck of the steamship as it plowed the Caspian Sea toward the port of the strange city of Baku. In the distant cityscape, the single gilded cupola of the Orthodox church was the only evidence of Russia's Western roots. All else—the eight-hundred-year-old mosque, the citadel, and the palace of the khans who ruled Baku in the seventeenth and eighteenth centuries—spoke of the East. Already by the time of the father-and-son visit, pillars of black smog rose from the many refineries. The scaffolding of the wooden derricks crowded the hills like an army of miniature Eiffel Towers. Oil and smoke hung thick in the air and scented every breath.

As they slowed in the harbor, Emanuel saw that a thin layer of crude enameled the water so that a swimmer would emerge coated with globs of it. Floating patches of oil sometimes sparked into a short burst of flame. The presence of petroleum dominated the senses.

As Emanuel inspected the oil fields with his father and uncle, he found that the area was difficult to travel. The constant wellspring of geysers created a slurry of sand and oil, too wet to walk and too dry to swim.

Ludvig and his son became resolved that under their management, a larger investment in Baku would create a global enterprise. Ludvig envisioned a goal that was far grander than what he and Robert had initially planned. He saw enormous opportunity at each stage of production, and he knew that he needed far more than his own capital to achieve his goals. In April 1876, from Baku, he wrote a letter to persuade Alfred to invest in the business alongside him. "In America such a business has already been carried out on a large scale. . . . The model is to hand—calculations easy to make and clear as day."

Through 1877 Robert and Ludvig persuaded several outside investors, including Alfred, to join the investment group. Then, on August 31, 1878, they submitted an application to the Tsar's minister of finance to set up a limited company operating under the name Nobel Brothers Petroleum Production Company.* The Russian name was Tovaristjestvo Neftjanovo Proizvodsta Bratjev Nobel, which locals abbreviated to Branobel, meaning "Brothers Nobel."

With a slate of new investors, the capitalization of the company consisted of six hundred shares at five thousand roubles for a total of three million roubles, with the following holdings:

Ludvig Nobel: 1,610,000
Pyotr Bilderling: 930,000
Ivan Zabelsky: 135,000
Alfred Nobel: 115,000
Robert Nobel: 100,000
Alexander Bilderling: 50,000
Fritz Blomberg: 25,000
Mikhail Beliamin: 25,000
Albert Sundgren: 5,000
Bruno Wunderlich: 5,000

---

* Royal permission for the company, which required the signature of Alexander II himself, arrived on May 18, 1879. Of the investors, Zabelsky and Beliamin were Russian; the rest were a mix of Swedish, Finnish, and German.

Alfred was the fourth-largest investor and actively consulted with Ludvig on business strategy. Alfred, a vastly wealthy man due to his international dynamite business, was capable of much greater investment in the future should the business need it. So, for both personal and professional reasons, Ludvig and Emanuel kept in close touch with Alfred. The Nobel family was geographically spread out at this point. Robert ran the petroleum operation in Baku, Ludvig and Emanuel worked primarily in the Saint Petersburg headquarters of the family business, and Alfred lived and worked in Paris.

In October 1878, nineteen-year-old Emanuel traveled to Paris to visit his uncle at his mansion at 53 Avenue Malakoff.* Ludvig joined them a few days later. The three men toured the city and visited the ongoing World's Fair. Alfred also introduced his new female companion, Sofie Hess, to his brother and nephew. Chronically unlucky in love, though apparently managing any symptoms of syphilis, Alfred had begun a romantic relationship with Sofie after encountering her while making a purchase in the flower shop where she worked.

Alfred's relatives were immediately troubled by the ease with which Sofie accepted Alfred's financial generosity and suspected that she was only after his money. Having met Alfred less than two years prior to Ludvig and Emanuel's visit, Sofie was by then already living in a comfortable apartment, paid for by Alfred, that was conveniently located between Alfred's home and the Champs-Élysées, known for some of the best shopping in the world. Naturally she made regular shopping trips there, with the bills sent to Alfred.

At the time of the visit, Alfred was forty-five. Historians' best guess at Sofie's age is twenty-two, only three years older than Emanuel. On Emanuel's last full day in Paris before returning to Saint Petersburg,

---

* The city renumbered the home as 59 Avenue Malakoff in 1891, and today the street is called Avenue Raymond Poincaré. The home was demolished in 1910 and replaced with a famous house in the Art Nouveau style that has been classified as a *monument historique* and since 1994 has been the site of some of Paris's most prestigious restaurants.

despite his reservations about his uncle's relationship, the dutiful nephew went to pay his respects to Sofie, as was expected of him.

The two young people spoke in Sofie's apartment for a short time. The conversation was unremarkable and a light rain had started. As Emanuel prepared to leave and return to Alfred's home where he and his father were staying, he was stunned when Sofie suggested that Emanuel should spend the night.

To Emanuel, the message was clear. Alfred's biographer Ingrid Carlberg writes, "It was impossible to interpret this as anything other than an erotic solicitation." Unsettled, Emanuel promptly left for Alfred's home, where he told the whole story to his father.

Ludvig became extremely alarmed and refused to call upon Sofie before leaving Paris (the snub was a clear social breach) and decided to warn his brother. Ludvig wrote to Alfred, "Happiness is not to be found where you currently seek it."

Alfred eventually came to learn the details of Emanuel's story and confronted Sofie, who denied Emanuel's interpretation of events. Her denials led to an exchange of letters between Emanuel and Sofie, and Emanuel soon decided to let the matter drop, attributing it to a misunderstanding, which seemed an important resolution to reach for Alfred's peace of mind.

Ludvig also apologized for having snubbed Sofie in Paris, writing to Alfred that he had avoided her so as "not to strengthen her in her hopes and strivings to bind herself to you for her whole life. Please forgive me this indiscretion, but my fraternal heart means well."

The affair was yet another source of tension in the complex Nobel family web, but both the personal and professional relationship between Alfred and the father-son team of Ludvig and Emanuel survived intact, and Alfred's investment would continue to prove useful.

With Alfred and a group of new investors on board, Nobel Brothers had money to pursue the opportunity before them in full. Given the degree of inefficiency in the current Baku oil business, the potential was enormous.

The resources in the ground were so massive and under so much pressure that once disturbed they became an unbridled beast on the surface. By the late 1870s in Baku, oilmen were no longer using shovels but had adopted the rotary drill, a technology first used in salt mining. Encased in a metal pipe, the drill bored into the ground while a wood-framed derrick housed the aboveground equipment and small steam engine to power the rig.

When a drill connected with a subterranean reserve, the release of pressure sent out a dull tremor felt throughout the city. This began the most lethal part of the operation. The initial blast of a gusher sent not only crude oil hurtling skyward but also sand, rock, and poisonous gases. The spectacle of dark liquid spurting in the air has become a symbol of wealth, but these large gushers—called blowouts—killed workmen, destroyed equipment, and painted the landscape black. The concussion from the initial strike caused nearby oilmen to lose their hearing permanently, and there was the constant danger that the slightest spark could turn the well into a giant bomb that would continue to rain fire for days in the form of lit petroleum.

Once tapped and with the gusher underway, a team of oilmen needed to fasten a valve to the casing, typically a pipe about eight inches in diameter. Most found it prudent to wait until the well settled down a bit and was no longer blasting rock into the air. An experienced oilman from Pennsylvania who'd been capping gushers for decades would have looked on with horror at this untamed spectacle, because in Baku, a week could pass before the rudimentary implements used by the oil crews could bring a gusher under control. Fortunes of black gold were lost by the hour.

Americans had learned these lessons the hard way. In April 1861, seventeen years before the Nobels raised capital and founded their company, the Little & Merrick well struck a massive petroleum reservoir in Oil Creek, Pennsylvania. It was the world's first true gusher, and with limited technology to control the pressure, three thousand barrels of oil per day shot into the sky and then returned to seep back into the dirt. A joyous crowd formed, many becoming soaked with oil. Possibly ignited by the steam engine, the well suddenly erupted in fire. Flaming oil engulfed the scene like a medieval weapon, resulting in nineteen deaths.

The Nobels sent engineers to America to study advances in drilling and capping wells. There was no need to reinvent technologies that already existed. Other stages of the oil business in Baku were similarly outdated. The main oil fields of the Caucasus were about six miles from the refineries surrounding Baku. The traditional method for transporting the oil from the wells to the refineries was to fill leather sacks or wooden barrels with crude, then load these onto a two-wheeled cart called an *arba* that was pulled by a mule. Thousands of locals made their living by providing this transportation, but it was slow, expensive, and fraught with vulnerabilities. Transportation relied on decent weather and the supply of oak to make the barrels, most of which was imported. The barrels were constantly degrading, leaking, and needing repair. The mules needed to graze, and the unreliable transportation workers were prone to stealing, damaging inventory, and, worse yet, strikes. The cost of freight was variable and frequently more expensive than the cargo itself.

A mule cart, or arba, *the traditional means of transporting oil in the Baku region, circa 1870s.*

Initially the Nobels had established their own cooperage to build high-quality barrels, but their long view was to connect the fields to the refineries with a network of pipelines. Conveniently, the oil fields were almost two hundred feet higher than Baku's port at sea level, eliminating much of the need for mechanical pumps to move the oil.

The Americans had been using oil pipelines since 1863. Ludvig began the construction of his pipeline network in the spring of 1877, and though the work was violently harassed by both coopers and carters (the Nobels had to build eight watchtowers along the network to protect the pipelines), they completed construction by the summer of 1878. The Nobels had enhanced one important link in the value chain of their business.

Robert had already made terrific improvements to the refining process so that the Nobel petroleum was competitive in quality with the premium product of Standard Oil. Ludvig, meanwhile, focused his efforts on a grand innovation that would not only make Nobel Brothers equal to Rockefeller but would surpass him.

Refined oil sitting in storage in Baku didn't do the Nobels any good, no matter how high its quality. While they had solved for the inefficiencies of getting crude oil to the refinery, they had not yet solved for the inefficiencies of getting finished product out to consumer markets, which were distant in the extreme.

The traditional method in Baku had been to store the oil in oak barrels that were loaded onto the decks of ships. These ships sailed or steamed across the Caspian Sea, then traveled north up the Volga River and through a system of canals to ports where the barrels would be unloaded and sold to provide illumination in Moscow, Saint Petersburg, and Tsaritsyn. But using the oak barrels for maritime shipping presented all the same problems as did the cart and mule, only worse. With the loading and unloading of cargo in ports and the long duration of rough seas, the barrels often cracked, spilling all their contents.

As an experienced engineer and metalworker, having built boilers and steam engines for the Russian navy and all manner of munitions, Ludvig had designs for a better method of reaching global markets. He abandoned wood altogether and designed a ship with eight separate cisterns made of Bessemer steel, strategically placed in the ship's hull for ballast, each cistern surrounded by an envelope of water for fire prevention. He designed a series of twenty-one vertical watertight compartments (more than thirty years before the *Titanic*) to ensure the ship would stay afloat in the sudden storms and squalls for which the Caspian Sea was famous.

Ludvig had a manufacturing plant and had built plenty of marine engines, but he was not in the business of building ships. He approached several shipbuilders with his design, and all declined the proposal, believing Ludvig's concept to be impractical. Undeterred, he built the ship himself. Ludvig had invented the world's first oil tanker.* Nobel Brothers named the ship *Zoroaster*, after the prophet of the world's first monotheistic religion. The ship was 184 feet long and 27 feet wide and held 242 tons of petroleum cargo.† In June 1878 the *Zoroaster* began service. By September, Ludvig had ordered two more ships, and by the end of the decade he had a fleet of tankers with names that reflected the religious and philosophical diversity of Baku and the Nobels' expanding workforce: *Buddha*, *Nordenskjöld*, *Moses*, *Mohammed*, *Tatarin*, *Brahma*, *Spinoza*, *Sokrates*, *Darwin*, *Koran*, *Talmud*, and *Kalmuck*.

Robert's hard-earned groundwork and Ludvig's ingenuity‡ in Russia's increasingly friendly business environment had brought Baku onto the world stage. Standard Oil found itself getting squeezed out of the Russian market. And Nobel Brothers wouldn't stop there. The

* Globally, as of 2023, there were 7,500 oil tankers that ship more than two billion tons of oil annually.

† The Nobels later built much larger oil tankers designed for the oceans, but the *Zoroaster* was designed for the Volga's lock system and tributary canals to reach Saint Petersburg.

‡ Ludvig also designed the first commercially viable oil-burning stove for domestic heating. He introduced his model to the Russian market in 1882, three years before a similar model appeared in America. Ludvig rarely pursued patents, unlike his brother Alfred, believing operational advances should be of general benefit.

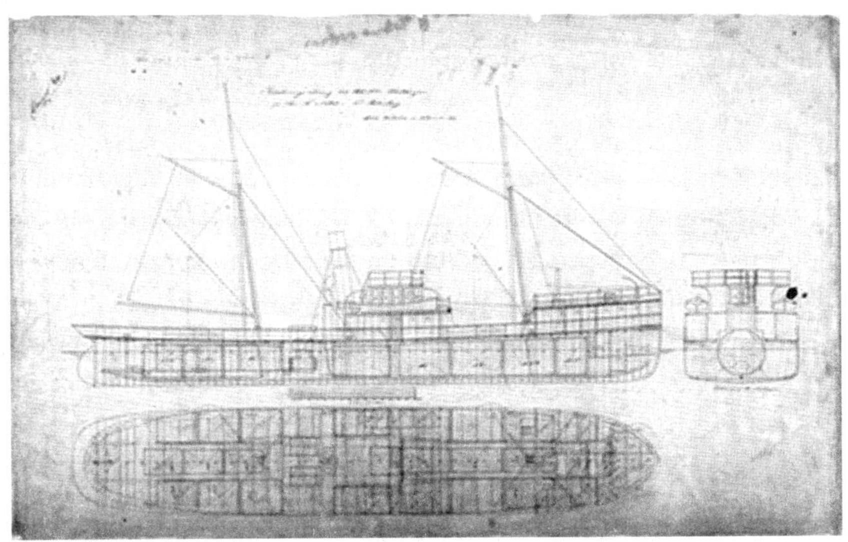

Ludvig Nobel's design drawings for the Zoroaster, *the world's first oil tanker, and the ship photographed at sea, 1878.*

young firm had additional markets in mind, but it would be a difficult road ahead. Their astounding and rapid successes would bring new competition that was ruthless, sophisticated, and well funded.

The Nobels had an uncommon but very logical view of how to build a successful relationship with their employees. They understood that a highly motivated workforce within a burgeoning capitalist system was the best outcome of all. Ludvig wanted his employees to take pride in Nobel Brothers, to have his firm be a place where jobs were coveted, and he went to great lengths to achieve this status with his workers.

In addition to sharing ownership equity with his employees, he founded a bank to help them accumulate savings. He believed in compulsory, free education for children and founded two schools in Baku while vocally supporting a national ban on the employment of children under twelve.* In a savvy this-for-that, he persuaded his employees to accept a reduction in the number of annual holidays to sixty-five (still an absurd number of observed holy days that engendered management complaints of a lazy Russian workforce) and in return reduced the workday to ten and a half hours. For married workers and engineers, he built a settlement of houses, and for the unmarried he built communal residences that were far nicer than any accommodations available in the town.

To set Nobel Brothers further apart, Ludvig began construction of an appealing park in Baku's arid landscape. He shipped in rich soil from the Volga region to lay over more than twenty-five acres of the oil-soaked sand. He acquired more than eight thousand trees and plants to landscape the park and arranged for the oil tankers, which would otherwise return empty, to come back with tanks of fresh water from the Volga that he used to irrigate the park. On the grounds he added a library, a communal dining hall, a billiard room, a skittle alley

* Later, the 1881 reforms of the Tsar banned the employment of children younger than twelve years old.

(similar to bowling), a medical facility, and numerous homes for managers—all sturdily built in stone and designed in the Byzantine style that incorporated domes, arches, and mosaics.

Ludvig named this resplendent park Villa Petrolea, and word of it spread to Saint Petersburg and beyond, even reaching the ear of the Tsar. And of course within Baku, with the luxuries the company provided its workers, Nobel Brothers was held in the highest esteem. Employees began happily to refer to themselves as "Nobelites."

The British journalist, author, and nineteenth-century expert on the petroleum industry Charles Marvin observed at the time that, in a region famous for bribery and corruption, "the brothers Nobel have acquired their wealth by honorable means, and by enterprise and vision such as is uncommon even in the England of our time. The benevolence they show their workmen is remarkable. A fine suburb has been built near Baku on the coast of the Bay. . . . The name of this suburb is *Villa Petrolea* . . . and might serve as an admirable example for many an English capitalist."

Ludvig's generosity extended beyond his employees. Through the 1860s and 1870s, even when his fortune was not secure, he made numerous substantial gifts to scientific, trade, and educational organizations, and nearly all the gifts were made anonymously. Emanuel observed his father's example of generosity and humility and would continue the tradition within the community. The anonymous giving of the Nobels makes an interesting contrast with their American counterpart, John Rockefeller, whose philanthropy began in earnest only after his retirement and whose gifts were made with the transparent purpose of gilding the legacy of the Rockefeller name.

Much of the credit for the development of Nobel Brothers during these years has gone to Ludvig rather than Robert. Ludvig was the natural leader, the more talented executive, and the largest contributor of capital. He was the more gifted engineer, whose vision delivered most of the technical innovations the firm achieved.

But Robert's contribution was also significant. He was the first of the Nobels to recognize Baku's potential and the first with a vision to shape the Russian oil industry. He acquired the family's first land in Baku, the first refinery, and developed techniques to produce the first quality refined petroleum in the Caucasus. He advocated for the expansion of the business and served as the firm's managing director. Ludvig was second to arrive, and thanks only to his brother's persuasion. Robert felt a degree of resentment that most of the credit went to his better-liked younger brother.* But Robert also recognized that of the three brothers he was the least gifted as a scientist and businessman. In a letter to Alfred he wrote, "If I had your knowledge and your capacities, I would spread my wings . . ."

During the first years of the venture, the two brothers had divided responsibilities such that Ludvig was mainly in Saint Petersburg overseeing the direction of the petroleum company, as well as running the Saint Petersburg–based manufacturing company, while Robert was looking after the day-to-day operations in Baku. Compounding Robert's frustration with his role in Baku, he complained that his health was beginning to fade. In 1879, after the launch of the *Zoroaster* and her sister tankers, Robert left Baku for a period of rest in the cooler and healthier air of Switzerland.

Ludvig told associates and employees that Robert had fallen seriously ill with typhoid, which required that he leave his post at the company, perhaps indefinitely. Likely this was a polite cover story for the dismissal of his cantankerous brother, who could no longer collaborate effectively with colleagues or lead the Baku workforce. As Ludvig observed of Robert's paranoid and repressive management style, "Independent natures did not thrive in his vicinity."

According to a different account, Robert was not dismissed but left Baku suddenly, by choice, during the fall of 1879, not telling anyone where he was going. Only months later did he inform the family

* Robert's numerous personal conflicts included a difficult relationship with Ludvig's second wife, Edla. Robert's own wife, Pauline, took Edla's side in the conflict.

that he was in Switzerland, at which point Ludvig offered the invented story to the employees. In any event, leadership of both Russia's largest petroleum producer and largest machine factory fell on the shoulders of Ludvig and his son Emanuel, now twenty and prepared to take on a larger role.

Ludvig was a committed family man, and already under the enormous strain of vast management obligations. Though he worked shoulder to shoulder with Emanuel, Ludvig's exhausting responsibilities kept him constantly at the office late at night or traveling far from his family, which inspired a letter to his daughter. "Today I am asking you to give Mamma a little pat and a kiss on my behalf," he wrote. "You are to kiss her on both eyes and on her ear, and there you must whisper very quietly that the kiss comes with a very tender greeting from someone who loves her endlessly. . . . I have chosen your rosy red lips as my interpreter."

Alfred, through his dynamite business, had the most experience of any of the Nobels in managing a multinational manufacturing and marketing organization. From France the concerned brother (and shareholder) wrote to Ludvig, "The fact is, none of us has health enough to manage such a gigantic mechanism as Baku."

Russia's massive oil reserves were now roaring to the surface of these ancient lands. In a feat of industry never before seen in Russia, the Nobels had put drilling, refining, and distribution assets in place that were as good or better than any in America. They had put Baku on the map of the modern world, a fact that could hardly go unnoticed in Standard Oil's boardroom at 26 Broadway in New York City.

Ludvig's leadership and innovation were not the only reasons the Nobels found success. Tsar Alexander II's market-based reforms had unleashed an industrial surge. Free markets flourished, as Alexander intended. But as millions of serfs flocked to urban centers like Baku, many found work while many did not. These growing mobs, though disorganized and shapeless, continued to pour into a cauldron of discontent. While capitalism led to rapid growth, it was plagued by corruption and abuse, and nowhere was the corruption greater or the divide wider between the wealthy and the poor than in Baku.

Baku, in particular, became ripe for Marxist ideas and the growing socialist movement in Russia. The first social democratic party in the world began in Germany in 1869 with the founding of the Social Democratic Workers' Party, which espoused the socialism defined by Marx. Socialism spread internationally over the next decade and spawned a range of doctrines that had mostly subtle differences.

A point of difference that was not subtle was the method by which the socialist movement would replace an existing form of government with a Marxist system. In Russia, the more extreme of the socialist political left advocated for violent revolution and a complete overthrow of the monarchy, even death to the Romanovs. The moderate left advocated for gradual reform, even accepting that a constitutional democracy coexisting with a reformed monarchy could be an intermediate step to socialism much further down the road.

With a growing mob of the unemployed in urban centers, the voices of the extreme socialists became louder and fiercer. The Tsar's police uncovered numerous plots against his life. Making matters even more precarious, the moderate liberals who had anchored discourse closer to the political center began to open their minds to more extreme views and began to see the revolutionary terrorists not as murderers but as fighters against the regime. Literature of the time reflected the turn against autocracy as well. Dostoevsky, who had been sympathetic to Alexander from the time of his 1861 reforms, adopted more incendiary themes in his work. In 1874 he began chapters that he would use in his masterpiece and final novel, *The Brothers Karamazov.* When later speaking to the Russian publisher and journalist Aleksey Suvorin, he told of his intent, which was never realized, to write a sequel in which his hero Alexei Karamazov "is brought to the idea of regicide."

Once widely praised as the Tsar Liberator, Alexander II now

found himself in a terrible paradox. The conservatives were against him because there had been reforms, and the liberals were against him because the reforms hadn't gone far enough. The most violent faction of the left was not interested in reform at all, but only blood and revolution. They felt that dialogue of any kind with the Tsar's government would undermine their more radical goal of total rebellion. They believed the system could go not by peaceful diplomacy but only by savagery. As Marx had preached, "Violence is the midwife of history."

Threats to Alexander's safety were growing more common. The Tsar determined he needed to rally the public around his government. As Russia was largely a Slavic empire, Alexander endeared himself to his people by coming to the aid of fellow Christian Slavs in Serbia, who had been under Ottoman rule for centuries. On April 12, 1877, Alexander sent his army to fight the Ottoman Empire, which brought throngs of cheering crowds to the streets of Moscow.

Alexander's 200,000 troops, called the Danube Army, went south to war, which raised the hackles of the British, who had their own interests in the region. Alexander sent word to Queen Victoria that he was merely protecting the Slavic people and would never go so far as to conquer the strategic port city of Constantinople (as the Russians called it; it was known as Istanbul by the Turks) on the Black Sea, or to move toward India, the jewel in Britain's crown.

The Russians were assisted by Romanian and Bulgarian troops, and the combined force won a series of brutal battles against the Turkish army. By January 1878 the Turkish government asked for a truce. Alexander's army was only seven miles from the Turkish capital, and the Russian people were ecstatic, many feeling this was literally a divine opportunity. Dostoevsky himself had said in 1877, "Constantinople sooner or later must be ours!"

But the British would not have it. Queen Victoria, whose second son, Alfred, had married Alexander II's only daughter just four years earlier, declared that "she would sooner abdicate than allow the Russians to enter Istanbul." Her prime minister, Benjamin Disraeli, sent a fleet up the Dardanelles to the Sea of Marmara in view of the city walls and threatened war if the Russians attempted to advance. The regional tension that Kipling described as the Great Game had been festering since the Crimean War and was as fraught as ever.

Alexander II's son, whose education had been shaped by conservative-minded tutors and politicians, wanted to take the ancient city that was so valued by the Russians. Many of the empire's generals also wanted to take Constantinople. But the Tsar understood that Austria and possibly others would likely join the British in opposing him and he'd be outmatched as his father had been in the Crimean War twenty years before. Alexander II stood down. It was the first time that he and his son, now thirty-two years old, found themselves in significant political opposition to each other.

The Treaty of San Stefano was signed on March 3, 1878. Serbia, Romania, and Bulgaria (Balkan nations that are west of the Black Sea and north of Constantinople) became independent of the Ottoman Empire. The Ottomans gave up additional lands in the Caucasus to Russia, including the key trading city of Batum on the Black Sea. Though Russia did not take Constantinople, the war was undoubtedly a success. The Russian peasantry, who had always made up the Romanov armies, were happy with the Tsar's decision to end the war.

Alexander enjoyed a second wave of popularity with the Russian people, but it was short-lived. At eight a.m. on April 2, 1879, Alexander was enjoying his usual morning walk around the grounds of the Winter Palace to take in some fresh air. The Tsar's bodyguard followed at a respectful distance. As Alexander walked, deep in thought, a plainly dressed man strolled up to within a few feet of the Tsar, nodded in greeting, then pulled a pistol from his coat and shot at him.

Incredibly, the shot missed. Alexander fled and the assassin chased, firing four more shots that all missed before he was tackled by guards and taken prisoner. Bullet holes in the walls of the palace from the failed assassination became a tourist attraction.

Maria Frederiks, a royal lady-in-waiting, summed up the conservative view of the results of Alexander's shift from his father's strict regime:

> *He gave us freedom of thought and freedom of action and freedom of the press; everyone breathed it in and rejoiced, and everyone rushed for everything at once, hoping to speed up Russia's development. The wild flow that was suddenly unblocked . . . poured over its banks quickly and wildly; it broke and burned everything in its path. What was the end result? A handful of morally deformed degenerates who made their goal, under the guise of loyalty to the Homeland, to change the entire order of Russia.*

Alexander reacted to this attempt on his life with fear and outrage. He took his generals from the recent war with the Turks and reinstalled them as governors-general to exert military force domestically. Russia entered a stage of siege with itself, a tense form of martial law meant to shock and kill a metastasizing cancer of dissent.

The ramifications of Alexander's reforms had been chaotic and uneven. Industry was surging and Russia claimed technical feats like the *Zoroaster* in June 1878 that brought global acclaim. Yet his economic and social reforms had also catalyzed political upheaval and unprecedented opposition to the Tsar that led to the second attempted regicide in April 1879.

In the months between the launch of the *Zoroaster* and the plot against Alexander II, a child was born to an impoverished family in Georgia. On December 18, 1878, Ioseb Besarionis dze Jughashvili was born in Gori, a small town along the trading route between the Caspian and the Black Sea. Only five years before, Robert Nobel had passed through this way to see Baku for the first time, and in 1876, Ludvig and Emanuel Nobel had made their first trip to the region.

Ioseb, nicknamed Soso, grew up on the hardscrabble streets of

Gori, then part of the Russian Empire. The city was marked by gangs, poverty, and alcohol. Many of the inhabitants found work a short distance to the east in the oil fields of the Caucasus where the conditions, even in the more enlightened employ of the Nobels and especially if not, were grueling and treacherous.

In time, this child would change his name to Joseph Stalin, and his path would become inextricably linked with that of Emanuel Nobel.

CHAPTER 4

From Well to Wick

As THE NOBELS navigated Russia's tempestuous economic environment, the main tension between Alfred and Ludvig was over the pace of investment in the petroleum business. By 1880, Robert was no longer in an operational or even serious advisory role. Whether Robert's declining health or his difficult personality was the primary reason for his absence is unclear. Regardless, Ludvig ran the company with Emanuel learning at his side while Alfred, still living in France, was an active advisor and crucial deep-pocketed investor.

In his own field, Alfred had demonstrated great skill in finance and product licensing, but his experience came from a business that was insulated from competition by patent protection. As the owner of proprietary technology, he could control the terms of how his dynamite business entered new markets. Conversely, petroleum was a commodity business, and what Ludvig understood that Alfred did not was that the key to success in the oil business was to reach massive scale, and to be the first to do it. There were no patents to protect Ludvig from competition in the oil business. The only way he could keep his advantage was to control a greater volume than any other producer.

Ludvig had an ambitious plan to reach this scale, but the plan required putting enormous amounts of capital in harm's way. He tried to persuade his more cautious brother to put forward the millions of additional roubles that he believed were necessary. He wrote to Alfred, "I see that day approaching when our products will go out over Russia's borders in great quantities and secure a world market for us. Then, but only then, will the victory be complete."

Ludvig wanted to control the entire vertical production chain of his petroleum business, from the oil derricks drilling in the sand to the refineries that made the end products to the storage and transportation network that delivered products all the way to the very wicks of the customers' lanterns that burned refined kerosene. A critical, and still primitive, component of this vertically integrated business was distribution. Ludvig's tanker fleet was a success, but the Volga was frozen and impassable for months during winter. And in the populated cities of northern Russia, winter came with long nights, precisely when illumination was most in demand. Ludvig needed transportation over rail to serve markets year-round. He spoke to fellow oil producers about investing together in a rail system, and he pitched the idea directly to the privately owned Griazi-Tsaritsyn Railway Company. As it had been with the *Zoroaster*, all declined to participate. Once again, he was undeterred and struck out alone.

Ludvig had a model for this operation in the American oil industry. Standard had been shipping oil over the American railways for a decade. Acting as his own engineer, Ludvig designed railcars with steel tanks that held twenty-six hundred gallons (smaller than the American railcars) and fabricated the parts for the cars in his Saint Petersburg plant.

He acquired land along the rail lines and built strategically placed repair yards for the Nobel-owned railcars. He then turned to his parallel project of constructing storage depots throughout the region. In 1880 he completed the first depot in Tsaritsyn, a city almost halfway between Baku and Saint Petersburg, that he reached by the Volga River. (The city was later called Stalingrad and today is called Volgograd.) He built nine steel tanks that could hold a total of five million gallons—a scale unprecedented in Russia at the time. The tanks were then connected by pipelines directly to the wharf along the Volga.*

He built similar depots strategically located in riverside cities throughout the empire: Riga, Moscow, Saint Petersburg, Domnino, Nizhny Novgorod, Warsaw, Rybinsk, Yaroslavl, Samara, Saratov, Kazan, Perm, Tver.† The construction cost of the Domnino plant alone was nearly one million roubles.

Massive storage capacity gave Nobel Brothers supply flexibility and a strategic business advantage over competitors who lacked similar infrastructure. On occasions when gushers were hit and supply skyrocketed, the price of oil would plummet. Now, Ludvig could store his product to wait out the poor sales environment or even purchase additional oil from other producers at these low prices, then wait until supply became scarce and turn around and sell the oil at a profit.

Ludvig and his engineers also attacked inefficiencies in the distillation process. He modified the industry norm of "batch distillation," which required the process to be stopped while new chemicals were added, and pioneered the method of continuous distillation, allowing for the constant flow of crude and the required chemicals in the process. The constant flow in Nobel's process eliminated the timely and costly step of emptying and cleaning the vessels at each interruption of batch distillation. Ludvig found that he was able to refine a far greater volume of kerosene at a higher grade of quality, all at a lower cost.

With the advent of continuous distillation in 1881, Ludvig's production surged to the point that his oil output was greater than the next five Baku refiners combined. He immediately invested in the upgrade and expansion of each of his refineries to use the continuous distillation method. Though he generally felt inventions should belong

---

* By 1900 Nobel Brothers expanded the Tsaritsyn storage depot capacity to twenty million gallons.

† By 1885 Nobel Brothers had built forty depots, and by 1900, under Emanuel's leadership, one hundred twenty-nine. By the time of the Great War, the company had approximately three hundred petroleum storage depots.

to all and refrained from patents—unlike his brother Alfred, who earned 355 patents over his career—Ludvig filed for and won a patent for continuous distillation. The process was not adopted in America for another twenty-five years.

Ludvig's efforts to finance new initiatives became an increasing part of his overall responsibilities. Emanuel was gaining an early education in finance and capital markets at a scale that previous generations of Nobels had not. Together, father and son developed strategies to fund growth, fervently reinvesting profits into the expansion of the Nobel business. Gustaf Törnudd, who became Ludvig's director of Baku operations after Robert left, remarked:

> *When I first came down here I feared that I was making plans on too large a scale but I soon found out that, no matter how large my scale, Ludvig Nobel outdid me. Every time his plans are still more grandiose, and they aren't just words. He acts, and with such speed that I sometimes find it difficult to bring to completion one bold idea before the next has been worked out. Money, which everywhere else constitutes a terrible problem, he seems to conjure up from the ground. In the final analysis, I guess that is where it truly does come from.*

Ludvig created everything he needed for a world-class petroleum business that could bring his product from the oil well in the fields to the wick of a customer's lantern. If he could copy the Americans, he did so. If the Americans hadn't yet figured it out, he invented it himself. He drew the engineering schematics for oil tankers, barges, and railroad cars; planned the layout for freight yards, storage tanks, and warehouses; pioneered the chemistry of distillation; improved the drilling and capping of wells; arranged multiple networks of pipelines as well as the required pumps and engines; organized sales territories; and oversaw the company finances.

Perhaps above all else, the most important thing Ludvig built was the sense of pride in working for Nobel Brothers. In 1882, Törnudd wrote to his young niece back in Finland of the near-magical aspect of Villa Petrolea and his home in the desert sands that included a telephone (the first in Baku), electric lighting (also the first), gas piped into the rooms for heating and cooking, an orangery, stables, henhouses, duck ponds, and daily fresh water from the Volga. He closed the letter, "What do you think, doesn't the whole thing sound like a story from *The Thousand and One Nights*?"

Of course, Ludvig couldn't simply conjure money from the ground. He needed bank loans as well as periodic infusions of capital from Alfred, who was increasingly concerned about his exposure to a business that was so vulnerable to price volatility. But 1881 brought more good news. Nobel Brothers hit its first true gusher at well No. 25. At a depth of 582 feet, the Nobel crew hit a gusher that shot a ten-inch-diameter stream of sand and oil more than two hundred feet into the air, sending the derrick and boring gear hurtling into the sky with it. The oil and sand fell back to the earth over a two-hundred-foot radius. Anything within twenty yards was buried five feet deep. Once capped, No. 25 delivered four thousand tons of oil per day for six months until the output gradually slowed. This was as large as the record-holding Pennsylvania gushers of the time, and the Nobels would have even larger strikes to come.

Just as Ludvig was developing industry-leading infrastructure and hitting gushers in 1881, a political earthquake was happening.

By the late 1870s, Alexander II had returned to his reformist tendencies. He became convinced that a strict autocratic government would lead only to revolution, and that the way ultimately to preserve the monarchy was to limit its powers. Alexander appointed one of his more liberal-minded advisors, Mikhail Loris-Melikov, as the new minister of the interior. The two then traveled to Livadia Palace, a summer retreat of the tsars on the Black Sea, to begin work on what became known as the Loris-Melikov Constitution. It was not really a constitution, not by European standards, but as Alexander encouragingly characterized the legislation to his son, it was a movement toward constitutional monarchy and away from Russia's autocratic past.

The plan allowed for elected representatives from the towns (the *zemstvos*) to participate in the legislative work of the State Council, with a direct line to the Tsar. Though there was no real substantive transfer of power in this reform, the mere introduction of the principle of popular representation and elections subverted the empire's long-held concept of autocracy.

In January 1881, Loris-Melikov delivered a revised draft to Alexander. The Tsar had no changes to make. He then turned his energies to persuading his ministers and conservative-minded son to support the legislation. His son opposed the changes but eventually acquiesced to Alexander's wishes for reform. By March, Alexander was ready to sign the Loris-Melikov Constitution into law. It was a mere baby step toward a true parliamentary system, but a bloodless one, unlike the tumultuous English Civil War of 1642–51 that led to their constitutional monarchy, or the ongoing and brutal transitions of French government. Perhaps Russia, though later than much of Western Europe, would achieve the most graceful transition to democracy of all.

Alexander II's optimistic gesture toward more enlightened governance came to an abrupt and horrific halt. On March 1, 1881, in Saint Petersburg, the social revolutionary Ignacy Hryniewiecki stepped from the crowd toward Alexander's approaching horse-drawn carriage. As Alexander often did on Sundays, he traveled his usual route through the city, over the Pevchesky Bridge via the Catherine Canal to view military roll call at the Mikhailovsky Manège. Hryniewiecki's partner was the first to throw a bomb under the carriage. The explosion of dynamite injured the driver of the Tsar's carriage and killed a Cossack guard on horseback who was an escort. The Tsar emerged from his stopped carriage.

Alexander stood exposed on the street while he examined the injuries to his men who had been riding alongside in an adjacent carriage. Hryniewiecki, who would become the second bomber (there was a third in the crowd who proved unneeded), tossed a crudely wrapped bomb at the feet of the emperor that, with metaphorical perfection, blew both the bomber and his target to pieces. In that moment, the most significant reformer in the history of the Russian Empire was dead at the age of sixty-two. What might have been . . .

Tsar Alexander III succeeded his father. Only three days before his father's assassination he'd celebrated his thirty-sixth birthday. The new Tsar was loud, had an aggressive disposition, and, according to his ministers, was socially unrefined. A reason for the lack of attention to his refinement and education is that the family had believed his older brother Nicholas would succeed to the throne. But the Tsarevich Nicholas died unexpectedly of complications from meningitis (a terrible blow to Alexander, who loved his older brother),* and so the unprepared younger brother suddenly found himself the new Tsarevich at the age of twenty.

In stature, Alexander III was the size of a Russian bear. He enjoyed asserting his enormity to intimidate foreign dignitaries, which was easy to do. Many of Europe's sovereigns were quite short. Austria's Emperor Franz Joseph was tiny, and Germany's soon-to-be leader Kaiser Wilhelm II was also small, about five seven. But for the sheer girth she attained later in life, Britain's Queen Victoria would be described as diminutive, standing only four eleven.

Unlike the British and other royals of the time, the Russian tsars had height. Reports of Peter the Great range to the fantastic, but reliable accounts put him at six eight. Nicholas I was six two, Alexander II was six one.

Even more imposing than Alexander III's six-foot, three-inch frame was his broad and powerful physique. On several occasions while meeting with foreign diplomats, he was known to take a piece of metal in his massive hands and bend it into new shapes, leaving his audience speechless.

---

* Tsarevich Nicholas was engaged to Princess Dagmar of Denmark, with whom he'd been besotted from first sight. On his deathbed Nicholas expressed the wish that his fiancée should marry his younger brother, the future Tsarevich, Alexander. Alexander and Dagmar married in 1866, the year after Nicholas's death.

Alexander III had voiced opposition to his father's social and political reforms throughout his adulthood. Not coincidentally, his primary tutors were monarchists who had instilled in him this worldview, as did many influential ministers who had surrounded his father. The opposition to Alexander II's reforms inside the palace had been so rampant that rumors circulated that the assassination had been facilitated by someone in his inner circle.

The deputy minister of internal affairs (and close friend of the new Tsar), General P. A. Cherevin, remarked soon after the assassination of Alexander II, "I owe my entire career to Alexander II, but I still say: it's a good thing they got rid of him, otherwise where would he have led Russia with all his liberalism?!"

Despite their political differences, Alexander III felt no relief at the elimination of his father, but experienced the genuine trauma of the sudden loss of a parent. His reaction, partly due to the grief and outrage following the murder, was a resolute departure from reform and a return to the iron fist of the prior generation of Russian rule. Alexander III abandoned the Loris-Melikov Constitution and instead enacted laws to suppress the media and forbid assembly. As antisemitism was rampant in the Russian Empire and there were rumors of a Jewish conspiracy behind the assassination, he signed legislation that forbade Jews from owning or leasing Russian natural resources.

In general, Alexander III was very pleased with the industrial boom that his father's reforms had catalyzed. He believed that aspects of capitalism could coexist with his absolute rule. He liked what he saw of the Nobel businesses in Saint Petersburg and Baku and did nothing to hamper them. In fact, quite the opposite. In March 1883, when Ludvig was trying any and all means to conjure up the capital to fund his firm's frenetic growth, a private banker in Saint Petersburg tried to bleed him for loans at a fifteen-percent interest rate, knowing how scarce sources of capital were.

But the new Tsar believed in the progress and entrepreneurial drive of Nobel Brothers, and in a show of faith, the Russian State Bank stepped in to grant a personal line of credit for two million roubles at

7.5 percent. Emanuel, who was deeply involved in securing the terms of the loan, later wrote to a friend that if the loan from the bank had not come in, the firm would likely have gone bankrupt.

However, another law enacted by the new Tsar did place a significant restriction on the Nobel businesses. Ludvig and Alfred had planned to establish a dynamite factory in Saint Petersburg. Ludvig had already taken meetings with leaders of Russian construction firms and the military, who had indicated great demand. As much as anywhere in the world, in Russia there was mining and construction of railroads that required blasting through the sides of mountains. But Alexander III put a halt to Ludvig and Alfred's plans. In the wake of the assassination, in order to curtail a clear pattern of terrorists using dynamite as their weapon of choice, the new law forbade the fabrication of dynamite on Russian soil. Alexander wanted tighter controls on the raw materials, and the finished product imported for military or industrial use would be closely tracked at the border.

While Alexander's law made the acquisition of dynamite more difficult, dynamite was of course merely an implement available to terrorists, not the root cause of the terror. Another of Alexander's new laws inadvertently exacerbated homegrown terrorism at its source, in particular the growing breed of agitators in Georgia who could count among its numbers the young Joseph Stalin.

Alexander mandated that all subjects of his empire learn and speak Russian. The proud Georgian people viewed this as gratuitous scorn from a colonizing power. Resentment of the Tsar grew.

Georgia is a Christian nation dating back to the fourth century that was subsequently conquered by the Mongols, Persians, and Turks. The Russian Empire annexed the Kingdom of Georgia from the Turks in 1801, by which point the demographic makeup consisted of Assyrians, Greeks, Jews, Ukrainians, Russians, Azerbaijanis, and a majority of ethnic Georgians. About half the country was Eastern Orthodox and about a third Muslim. Georgian was the dominant language.

Feeling like second-class citizens within the empire, Georgian nobles came both to envy and begrudge the Russians. In 1832, a group of these nobles conspired to restore the Georgian monarchy by inviting the local Russian overlords to a ceremonial ball at which the unsuspecting guests would be murdered. The conspirators were found out and exiled. Though the Georgian people and culture were not esteemed by the tsars, their territory was. To the northwest of Azerbaijan, Georgia sits at the heart of the Caucasus with abundant natural resources and critical warm-water ports on the Black Sea.

Alexander III was determined to keep this territory and to Russianize its people. This would include forcing them to learn Russian in their schools and speak it in the streets. When Joseph Stalin turned five in 1883 and began going to school, he was forced to learn Russian and was forbidden to speak Georgian to his friends in the presence of a teacher.

A short, skinny, weak child with webbed toes on his left foot, Stalin came from a broken home. His mother, Keke, was sexually promiscuous, with numerous lovers in Gori. Her behavior with her son was obsessive, sometimes turning physically abusive. The boy fared no better at the hands of his father, Beso, a rage-filled alcoholic whose bouts of drinking and physical abuse toward his wife and child were fueled by the humiliating and persistent rumors that he was not the boy's father.

The parents of both Beso and Keke, Stalin's grandparents, had been serfs to a local lord near Tiflis who were freed by the Tsar Liberator, Alexander II. Beso, still quite handsome years into his marriage, worked as a cobbler to keep a roof over the head of his remarkably pretty wife. Their first two children had died within months of birth. Their third, though small and weak, had a stubborn will to survive. A feistiness that he demonstrated on the streets, even among his larger friends. He seemed naturally to find himself the leader of his peers.

This feisty child, still going by the name Soso, went off to school, where he complied with the mandate to learn Russian. A useful language to know if one should want to rule the empire.

CHAPTER 5

The First Oil War

As JOSEPH STALIN'S education began on the streets of Gori, Emanuel Nobel's education progressed from tutors to the corporate boardrooms and banking centers of Saint Petersburg. Emanuel turned twenty-five in 1884. Unlike the prior generations of Nobels who had endured bankruptcies and ruin, Emanuel was raised in an established family among Russia's elite. What's more, he had a natural grace in dealing with aristocrats and the heads of banking institutions. The third generation of Nobels was fortunate in having the perfect ambassador for the family business.

Gustaf Törnudd, who directed all Baku operations for Nobel Brothers in the 1880s, wrote fondly of Emanuel in a letter home: "Mr. Ludvig Nobel's young son, Emanuel, came here and left for Petersburg a couple days ago. He is a very likeable and serious man who will someday be head of the firm, God willing."

Emanuel's wide-set blue eyes and his broad, friendly face made people ready to be charmed by his earnest and direct manner. A common adage in reference to family businesses is "shirtsleeves to shirtsleeves in three generations," which means that the first generation creates the wealth from humble beginnings, the second stewards the wealth, then the third spends it all away. Emanuel was the rare third-generation owner who seemed unlikely to deliver on this curse. Not only did he have the good judgment to take care of the wealth he inherited, but he had the intellect and skill to create much more of it.

Alfred had officially joined the board of directors by this time. Though persistently cautious and often at odds with Ludvig regarding how much to spend in pursuit of growth, Ludvig and Emanuel welcomed Alfred's involvement. His connections and experience in dealing with bankers to build his international dynamite empire were needed once again as Ludvig became determined to get more deeply involved in another expensive endeavor.

The most capital-intensive industry in the history of the world—the railroad—had become critical for the Baku oil business. Ludvig not only needed additional railcars; he needed a new railway system altogether. Railroad construction required so much money that in America the need to pool investment capital for the industry led to the innovation of the modern corporation and the stock market.

The work to construct a five-hundred-mile rail line that would connect the Caspian with the Black Sea began once Batum (an active trading port on the east coast of the Black Sea reaching the Mediterranean) became part of the Russian Empire in 1878. Once Baku and Batum, as the endpoints of the railway, were both under Russian control, the entrepreneur Sergei Palashkovsky negotiated with the government to acquire a land concession to lay the line. Palashkovsky also owned a small oil refinery in Baku. He faced enormous capital requirements and pitched his fellow oil producers to join the investor group.

Ludvig was already capital constrained and faced other internal challenges. There had been several costly fires at his refineries and the *Nordenskjöld*, a prized tanker, had just exploded, resulting in the full load of cargo burning through the night. Ludvig also faced downward pressure on oil prices. A gusher in the fields could be a double-edged sword. Tapping a new reserve would refill his tanks, but news of a gusher, and a pending glut of supply, would spread quickly and could immediately depress market prices. At the same time, competing refineries, though much smaller, had observed Nobel's superior distribution tactics and were copying them, putting more of the commodity on the market, which further depressed prices. The disorganized competition was prioritizing the acquisition of market share over short-term profitability.

Because petroleum is a commodity business, the main point of competition is price rather than quality or service, and as Ludvig had been preaching, the key to success was in having massive scale to drive efficiencies that allow a company to maintain a profit margin even at lower prices. The pitfall is that companies try to gain market share by artificially (and temporarily, they hope) lowering prices to attract customers. These price wars become suicidal for companies without enormous cash reserves. This was true for all the commodity industries of the era, including sugar, steel, cotton, and tobacco. Entrepreneurs could win, or quickly lose, vast fortunes.

When Palashkovsky approached Nobel and the other Baku producers for investment, none had the available cash to seize the opportunity. Palashkovsky himself was struggling to keep his head above water, and it wasn't long before the most famous family of financiers in Europe entered the game.

The Rothschilds were a family of Ashkenazi Jews from Frankfurt, Germany, who rose to prominence when Mayer Rothschild established his banking business in the 1760s. Mayer ensured an international banking presence by deploying five sons to establish banking offices in Paris, London, Vienna, Naples, and Frankfurt. By the 1870s, Mayer's grandsons Alphonse de Rothschild and his younger brother Edmond headed the Paris branch of the family. They had already financed railroads in Austria, France, and elsewhere on the continent. They also had already dipped a toe into the petroleum business as the owners of refineries in Fiume* and Marseille.

* On the Adriatic Sea. At the time of this story it was the Free State of Fiume, existing within the Kingdom of Hungary. Now called Rijeka, it is part of modern-day Croatia.

As part of his race to keep up with Western Europe, the new Tsar encouraged foreign investment in the empire, provided these investments complied with a series of laws mandating that Russian citizens be involved in directing the Russian companies. Alphonse de Rothschild took the opportunity to invest in the Baku-to-Batum railroad.

The Rothschilds faced antisemitism throughout much of Europe, and Russia had particularly strict anti-Jewish business laws at this time. However, Russia was desperate for foreign investment. In order to coax massive sovereign loans from the Rothschild banking empire, the government would attach special concessions that were favorable to Rothschild businesses in Russia. These concessions somewhat, though not entirely, leveled the playing field with non-Jewish-owned businesses in Russia.

Rothschild initially invested alongside Palashkovsky, then bought out his interests entirely, including Palashkovsky's refinery. Rothschild completed the railway line and opened for business in May 1883. In December, he founded the Caspian & Black Sea Petroleum Company within the borders of the Russian Empire. This represented a neighboring and formidable competitor for the Nobels—one with deep pockets, a successful track record in rail construction, and a reputation for remarkable business savvy.

The competition didn't end there. With a railroad to connect the oil fields and refineries of Baku to the warm-water port of Batum, where Nobel and Rothschild tankers could ship product to ports anywhere in the world, the Caucasus was an increasing threat to Rockefeller's Standard Oil. Rockefeller controlled ninety percent of America's refineries, which produced an astounding seventy-seven percent of the global supply. Aside from a negligible amount of oil from Romania, the world's supply came from either America or the Caucasus. Commercial production of oil in Mexico did not begin until 1902, and the first discovery of oil in Persia (modern Iran) was not made until 1908, with commercial production beginning a few years after. With Rothschild operating in Baku, there were now three significant oil refineries in the world. The French family's entry set Standard Oil, the world's market gorilla, against two powerful firms that had now established business in the only known region on earth that held an abundance of petroleum to rival America.

The Rothschilds had a history of entering commodity industries (they had successful investments in copper, mercury, lead, and nickel) and either acquiring or negotiating with competitors to resolve price wars and stabilize profit margins. In America, Standard Oil overcame competitive price pressure by arranging advantageous distribution agreements for its oil with a consortium of railroad companies (ultimately ruled to be unfair and illegal by the US Supreme Court), which gave Standard a cost advantage over all other oil refiners. With this advantage, Rockefeller suffocated his competitors to the point that he either acquired them cheaply or ran them out of business entirely.

In the Caucasus, similar market forces were at play. The Rothschild strategy had been to establish a monopoly position, or, failing that, to negotiate a market division among a reduced number of competitors to maintain price levels. Nobel Brothers was the clear market leader by volume, but Rothschild had vast capital reserves and a secure foothold with oil wells, refineries, and distribution in the region. Each would also have to contend with the established power of Standard Oil selling to European markets. The first great oil war was coming.

A cautious Alfred had no desire to tangle with the Rothschilds. He encouraged a diplomatic approach and a settlement with his French adversary. In May 1884, Ludvig sent two of his top executives, Mikhail Beliamin and Ivar Lagerwall, to Paris for a series of meetings.

Jules Aron, known as "Mr. Oil" in Paris, represented the Rothschild interests. Aron recognized how damaging direct competition and a price war with Nobel would be. In the first meeting, he pitched the Nobel representatives on a coordinated approach to the market and even suggested some form of merger.

Beliamin briefed Ludvig back in Saint Petersburg, and within weeks Ludvig counter-proposed that the Rothschilds acquire a twenty-five-percent interest in Nobel Brothers for approximately five million roubles (valuing the company at approximately $300 million today).

With optimism that this proposal would be acceptable and bring a new capital infusion from the Rothschilds, Ludvig began expansion plans for the business.

But when Beliamin returned to Paris to conclude the arrangement, Aron did not even attend the meeting. Instead, he sent two lieutenants who flatly rejected Ludvig's proposal with the accompanying message that the Rothschilds would never enter a business partnership without a controlling position of majority ownership. As a departing message, the executives boasted that the Rothschild family was far too powerful globally to have as a rival. Still, Ludvig did not bend.

With the negotiation having failed, Ludvig prepared to fight. He had a head start of several years and felt he had a lock on distribution to the Russian market. Maintaining the headquarters of his petroleum business in Saint Petersburg, near the ministries of government where he had developed close relationships, had advantages too. With sales to his home market generating a reasonably secure revenue stream, what was at stake was some portion of international markets.

Then a telegram arrived from Aron suggesting another meeting in September. In the weeks leading up to the meeting, the French firm indicated a willingness to agree to terms similar to those that Ludvig originally proposed. Aron claimed that Alphonse de Rothschild was personally reviewing the terms of the offer. However, September came and went and the negotiation was still stalled.

Though Aron had signaled enthusiasm for a deal, Ludvig sensed it would never happen. Just as Ludvig pulled away from the negotiations, a senior executive from Standard Oil named F. W. Lockwood visited Baku. A recent report from the American business journal *Bradstreet* declared that the Russian business environment under the tsarist bureaucracy was clumsy and that the petroleum transportation and production facilities of the Caucasus were "wretchedly inadequate, posing no threat to American domination of global markets." Lockwood wasn't so sure and wanted a closer look for himself.

After an inspection of Baku operations through the fall of 1884, Lockwood approached Ludvig suggesting that the Americans would like to reach an accommodation with Nobel Brothers. Though the Tsar would never allow Standard to acquire Nobel Brothers outright, senior executives at Standard internally advised the acquisition of a large ownership stake, writing to Rockefeller of the good sense to partner with Ludvig, whose "shrewd ability, . . . knowledge of Russian business, . . . high connections and experience dealing with the Tsarist bureaucracy, make him invaluable."*

The Rothschilds, meanwhile, had given up on the idea of reaching an amicable settlement and prepared for direct competition instead. They continued to acquire wells and refining capacity. The name Caspian & Black Sea Petroleum Company, when translated to Russian, had the initials BNITO, which is how the company would become known globally under Rothschild ownership. With the Rothschilds now on a war footing and no cooperative agreement yet established with Standard Oil, Ludvig began 1885 resolved to engage in a great three-way struggle.

With his son Emanuel increasingly directing financial strategies for the family business, the Nobels decided to bet on themselves. As the Russian Empire became increasingly capitalistic in the last decades of the nineteenth century, Emanuel knew that a joint-stock company, such as Nobel Brothers with its transparent accounting practices, could raise capital to fund growth and defend the business from competition, and Emanuel had already developed close relationships with Russia's largest banks. As Rockefeller and the Rothschilds made entreaties to negotiate a market arrangement that the Nobels believed undervalued their company, the message back from Ludvig and Emanuel was *We don't need you*.

Emanuel reconstituted the European sales organization and increased investment in distribution capacity, including new tankers for the Baltic Sea that could better service Western Europe, new railcars

---

* Ludvig's long presence in Saint Petersburg as the largest manufacturer of engines and armaments was synergistic with his petroleum business. His close relationships with government ministers, which typically involved graft as a common and accepted business practice, opened doors for Nobel Brothers as a domestic firm and provided advantages over foreign firms.

along with more powerful locomotives that could haul greater quantities of kerosene up the steep inclines of the Transcaucasian Railway to reach ports on the Black Sea, and new pipelines from the wells in the oil fields to the Nobel refineries in Baku.

As the three corporate titans waged the oil wars, Tsar Alexander III certainly recognized the enormous value of the natural resources in his lands over which they fought, and he decided his petroleum region needed military protection. The Russian Empire had first acquired Batum and other regions of the Caucasus near the Black Sea when defeating the Turks in 1878. In order to gain international support of the treaty that brought these lands under Russian rule, Alexander II had agreed that Batum would remain a free port with no military presence. But that was five years before the completion of the Baku-to-Batum railroad that crossed the Caucasus with millions of tons of petroleum products. In 1886, Alexander III simply abrogated the term of the treaty that required a demilitarized Batum port. He dredged the harbor to a depth of thirty feet, sent several of his most powerful ships of war, and directed construction of fortifications for the port.

Alexander III's paranoid and militaristic regime put Europe on edge. His focus on foreign policy was accompanied by neglect of his family at home. The Tsar had five children, three boys and two girls. His eldest son and heir, Nicholas, was a small,* frail, thin-necked, and unscholarly boy. Nicholas was not the favorite son, nor was the second son, George, who was stricken with tuberculosis. The Tsar favored his precocious third son, Michael, who turned eight in 1886. Alexander bounced the little boy on his knee and laughed at his impudent jokes that would have earned Nicholas a beating. The Tsar devoted little time to the mentorship of his eldest. He was far too preoccupied with the suppression of the revolutionaries in his empire.

This preoccupation extended to the Tsar's choice of living quarters. He decided to make the primary residence for his family twenty

* Though Nicholas's father was six three, his mother was not quite five four, and Nicholas apparently inherited his stature from his mother's side.

miles outside Saint Petersburg in the more fortified town of Gatchina. The tsars had a palace there too, but Alexander decided not to live in the luxurious and spacious rooms of the Gatchina Palace because he felt he and his family could not be well protected there. Instead, he moved the family to the less exposed basement quarters that had once been occupied by servants under Tsar Paul I almost one hundred years earlier.

At each meal he had food tasters eat a few bites first, then all the Romanovs would wait a few minutes to observe whether the tasters would drop dead from poisoning. It was an extraordinary but necessary way to live. The threat was real.

Alexander's reactionary and politically conservative posture engendered an extreme reaction from the socialist revolutionaries of the political left. He received constant death threats, and his police uncovered several sophisticated assassination plots, including one planned for March 1, 1887—the sixth anniversary of his father's assassination.

On that day, Alexander III visited the Gatchina church in observance of his father's death. As he prepared to pass from the church down the main road, the Tsar's police apprehended a group of revolutionaries positioned along the street. Inside the coats of each of the conspirators were homemade bombs loaded with dynamite and lead pellets dipped in strychnine. The leader of the group, and the bomb-maker, was Aleksandr Ulyanov, a twenty-year-old activist with a degree in zoology from Saint Petersburg Imperial University.

Police investigated and routed the entire conspiracy. Ulyanov's mother begged for mercy from the Tsar. Though all conspirators had been sentenced to death, incredibly, Alexander III offered to spare the lives of those who were willing to repent. Ulyanov and four others refused, and on May 8 they were hanged. Ulyanov's death devastated his mother and younger brother Vladimir. The Ulyanov family was ostracized in their hometown due to the family connection to the assassination plot.

Vladimir, who adored his older brother, had just had his seventeenth birthday. He was only two years younger than Nicholas Romanov, heir to the throne. Thirty years later, these two boys would cross paths as men under very different circumstances. By that time, Vladimir Ulyanov would be using the name Vladimir Lenin.

At the time that Lenin's brother was hanged and the Ulyanov family was in despair, Soso, the boy who would become Joseph Stalin, was experiencing an appalling childhood in Gori. By 1887, eight-year-old Soso's alcoholic father was four years gone, having walked out on his family. The destitute mother and boy were forced to move to new homes a total of nine times during these years. Keke turned to prostitution, making just enough to keep them fed and sheltered. But there were other challenges. Soso barely survived the fevers of smallpox, and the disease left his face ravaged with scars that he carried the rest of his life and that earned him the nickname "Chopura" ("Poxy").

Worse, Soso's left elbow and shoulder began to develop abnormally due to an injury he suffered. Accounts differ as to whether the injury was the result of a fight or an accident with a horse-drawn carriage. As he grew, the arm had less functionality and acquired a withered look—a significant problem for a boy surviving gang life on the streets of Gori.

Keke worked, begged, and borrowed to support her ambitions for her son. She and Soso eventually moved into a room on the upper floor of the home of the family's priest, Father Charkviani, a former drinking friend of the boy's father, who was also one of the men rumored to be Soso's biological father.*

Keke constantly struggled to provide any advantage for her son. She encouraged Charkviani's teenage children to tutor Soso in Russian so as to elevate him from the common Georgian tongue. Keke's primary goal in these years was a quality education for Soso because her ultimate plan for him, fantastic as it may seem in retrospect, was a life in the priesthood.

Adjacent to the poverty in Gori, the petroleum business thrived.

---

* In the Russian Orthodox Church, the priests ("White" clergy) are expected to marry and have children, while the monks ("Black" clergy) do not marry and take a vow of chastity. Traditionally, only the monastic life of chastity can lead to sainthood.

Gori was located between Baku and Batum, close to the railroad that connected these two cities that brought oil to global ports. Soso had a close-up view of the industry as many of the adult men of Gori and Tiflis who had once driven the mule carts to transport oil now performed the extremely perilous work in the oil fields. Many men died attempting to drill deep into the earth, or else came home with horror stories. The journalist Essad Bey wrote of working the oil derricks, "Several times during the day one of the workers, sitting in an ordinary pail, would have to dive down into the bore-hole, a procedure which meant death nine times out of ten."

Life in the oil fields was near lawless, and there were risks beyond just the job itself. Bey wrote, "The bandits of the country could unobtrusively throw anyone into the shaft." Owners lived in newly built homes on the outskirts of Baku, miles from the oil fields. When the owners came to inspect their wells, they traveled with a team of armed security. "For the journey [the owner] equipped himself as for war, for his way led through the desert, where enterprising bands would lie in wait for an unarmed traveler."

To manage theft and maintain the security of property, there was a Mafia-like protection racket. Each owner hired a *kotschi*, a local man who acted as a chief of security, for about a thousand roubles per month. Each *kotschi* would have between five and ten clients, and in return for the monthly collection, he and his armed thugs would enforce the protection scheme.

Initially the Rothschilds turned their nose up at the *kotschi* system, believing it to be a debased way of doing business, and that their name would be protection enough. After near-nightly theft and damage to their holdings, they hired a *kotschi* of their own—at double the market rate.

The Nobels and the Rothschilds were by far the leading industrialists in the region. The makeup of the second tier of oil magnates ranged from Armenians, Turks, and Russians to Poles, Georgians, and Swedes. They were smugglers and former prisoners, princes and dukes.

Apart from the disciplined Nobels and Rothschilds, for many of the owners the sudden windfall of massive wealth led to lives of debauchery and the construction of extravagant palaces. One owner built a mansion in the form of a dragon. Another commissioned a palace made of solid gold; only when architects persuaded him of the impossibility of his design did he settle for a gold-plated palace.

By 1887, Baku producers had worked through a glut of supply and oil prices had normalized. Nobel Brothers returned to paying a lucrative dividend to investors. The enormous capital outflows to fund the expansion of infrastructure were now bearing fruit. In 1885 the dividend had been only two percent, and in 1886 there was no dividend at all. The infrastructure spending, combined with downward price pressure due to the competition from Standard and the Rothschilds, which increased supply, had resulted in lean years for the Nobels. But in 1887 the dividend was back at six percent and poised to go higher. Nobel's growth in productive capacity was staggering, and its business efficiencies were market-leading.

In June 1887, Ludvig updated his retired brother Robert, convalescing in Europe, with a letter declaring, "Our business is fully built. Technically it is so perfect that surely nothing can surpass it. Our rivals cannot create anything better. It needs only hard work, care, goodwill and sound commonsense to prosper; it is for the younger generation to complete this program."

Ludvig and Emanuel had dominated the Russian market and were beginning to realize their global potential. Rockefeller had been a global force for years with a relatively smooth, robust, vertically integrated operation and, critically, immediate access to a deep pool of skilled labor. The Rothschilds had unparalleled business expertise, connections throughout Europe, and seemingly endless capital reserves. Dozens of meetings between the three competitors had failed to deliver an amicable division of the market. Though a balance between global supply and demand had led to a quiet period among the three rivals, the true oil war was yet to be fought.

This was to say nothing of the political challenges the next generation of Nobels would face that were specific to Russia. As Ludvig noted in the same portentous 1887 letter to Robert, the Nobel business objectives could be satisfied "as long as no revolution sweeps away all wealth and all private ownership in one go."

Karl Marx had died only four years before Ludvig's letter, stateless at the time of his death and buried in England. In Germany, Chancellor Bismarck had passed anti-socialist laws, which he renewed in 1886, to combat the social democratic movement that was taking root there. Marxist doctrine was taking new root in the years after its messiah's death. Russia's liberated serfs were creating swelling numbers of urban proletariat that seemed the most fertile ground. Baku, the base of Nobel's petroleum fortune, was the fastest-growing city of all.

CHAPTER 6

Emanuel Leads a Russian Deluge

LUDVIG AND EMANUEL'S success was attracting attention from as far away as the US State Department. On October 6, 1887, George Lothrop, the American ambassador to Russia,* delivered a stunning report to Congress that highlighted the new Russian threat to American interests.

Lothrop relayed that the combined analysis of Charles Marvin (a British journalist and petroleum expert), Russian industry experts, and the consul of the United States at Baku had concluded that "the entire expulsion of American petroleum from European markets is confidently looked for." Lothrop then stated the obvious feeling that this result "can not but cause some solicitude respecting the future of a business which has hitherto been so valuable to the producers in the United States." By producers, he meant John D. Rockefeller of Standard Oil.

Lothrop included in his report a newspaper article that had

* The more formal title at the time was Minister Plenipotentiary to Russia. Lothrop served in the role from 1885 to 1888.

appeared a week prior in the *Journal de St.-Pétersbourg*. Congress then read several staggering facts reported from Baku.

The article opened by saying that the petroleum industry in Russia was developing at a breakneck pace while the American wells showed signs of becoming exhausted. "In Pennsylvania, for instance, in order to obtain naphtha [oil], it is necessary to bore into the earth to the depth of 2,000 feet, whereas in Baku the deepest wells are only 700 feet."

The article conceded that the Russian petroleum business had been stagnant for many years and attributed the lack of growth to tsarist tax policy and regulations. Back in 1872, there had been a very modest 750,000 gallons of oil extracted from Baku. Then things changed dramatically. The change was due in part to the abolishment of the Tsar's tax policy and in part due to one entrepreneurial and innovative new firm. The flurry of activity and astonishing growth of the Russian oil industry began "especially since the arrival of the Nobel Brothers, today called the *naphtha kings*."

The article spoke admiringly of Ludvig and Emanuel's achievements. "The firm of Nobel Brothers owns thirty-two wells which work permanently and *daily* furnish from 150,000 to 500,000 hectoliters [4 million to 13 million gallons]. It owns also the best organized and largest petroleum refinery in Russia, thirteen maritime constructions especially arranged for the transport of petroleum, also a great number of cistern-wagons to be met with on all our railways."

The article then recounted a series of stories and statistics that put true fear into the government and Standard, including verified reports of numerous colossal gushers, one tapped on October 6, 1886, from which "30,000 pounds of oil were emitted *every hour*, to the point when it became necessary to put out all the fires of the factories of the 'black city' in order to prevent terrible conflagrations." For perspective, in 2018, with the benefit of modern advances, the majority of wells in the United States produced between 2,500 and 20,000 pounds per hour.

The ancient city of Baku had come to a second life. Though it had been known as the city of eternal flame for more than a thousand years, Baku was suddenly an urgent topic in boardrooms and government committees from Saint Petersburg, Berlin, Vienna, Paris, and London to New York and Washington, DC.

The article concluded, "Mr Marvin speaks of the deluge with which Russian petroleum threatens Europe, definitively ruining the oil trade of North America."

Six months after Ambassador Lothrop's report stunned the State Department, tragedy struck Nobel Brothers. On April 12, 1888, Ludvig Nobel died, age fifty-six. Emanuel was twenty-eight and had already taken a leading role in the financial oversight of what had become a massive family-run concern. The father and son had worked closely together, and the succession plan was ordained. Emanuel was about the same age Ludvig had been when he'd cleaned up Immanuel's bankruptcy and founded a new business in Saint Petersburg. But for this generation, the task was not to wind down a failure but to take up the torch.

Ludvig's health had been failing for months, and he'd spent the entire winter in the South of France, hoping to recover while Emanuel oversaw the businesses between visits to his father's bedside. Both Robert and Alfred managed to visit Cannes to see their sick brother in his final weeks.

The death of the industrialist generated enormous press coverage in Russia and Sweden. In France the coverage was somewhat different and carried an inaccuracy with a lasting impact on the Nobel legacy. Ludvig was very well known in Russia and Sweden, but in France the surname Nobel was associated mainly with his younger brother, the dynamite millionaire Alfred, who had made Paris his home. The French press, including *Le Figaro*, enthusiastically reported the death of a Nobel. However, they had the wrong Nobel. On the morning of April 15, 1888, Alfred woke to the morning issue of *Le Figaro*, which was delivered daily to his home, and read his own obituary. It was not pleasant reading. The French paper wrote, "A man who only with great difficulty can be regarded as one of humankind's benefactors died yesterday in Cannes. The deceased is Monsieur Nobel, the inventor of dynamite." The paper went on to state that the world should remember Alfred and his invention chiefly for having brought death and destruction.

The origin of the Nobel family wealth, many years before the petroleum business even began, was indeed from the manufacture of munitions, but Alfred was so alarmed at this potential posthumous remembrance that he later rewrote his will to bequeath the majority of his assets to the founding of an annual prize awarded to the individual deemed to have created the greatest benefit to humankind.*

Ludvig Nobel—the brother who had actually died—was buried in Saint Petersburg on April 16. At the funeral service, Emanuel tearfully spoke to the large gathering of a son's love for his father. "I will miss in him not only a loveable and tender father, but I lose in him a loyal and wise and thoughtful friend, from whom I have had no secrets."

Emanuel and members of the Saint Petersburg Technical Society announced the founding of an annual prize in Ludvig's name to award "the best work in metallurgy or the petroleum industry." This was the first prize to bear the Nobel name, established years before the other and years before the death of Alfred or the update to his will.†

Ivar Lagerwall, a Swedish doctor of philosophy and advisor to Nobel Brothers, wrote that despite "his prominent position as head of Russia's largest industrial enterprise Ludvig Nobel was modest and unpretentious like few others . . . [I]n the promised land of titles he went all his life without a title . . . [H]e was equally highly regarded by high and low."

---

* For decades historians have struggled to determine whether this origin story of the Nobel Prize is a myth. Swedish author Ingrid Carlberg reveals the truth in her terrific 2019 book, *Nobel: The Enigmatic Alfred and His Prizes*, by recovering the contemporaneous news articles for review. The French newspapers *Le Figaro, Le Matin, Le Gaulois*, and *Gil Blas* all erroneously reported that Alfred had died instead of Ludvig. Subsequent literature regarding this story has referred to Alfred as a "merchant of death," though Carlberg was unable to locate this moniker in contemporaneous newspaper accounts. There is no doubt, however, that newspapers wrote unflatteringly of Alfred in these premature obituaries.

† The nature of the Ludvig Nobel Prize has evolved substantially over the last hundred years. More recent winners include Vladimir Putin in 2008 for his contributions to Russia.

These qualities were Emanuel's most valuable inheritance. As for the other assets to be passed on, Ludvig drew a distinction between handing down cash and handing over the reins of a business. Shortly before his death, he wrote to Alfred, "Capital in pure money form left as inheritance to children is pure moral corruption. Capital in industrial form is a good weapon in the struggle for existence." In essence, Ludvig felt that to give away cash would promote laziness, but to give a business would promote hard work.

Emanuel would need all the good qualities that Ludvig had passed on to him to meet the challenges of the two businesses he now controlled. Emanuel's brother Carl, younger by three years and who had shown promise as an executive, would focus on the factory in Saint Petersburg while Emanuel assumed the role as head of the family and dedicated the majority of his time to the petroleum business. With Alfred as a distant advisor in Paris, Emanuel and Carl were the only Nobels to preside over the family empire.*

Their younger sister Anna was not involved in the operations of the businesses. Alfred had no children, so their only cousins were Robert's four children, who also were not actively involved. Emanuel and Carl had a total of seven half siblings by their father's second marriage, though all were far too young to be involved in the business at the time of Ludvig's death. Ludvig and Edla had Mina (the namesake of Ludvig's first wife, who had passed), then came Ludvig ("Lullu"), Ingrid, Marta, Rolf, Emil, and Gösta. Emanuel and Carl came to view their stepmother as a mother figure, but as was custom, neither Edla nor the half sisters took operational roles. Lullu, the eldest male, would much later serve as a board member for certain of the Nobel companies, but only the youngest three half brothers would take on significant operational roles. Yet at the time of Ludvig's death the boys were five, two, and one. Gösta, the youngest, was twenty-seven years younger than

---

* Carl operated the factory with some success but died a few years later in 1893 from diabetes at age thirty-one. Carl's share of the factory passed to his widow, Mary, who remarried in 1896 and moved to Stockholm. Emanuel disliked Mary's new husband and soon purchased her shares to become sole owner of the factory.

Emanuel, who was more of a father figure than a brother to the toddler. It would be many years before these half brothers would make an impact on the Nobel family fortune. For now, the family empire rested on Emanuel's shoulders alone.

Alfred remained on the board of directors of the petroleum company and was an advisor to Emanuel as he took the reins. However, the transition of executive power to the next generation was not entirely smooth. In part, the difficulties arose from the unenthusiastic welcome Emanuel received from members of his own family.

From Paris, Alfred wrote to members of the board to express his concerns about Emanuel's ability to lead such a massive enterprise. He raised the possibility that the Nobel family businesses in Russia had grown beyond what any single person could oversee, let alone a person as young as Emanuel. Compounding Alfred's dubious support, Edla voiced doubts that her stepson could fill the shoes of her deceased husband.

Emanuel faced these headwinds with calm and steely resolve and a maturity beyond his years. With no bitterness or grudge against the skeptics within his family, he humbly went about the work he knew he was capable of doing, because only one opinion truly mattered to him—that of his dead father. Only Ludvig had spent more than a dozen years in close confidence with Emanuel, years that were full of impassioned work and adventures great and small—from the breathtaking first-ever trip to Baku as father and son stood shoulder to shoulder on the deck of the passenger steamer traversing the Caspian Sea through pockets of flame that dotted the water, to supervising the refineries and the fleet of tankers in port, to countless hours in the Saint Petersburg factories, to late nights at the headquarters discussing finances and strategy. Ludvig had known Emanuel was not only up to the job but that he could lead the family to an even brighter and bigger future. Emanuel's humility and quiet confidence would be assets. Certainly, for such an important position, critical not only to the family but to the Russian Empire, he was young, without a single gray hair on his head or in his beard. But he had already spent years in training for leadership.

Within weeks, Emanuel faced two major events in quick succession that would test his abilities. The first crisis was a near civil war between the two top executives at Nobel Bothers, Ivar Lagerwall and Mikhail Beliamin, both longtime colleagues of Ludwig's and both much older than Emanuel. Lagerwall, who had spoken at Ludvig's funeral and was also a member of the board, felt that Beliamin, who was serving as president, was attempting to usurp power in the wake of Ludvig's death and that Emanuel needed to take a firmer approach with Beliamin.

Emanuel worked with a slow and steady finesse. Recognizing his youth and the fact that he was new to the role of chief executive, he didn't want to alienate his team by behaving like a corporate strongman. In particular, he didn't want to ostracize Beliamin, who was the only Russian citizen on the board, a legal requirement for the business.

Emanuel reviewed the company's finances and shrewdly reorganized the executive team in a way that was satisfactory to Beliamin yet limited his power. He managed this transition so skillfully that even Lagerwall returned to Emanuel singing a different tune only months after first lodging his complaints and warnings. Lagerwall praised Emanuel for his deft handling of Beliamin and said that the experience had made Emanuel "into a man." Even Alfred wrote from France with the emphatic compliment "Bravo, nephew!!!"*

With the brush fire of civil unrest inside the company put out, Emanuel faced the second crisis and hoped that with deft handling he might again turn a crisis into an opportunity. The staggering flood of petroleum in Baku that had intrigued Rockefeller and the State

---

* Beliamin was Jewish, and his prominent role as president of Nobel Brothers speaks well of the Nobels' treatment of Jewish people at a time of rampant antisemitism in Russia. In this period there was a high proportion of Jewish people working in the banking community—Rothschilds included—and the Nobels generally had an adversarial relationship with bankers over negotiated terms. In correspondence among the Nobel family, there are turns of phrase that would raise an eyebrow today, but these have the feel of being professionally motivated against bankers, not ethnically motivated against Jews. Emanuel was outspokenly critical of Russia's "medieval perception" of Jewish people as "vermin."

Department had also intrigued the government ministers in Saint Petersburg. Now Tsar Alexander III himself wanted to have a closer look at Baku.

For centuries, the main export from southern Russia had been grains (mainly corn and wheat). The Nobels had given the Tsar something of equal, if not greater, importance on the world stage.

It's hard to imagine the world before artificial illumination. For most of human history, the workday ended when the sun went down. Roadways were impassable at night—not because of floods or snow or fallen trees, but because on a moonless night a person couldn't see his hand in front of his face. The advent of reliable illumination was a paradigm shift in the course of human history. Light from a source other than the sun doubled human capacity for work.

Early forms of lanterns burned candles or natural gas or the oils from whales, nuts, or vegetables. Upon the discovery of distillation processes for petroleum in the mid-nineteenth century, companies like Standard Oil redesigned lanterns to burn kerosene, which worked remarkably better than any previous lighting device. Today we think of petroleum as the driver of human productivity because it's the fuel for the combustion engine. But in the decades before ubiquitous internal combustion engines and lightbulbs, petroleum was the driver of human productivity as the source of industrial lubricants and fuel oil (fuel oil increasingly replaced coal as the fuel for updated steam engines in ships beginning in the 1870s) and, primarily, as the fuel for illumination.

Alexander III wanted to see for himself this abundant resource that was a new and critical export for his empire. More than coming to see Baku generally, he was coming to see Nobel Brothers specifically. The royal visit was set for October 1888. The Tsar's massive entourage included his wife and his twenty-year-old heir, Nicholas. Emanuel had just turned twenty-nine and was still fresh in the top job. His prodigious diplomatic skills would be put to the test hosting Alexander III—anointed by God as the absolute monarch of the Russian Empire, perhaps the most powerful person in the world.

All of Baku eagerly awaited the arrival of Alexander, Empress Maria Feodorovna, and their son Nicholas. The city was cleaned up and beautified, grand arches constructed by the entrance to the rail station and at the city gates, streets newly paved. Dignitaries from surrounding towns and provinces arrived wearing extravagant attire adorned with silver, gold, and jewels. International press arrived from France, Britain, Germany, America, and elsewhere to report on the event.

The police presence was massive. Arrests in anticipation of the Tsar's arrival filled the prison cells. Authorities shut down rail traffic between Batum and Baku weeks prior to the visit, at significant economic expense.

There were many refiners in Baku, but it was the Nobel name that had been in the Tsar's ear. The Tsar and Tsarina led the procession as it approached Nobel's petroleum factory. Emerging from the factory to greet them was Emanuel's younger sister Anna, then twenty-two. She approached the Empress and delivered a bouquet of flowers held in a diamond-studded vase. For Alexander, the Nobels delivered the traditional Russian gift of bread and salt, presented on a silver tray engraved with the image of the factory. Anna also presented gifts to Nicholas and his younger brother, the Grand Duke George, including a case of twenty-four bottles of Nobel Brothers petroleum and miniature oil derricks complete with a pumphouse, all made of silver.

The robust Tsar was only forty-three-years-old and still gave the impression of indomitable strength. In contrast, his young heir appeared diminutive next to his bearlike father. Alexander III, seeming to believe he had decades more to rule, created no urgency at the Russian court to mold Nicholas into something fit for the throne. Nicholas was handsome in his military uniform, but within the royal entourage that came to Baku he was timid and unsure of himself.

Emanuel awaited the royals inside the factory. He greeted them as they crossed the threshold, then conducted a tour of the refinery, explaining the chemistry of the distillation process to a rapt audience. From there, Emanuel led them back outside toward the sea. They walked along the loading docks and boarded the Nobel tanker *Darwin* for the Tsar's inspection. Afterward, in a nearby pavilion, Emanuel had laid out papers that detailed the quantities of oil drilled, refined, and shipped to ports around the world.

Leaving the coast, Emanuel led Alexander and his troupe several miles by horse and carriage to the oil fields. Standing at a safe and dry distance, Emanuel and the royals observed an engineer release the cap of an active well so that Alexander could see the pageant of a gusher in action.

Then, in the elegant boardroom of Villa Petrolea, Emanuel handed the Tsar a silver-bound album with photographs of the Nobel Brothers' enterprises. Alexander instructed the opening of champagne and made a toast to Emanuel's generosity and success. To the chagrin of other refiners in Baku, Alexander spent so much time with Emanuel that he saw no other owners.

Emanuel had succeeded in utterly charming the towering Tsar as well as the Empress Maria Feodorovna, with whom he maintained a friendship and regular correspondence for decades. He exhibited the grace and deftness of a seasoned diplomat.

Upon leaving, the Tsar expressed his wish that Emanuel become a Russian citizen, and he formally extended the offer. As Emanuel was the owner of two of Russia's most significant enterprises, both of an increasingly critical nature to the military, the Tsar was eager to make him a son of Russia. Emanuel accepted. He became the first and only Nobel to be a Russian citizen, which came with legal benefits for doing business in Russia as well as prestige. Emanuel's reception of the Tsar, which cost the firm hundreds of thousands of roubles, was a tremendous success and cemented Emanuel's connections to the highest rungs of power in the empire. Standing on his father's shoulders, less than a year after his father's death, Emanuel reached a level of power greater than any of his forebears.

In November 1889, the State Bank of the Russian Empire granted the same credit rating to Nobel Brothers that it had set during the pinnacle of Ludvig's tenure. Alfred was filled with pride for his nephew and wrote that the action of the bank was an accolade that proved the "trust shown to the company and more so to you. You have charted a course through the difficulties like a true man, and as they say here [in France] 'à tout seigneur, tout honneur' [honor to whom honor is due]."

Under Emanuel's steady stewardship the petroleum business set new profitability records, and his brother Carl kept the munitions and engine foundry thriving. Nobel Brothers delivered a dividend of eight percent in both 1889 and 1890.

Yet Emanuel remained wary of the grumblings of civil discord among the empire's proletariat as well as the tactics of Standard Oil, which increasingly resorted to bribery, rumormongering, and sabotage. Nobel Brothers was producing by far the most petroleum in Russia, but as an overall concern it was still smaller than Standard Oil and had fewer financial reserves than the Rothschilds. Emanuel knew that the combination of the ruthless tactics of his competitors and the unstable Russian political climate were storm clouds on the horizon.

CHAPTER 7

Changing of the Guards

EMANUEL, ENJOYING THE favor of Tsar Alexander III and the perks of Russian citizenship, was now acknowledged throughout Saint Petersburg as the industrial chief leading two of Russia's most profitable and important companies. Finance Minister Ivan Vyshnegradsky made a follow-up visit to the Nobel Brothers facilities in Baku in 1890 and was also impressed with what he saw. Weeks after the visit, he appointed Emanuel to a coveted post with the State Bank of the Russian Empire, where Emanuel could influence commercial lending and monetary policy. This was a notable show of government support for Nobel and as a practical matter gave Emanuel greater influence in securing loans he might need to fund his businesses.

Support from the Tsar's regime was timely because 1892 ushered in what became known as "the hunger years." Crop failures in southern Russia led to grain shortages and severe famine. Amid this strife and economic slowdown, oil wells kept gushing and the resulting oversupply of petroleum led to a collapse in the price of crude and kerosene. Many of the smaller oil producers and refineries were unable to weather the storm and sold out to the cash-rich Rothschilds.

The Mazut Oil Company, the largest domestic competitor to Nobel Brothers, hit hard times and sold a majority interest to the Rothschilds, who were redoubling their interests in Baku. With the infusion of investment from the French powerhouse, the recharged Mazut sales agents crowded the market, further depressing prices. The Nobels had sound infrastructure and business planning but again found themselves in a cutthroat sales environment. Rothschild agent Jules Aron recognized that an ongoing head-to-head battle on price would be ruinous, even for the French banking giant. An organized sales syndicate comprising the major competitors, along the lines of what Emanuel and Ludvig had proposed years before, needed to come about. Talks between Nobel and the Rothschilds began yet again.

The hunger years were particularly hard on the Georgian town of Gori, where poverty and crime worsened. By 1892, young Stalin, nearly fourteen, had been a seminary school student for three years. At odds with history's perception of him, in these early years he was known for his studiousness and, according to biographer Stephen Kotkin, his "sweet alto singing voice."

At the same time he developed a reputation as a scrapper among his street-fighting peers. A son of Father Charkviani, the priest who had taken in Stalin and his mother, remarked that "there was hardly a day when someone had not beaten him up and sent him home crying or when he had not beaten someone else."

Soso challenged other boys to tests of bravery and made a game in the streets of latching onto the axles of fast-passing carriages. In one of his dashes into the roadway, the wheels of the carriage ran over his legs, causing a permanent limp and earning him another nickname: "Geza," meaning "crimped."

Though he succeeded in his schooling, even winning awards for his poetry, he maintained a rebellious posture in the seminary school. He bristled especially at the requirement for the exclusive use of the

Russian language. At school, young Stalin had a reputation as a rule follower—always arriving on time, always completing his assignments. Observing this, a Russian teacher named Lavrov pulled the boy aside to enlist him to spy and inform on the other boys. Lavrov felt that Georgian was a "language for dogs," and he instructed Stalin to report any students overheard to be speaking Georgian while on school grounds.

Instead, Stalin, about thirteen at the time, decided to give Lavrov a taste of Gori street justice. He told Lavrov he had information to share and arranged to meet him in an empty classroom. When Lavrov entered, Stalin followed behind, along with a handful of other students. When the teacher was surrounded by the Georgian boys, who threatened to kill him, he immediately broke down and pleaded for mercy. Lavrov survived and was much more permissive of his students speaking in Georgian going forward, but not all teachers were as lucky as Lavrov. Stalin and his friends viewed the Russians as occupiers of the Caucasus, and the Russian teachers were vulnerable while embedded in these resentful communities, especially if trying to enforce the heavy-handed policies of the Tsar. Several Russian teachers turned up murdered in alleyways, though none of the deaths was attributed to Soso.

Despite his savage start to life, the young Stalin seemed firmly on the path to priesthood. The seminary was a rough environment, but compared to his home in Gori it was an enclave. On one occasion his abusive father, Beso, appeared at the seminary, roughly grabbed the boy, and effectively kidnapped him. Beso had never agreed with the plan for his son to become a priest. He brought the boy back to Gori in the hopes of making him a cobbler's apprentice.

Whiplashed between two ruthless parents, Stalin seemed momentarily bound for a very different future until Keke interceded once again. When she heard what Beso had done, she stood down her husband, gathered the boy, and brought him back to the seminary, reasserting his religious education.

Then an unexpected shift happened. Around 1892, he acquired a copy of Darwin's *On the Origin of Species* and devoured it. According to the histories that Stalin later permitted to be written, it was at this point that he began to doubt the existence of God, and he began a slow turn away from a life in the priesthood that his mother had set out for him.

Stalin had acquired an education, could speak passable Russian, and had learned to navigate the hierarchies of the streets and institutions of learning. But he was no longer interested in devoting his life to the priesthood.

As young Stalin was discovering Darwin, a new era of Russian politics began in Saint Petersburg. The Tsar appointed Sergei Witte to be finance minister in August 1892. Emanuel knew that to succeed in business, amassing political capital was just as important as building efficient operations, and he made certain that the new finance minister became an ally. Witte was a brilliant statesman who favored the avoidance of war and worked to attract foreign investment to bolster Russian industry. His previous role had been transport minister, in which he presided over Russia's rapidly expanding network of railroad lines, and in this position he had become keenly aware of Emanuel Nobel's value to Russia's future. Witte courted Emanuel's involvement in oversight positions and ensured Emanuel joined the advisory board of the Volga-Kama Bank, one of the largest banks in the Volga region, with a new branch office in Baku. Emanuel wrote to his uncle Alfred that in this role he was able to "get a better insight into the position of our rivals."

The favor of the Tsar and his ministers for Nobel Brothers over their rivals was clear, especially now that Emanuel was a Russian citizen. Within the confines of Russia, Witte could stack the deck in favor of the Nobels against the foreign, Jewish Rothschilds.

When Emanuel began efforts to form a Russian oil syndicate with the Rothschilds to stave off the ruinous price pressure, Witte pulled him aside with a warning. A letter from Emanuel to his uncle reveals that Witte cautioned him not to partner with the "hateful Jew" Rothschild.

Emanuel was not put off by the powerful minister, however. With diplomatic finesse of his own, Emanuel kept a friendly relationship with Witte yet made a deal with the Rothschilds the following year. Nobel Brothers and the Rothschilds would lead a consortium that comprised sixty-two percent of all oil producers in the region. The alliance was formally approved by the government in February 1894* and was an important step in organizing the Russian oil industry and stabilizing prices. Cooperation between the rivals enabled them to compete more effectively for international markets against Standard Oil and block the American company almost entirely from the Russian market.

The show of unity caused distress among the Standard executives in New York City. Rockefeller recognized that the vast oil reserves of Russia had the potential to recast the global petroleum market and that if Nobel and Rothschild agreed on a coordinated approach, then Standard could be squeezed out of European and Asian markets. Rockefeller decided to dispatch his chief negotiator, William H. Libby, to Europe. Libby, Aron, and Nobel would sit around a map of the world and discuss how to divide it among them.

Amid these tense negotiations, a crisis struck the empire that was nearly the equal of another regicide. On November 1, 1894, Tsar Alexander III, who had seemed as strong as a bear, died of kidney disease at the age of forty-nine. The period from the onset of the disease to the Tsar's death was a matter of only months. There had been no time to remedy decades of neglect of the hapless Tsarevich. The sudden

* The consortium was called the Baku Paraffin Manufacturers' Union and managed to stabilize the downward price pressure, though Nobel and Rothschild were still locked in fierce competition for markets. Standard Oil was making similar types of combinations in the American market, albeit informally and without the express approval of the government. Not until 1902 did Ida Tarbell's journalism in *McClure's Magazine* expose Standard Oil's monopolistic practices to public scorn, eventually leading to the Supreme Court decision against the company in 1911. Supporters of Rockefeller argued that foreign firms, like Nobel Brothers, did not face such onerous government regulation.

passing of the autocrat launched the twenty-six-year-old and wholly unprepared Nicholas onto the throne.

One tenet that Nicholas held dear was that the tsars were absolute monarchs anointed by God. His regime continued his father's course as politically and socially repressive but economically open, which suited the Nobels just fine. Under Nicholas II, Emanuel would continue to enjoy the government's favor, which would strengthen Nobel Brothers for the three-way contest with Rockefeller and the Rothschilds.

In addition to government support, Emanuel's operational superiority separated his firm from the competition and enabled him to weather the storms—the acts of God—that affected all firms equally. The Baku region was suffering a horrific cholera outbreak through the early and mid-1890s. Cholera is an intestinal infection that spreads through contact with excrement, typically transmitted by contaminated drinking water, food, or soiled clothing. The disease was undemocratic, disproportionately harming the impoverished communities that lived in less sanitary environments. About half the people who contract the disease die of it.

At the first signs of the outbreak, Emanuel proactively brought in more doctors and cleaning supplies. The Nobel Brothers facilities were far cleaner to begin with than those of rival companies in Baku. Torbern Fegræus, a geologist for Nobel, wrote: "In the environs of the Nobel factory, where previously Swedish cleanliness was already the order of the day and therefore hardly requiring improvement in sanitary terms, they also do everything to protect the health of the workers."

The cholera outbreak was disastrous for many of the smaller and poorly operated oil producers in Baku and diminished Emanuel's competition further. Nobel Brothers emerged in a position of greater relative strength.

A decade earlier, Standard Oil had passed on making a partnership with the Nobels because the American firm felt that the Nobels had not sufficiently consolidated control of the Russian market. Standard had decided that the market was too fractured and could be won without a formal partnership. By 1895, the tables had turned. As Nobel, Aron, and Libby gathered together, it was Nobel who judged that Standard was not in control of its home market.

Years later, in 1911, the Supreme Court would rule against Standard Oil for having established illegal business practices in refining and distribution that created a monopoly position and suffocated free and fair competition. However, in Nobel's view, even by the mid-1890s Rockefeller no longer held a dominant monopolistic position in America. Discoveries of oil reserves in Texas, California, and elsewhere had led to powerful new entrants in the American market.

When Emanuel traveled to Paris in February 1895 for talks with Aron and Libby, he was not convinced Standard could deliver on their part of the arrangement. *Bradstreet* had written that Standard was negotiating with Emanuel Nobel and the Rothschilds to contrive "a scheme for parceling out between them the whole of the refined oil markets of the world." In the proposed division, Standard would claim markets in England and Germany while the Russian-based firms would share the Asian market.

By March, the deal was dead. In part, the breakdown was due to the opposition of the Russian and German governments—the Germans felt more safely supplied by Minister Witte and the Russians than by Standard and the Americans. But in larger part the deal never came off because Standard couldn't keep other American competitors out of Europe despite several aggressive price-cutting campaigns. Though Standard was still the largest petroleum company in the world, Rockefeller no longer dominated the supply coming from America in the way he once had.

Emanuel had no qualms about walking away from the negotiating table. His business was thriving even without the creation of a cooperative that would ease the market threat from the Americans. In 1895, Nobel Brothers paid a record ten percent dividend. All the hard work and infrastructure planning that he and his father had done to set the table were paying off. He didn't need a partnership with Standard. He intended to beat them.

As Emanuel focused on his main rivals, a new competitor slipped through the door. Marcus Samuel led the British firm "Shell" Transport and Trading Company.* The quotation marks around Shell were a part of the legal name of the firm, which was originally founded for the purpose of importing and selling seashells. Samuel, an expert in global distribution, arranged an exclusive deal with Rothschild's BNITO for a guaranteed supply of oil, then used British-built tankers and concession rights to travel the Suez Canal.† Samuel's tankers *Murex* and *Conch* (Shell named all its tankers for types of seashells) were the first to make the journey from the Black Sea through the canal to the Indian Ocean, where Shell would supply millions of tons of Rothschild's oil to Australia, Singapore, and parts of southern Asia. Rothschild had kept the arrangement with Samuel private, and these shipments through the canal surprised both Nobel and Rockefeller. The distribution play gave Rothschild a temporary advantage in Asia and introduced Shell as a substantial new player in the Great Game.

While Emanuel's petroleum and manufacturing businesses both accelerated in growth and profitability throughout the decade, 1896 came with personal tragedies and distractions. Emanuel lost two uncles in quick succession. On August 7, Robert Nobel died of heart failure at sixty-seven. Then, on December 10, Alfred Nobel died, the result of a brain hemorrhage, at sixty-three. Ludvig's generation of Nobels would not see the twentieth century.

Though Emanuel was not close with his uncle Robert, he had

---

* In 1907 Shell would merge with Royal Dutch Petroleum Company, which was founded in 1890. The combined company, called Royal Dutch Shell Group, led by Henri Deterding, became a major player in the petroleum markets prior to the Great War.

† The Suez Canal Company was a joint French-Egyptian enterprise that owned and operated the canal, and granted concession rights for passage, from its opening on November 17, 1869. The Egyptian government sold its stake in the company to Britain in 1875. Eventually the Egyptian government nationalized the canal in July 1956. Passage through the canal reduces the distance from the Arabian Sea to London by 5,500 miles. Construction of the canal took ten years.

maintained a personal and professional relationship with Alfred. The dynamite tycoon had left France and had been living in Italy for the last five years.* Emanuel had learned that Alfred was sick on December 8 and raced to San Remo but did not arrive in time to say goodbye.

Living far from Baku, both uncles had been removed from the operations of the business for years, though Alfred had been a steady source of counsel. Emanuel was saddened by their passing, but the real distraction for him was in handling the enormous fortune left by Alfred—33 million kronor, the equivalent of more than $2 billion today.†

To complicate matters, Alfred had taken the unusual step of completely rewriting his will in his own hand only a year before his death, without retaining a lawyer, in a document dated November 27, 1895, that he signed in Paris in front of four witnesses.

In what has become a famous and consequential term of the will, Alfred directed that the bulk of the inheritance should establish a fund, "the interest on which is to be distributed annually as prizes to those who, during the preceding year, have conferred the greatest benefit to humankind": the Nobel Prize.

Of Alfred's 33 million kronor, 31 million went to the prize. Two million went to private individuals, mainly spread among Robert's and Ludvig's children. All of Robert's children disputed the will, as well as Emanuel's sister-in-law Mary, the widow of his brother Carl.

---

* Alfred had sold patent rights to manufacture Ballistite, an explosive war material, to the Italian government in 1889. The sale started a press campaign against him in France, and in 1891 the government accused him of treason and threatened him with prison. Alfred bought a large villa in San Remo that same year and made it his new home.

† If simply adjusting for inflation, 33 million kronor equates to about $100 million, but adjusting for inflation always undervalues the historical amount. Methods that value wealth as a percentage of GDP, or that compare wealth to the average national salary of the period, value Alfred's estate at about $2.5 billion. Robert Nobel's estate was worth 1.5 million kronor and he left nearly all of the estate to family, so his heirs were already very rich at the time of Alfred's death. Alfred was still alive for the reading of Robert's will, and Alfred expressed his opinion of the dispiriting effects of inherited wealth and his disappointment that Robert did not leave a greater percentage of his estate to charity.

The family squabble turned ugly. As patriarch of the family, it would have been much easier for Emanuel to appease his relations, but he felt a responsibility to make certain that his uncle's clearly expressed final wish came to pass. The literal translation of the Russian word for the executor of a will is "agent of the soul." Emanuel took the duty to heart and intended on honoring his uncle's wishes. As a leader, Emanuel could be both lighthearted and firm. Within the family, he was a renowned practical joker, often presenting gag gifts and pulling pranks. Yet he was devoted to family in all ways, both playful and serious, and when it came to matters of duty and honor, he was fiercely committed.

Emanuel's cousins opposed his intention to enforce Alfred's terms. They wanted the fortune they had expected to inherit. The issue was so convoluted, and the Nobel family name was of such a high profile, that the allocation of Alfred's fortune became a media sensation. The details of the will leaked to the newspapers. On January 2, 1897, the Swedish newspaper *Nya Dagligt Allehanda* was the first to report Alfred's design for the prizes, which included the total amount bequeathed to establish the prize as well as the amount of cash dispersed annually for each recipient. The numbers staggered the public. Never before had a prize existed on such a scale. Reporters delighted in the comparison that Nobel's prizes would establish an Olympic Games for human achievement. (The first modern Olympics had been held in Athens the previous summer.)

While there was terrific excitement for the prizes, the family's legal challenge to the will had not been resolved. Emanuel was furious about the leaked information, as the dispute now had to play out in public. Alfred's prizes were already famous, yet they didn't exist, and until Emanuel could resolve the challenge to Alfred's will, there was no clear legal basis to create them. The contention became so hot, and was now a matter of such international interest, that the King of Sweden got involved.

Sweden's King Oscar II summoned Emanuel to the palace in

Stockholm on a frigid day in February. The King encouraged Emanuel to declare Alfred's will invalid, to take care of his siblings' and cousins' interests rather than fund Alfred's fantastical idea. The frustrated King complained to Emanuel: "Your uncle was influenced by peace fanatics." The King said that such fanatics argued for the establishment of international organizations to enforce peace and justice and that such organizations contravened a nation's sovereignty. (Oscar was referring to Alfred's correspondence with peace activist Bertha von Suttner, who was then editor of the international pacifist journal *Die Waffen nieder!* [*Down with Weapons!*]. In 1905 she would become the first woman to win the Nobel Peace Prize.) Despite the King's intimidating home-court advantage and his fervent wish to prevent the creation of the prizes, Emanuel held firm. Standing before Oscar II, he replied, "Your Majesty. I do not wish to expose my siblings to the risk of being reproached in the future by highly deserving scientists for having appropriated to themselves funds that rightfully ought to have come to the scientists." Emanuel departed the palace, leaving an extremely dissatisfied king in his wake.

Back at the hotel, Emanuel's Russian valet learned of the nature of Emanuel's unyielding response to the King. The valet knew how Russian tsars typically responded to subjects who did not yield—death or Siberia. Terrified by Emanuel's report, the valet immediately began packing bags for a hasty departure from the hotel and an escape from Sweden. But Emanuel did not flee the country, nor did the valet after a reassuring word from Emanuel.

Instead, Emanuel went on the offensive on behalf of his uncle. He gathered his extended family and made a persuasive speech in support of Alfred's design. He reminded them of Alfred's sense of charity, his intention to reward achievement, his wish to promote the betterment of humankind. Emanuel won them over. One cousin in attendance later recalled that "the young ones felt themselves inspired by Emanuel's idealistic view of their uncle's will and agreed . . . an agreement they never needed to regret."

As Emanuel played offense in his role as Alfred's "agent of the soul," he also needed to play a bit of defense. A letter had arrived soon after Alfred's death from a lawyer in Austria. Via Alfred's appointed law firm, the letter reached Emanuel, who read that the Austrian lawyer represented Sofie Hess, now forty-one, a divorced mother who had been pawning jewelry to make ends meet. Her near-eighteen-year relationship with Alfred had ended shortly before his death, and she naturally resurfaced amid the media craze surrounding Alfred's fortune.

Through her lawyer, Sofie informed Emanuel that Alfred had recognized her as his wife during their relationship, that she therefore had a rightful claim to a portion of the inheritance, and that she would pursue her claim in court. She also had come to understand Emanuel's character well enough to recognize his pressure points. Sofie had saved a trove of letters written to her by Alfred. Making a threat that could not be misunderstood, she expressed her concern that her financial situation was so dire that she might be forced to sell Alfred's letters for publication.

Sofie's threat worked. Emanuel had every reason to believe that these letters would be deeply embarrassing and possibly legacy altering to his uncle. Acting to protect Alfred, Emanuel wrote to Ragnar Sohlman, who was directing the purse strings of the estate, to pay twelve thousand Austrian florins (more than $100,000 today) for the acquisition of Sofie's stash of letters. Yet another step taken by the dutiful nephew to ensure that his uncle's name remained untarnished.

It is ironic that the entire world has come to revere the name Alfred Nobel over the last century while so few people know the name Emanuel Nobel at all. The Nobel Prizes and Alfred's shining legacy exist only because of the combination of Alfred's will and Emanuel's resolve to enforce it, a resolve that required him to defy family and a king, to resist personal greed and silence a hustler. When Emanuel had written to Sohlman to direct the purchase of Sofie's letters, he explained that he felt it was his obligation "to see to the good reputation of the deceased."*† Emanuel, though childless, was the father figure of the Nobel family.

The year 1896 also commenced the reign of a new leader for the Russian people, and for a moment the future of the empire seemed promising. The preparations for the coronation of Nicholas II took about a year. Over the course of those many months, the Russian public took warmly to the young, new Tsar. Unlike Alexander III, who inherited the throne due to the murder of his father and with the sound of exploding dynamite still ringing in his ears, Nicholas came to the throne after his father died of natural causes. In the absence of an assassination, the empire experienced a rare peaceful transfer of power. The public believed Nicholas might not rule with such repressive and paranoid intensity as his father had. The new Tsar's calm and gentle demeanor seemed to foster this hope.

Nicholas moved his primary residence back to Saint Petersburg. He walked freely in the streets of the city without pomp and ceremony, and without a massive retinue of guards. With his ministers he was affable, polite, and respectful and demonstrated polished manners that would impress foreign diplomats representing the great powers of Europe. But these were early and untested days.

The coronation took place in May 1896. Though the Russians seemed to embrace the new Tsar, they were suspicious of his German-born wife, Alexandra. She was born Princess Alix of Hesse and by Rhine and had initially refused to give up her Lutheran faith for

---

* Emanuel and Sohlman managed to keep Alfred's relationship with Sofie Hess a secret for more than fifty years. Only a handful of people had known of Alfred's intimate relationship. In 1948, years after Emanuel's death, Sohlman published his book *The Will*, in which he revealed the existence of Sofie Hess. News of a female companion was surprising to Nobel historians. The Hess letters had been sealed rather than destroyed (Emanuel's direction in his letters to the estate had been to destroy the letters). In the 1990s more of the Hess letters were published, which give a fuller understanding of the transactional relationship between Alfred and Sofie.

† Alfred had recently written a complete draft of a play called *Nemesis*. Alfred's ambition had been to write a published literary work, which he considered to be a great badge of honor. Emanuel saw to the publication of *Nemesis*, posthumously giving his uncle this distinction.

Russian Orthodoxy, a requirement of the marriage. Even Alexander III had opposed the match for his son and relented only in his final weeks as his health failed. In equal measure, Alexandra's grandmother, Queen Victoria, opposed the match because she personally disliked both Alexander III and his heir. But in the end, the two had fallen in love, and the marriage went forward.

The royal couple arrived at the Cathedral of the Dormition in Moscow for the coronation.* Camille Cerf, a Belgian journalist, filmed the event—the first-ever film produced in Russia. Muscovites painted and whitewashed buildings and draped the Russian flag from windowsills. The bells from every church throughout Moscow tolled, creating a celebratory atmosphere, the cacophony of chimes pealing through the air. God's appointed leader on earth crossed the threshold of the cathedral to the salvo of an eighty-five-gun salute.

Inside, at the center of the cathedral, Nicholas and Alexandra ascended twelve steps to a specially built platform where they sat on the imperial thrones. Nicholas sat on the Diamond Throne, nearly the entire surface area encrusted with gems, including 870 diamonds. The armrests alone boasted 85 diamonds, 144 rubies, and 129 pearls. Next to her husband, Alexandra sat on the Ivory Throne, acquired from Byzantium in 1472 by Ivan the Great.

Two metropolitans (the spiritual heads of the Russian Orthodox Church, similar to bishops) oversaw the traditions of the ceremony. Nicholas's coronation day would be the most lavish of any of the tsars. Of the several crowns from which to pick, the royal couple used the nine-pound Great Imperial Crown of the Russian Empire made in 1762 for Catherine the Great. The crown featured an enormous uncut ruby. Set in an arch spanning the top of the head and in a band around the circumference of the head were forty-four diamonds, each an inch across.

* Though Peter the Great moved the capital to Saint Petersburg in 1712, the coronation ceremony continued to take place in the ancient city of Moscow. The first ceremony, then called a "crowning" of the tsar, was in 1547. When Peter the Great established Russia as an empire, the ceremony became known as a coronation.

Nicholas wore the heavy necklace of the Order of Saint Andrew, a symbol of the tsar's omnipotence. The couple was surrounded by long-bearded priests wearing gold-laced robes while much of Europe's royalty looked on. By tradition, the tsar places the crown on his own head. As the metropolitan approached his majesty with the crown resting on a red pillow, the latch of Nicholas's heavy necklace gave out and the jewelry dropped to the floor with a clang that echoed through the cathedral. Both Nicholas and the metropolitan froze. Nicholas fell into a sort of trance, his eyes fixed on a spot above the heads of his subjects. After a painful moment, a courageous courtier gathered the necklace, then Nicholas came to, reached for the crown, and placed it on his head.

Russia's many believers in symbols and mysticism who saw this as a bad omen did not have long to wait for their dire predictions to take shape. Four days after the coronation, Russians enjoyed a national holiday in honor of the new Tsar, and Nicholas II sponsored a public celebration in Khodynka Field, an open expanse of several square miles just northwest of Moscow. Open-air theaters, circuses, carousels, swings, and music accompanied by free food and drink brought multitudes of people. By the afternoon, nearly half a million subjects packed the area on a hot and windless day.

The crush of people led to a panic, then the panic led to a stampede, in which throngs of terrified people were at the mercy of the current of the mob like a herd of wildebeest. Many fell and were trampled, and by the time the hysteria subsided more than a thousand people were dead (unofficial estimates were as many as four thousand dead).

Whether officials underreported the extent of the carnage to Nicholas, possibly so as not to spoil his happy coronation week, is unclear. What is fact is that a string of coronation events, including a ball at the French embassy that same evening, continued as planned with the Tsar in attendance. To the public, Nicholas II seemed unmoved by his subjects' tragedy, and popular sentiment began to turn against the newly crowned Tsar.

As Nicholas II faced these first tests of his reign, his ministers knew that behind the polite manners and simple charm Nicholas was an inept leader. Emanuel's relationships with the ministers surrounding the Tsar remained strong, but the overall competence of the government seemed suddenly compromised at a time that coincided with unprecedented popular unrest. Industrialists prefer political and economic stability. Nicholas II seemed poised to deliver neither.

CHAPTER 8

All Roads Lead to Baku

THE CORONATION CEREMONY in Moscow was a source of disdain to those living in the southern cities of Tiflis and Gori, which had become part of the Russian Empire only with the annexation of Georgia decades before.

Stalin, still going by either his birth name Jughashvili or by one of various nicknames that he'd taken or been given, was getting a bit old to be a student at the seminary in Tiflis, having repeated a year. Enrolled at the seminary in 1897 at nineteen, he began to show signs of evolving from a rebellious schoolboy into a true revolutionary. He smuggled in banned books by authors whose works explored themes of corruption and political repression, such as Hugo, Zola, Balzac, Thackeray, Gogol, and Chekhov. He read and heavily annotated Dostoevsky's novel of revolutionary conspiracy, *The Devils*. He became obsessed with Alexander Kazbegi's novel *The Patricide*, in which a ruthless Georgian bandit named Koba is the hero for fighting the Russians and defending Georgia's honor. In reference to the hero, Stalin began to call himself Koba and encouraged others to call him the same. Another identity added to his long list of aliases.

After reading the books and memorizing passages, he would share the books with other students, at great risk to all. The seminary priests were ever watchful, one in particular, Father Abashidze, whom Stalin had nicknamed "The Black Spot."

Through a series of quiet introductions within the seminary and beyond, Stalin met "Silva" Jibladze and Noe Jordania, who had just completed prison sentences for the crime of revolutionary activity. The two had founded a Georgian socialist party in Tiflis called the Third Group and published the newspaper *Kvali*, which espoused Marxist doctrine. Throughout Europe the autocracies and constitutional monarchies continued to resist socialist ideas and worked to marginalize the social democratic movement. There was still no example of a Marxist government in practice anywhere in the world.

Stalin began to take stealth meetings with Marxist activists around the city in out-of-the-way workshops and, frequently, inside a nearby cemetery. He sought to ingratiate himself with the fomenting Marxist movement in Tiflis, offering to write pieces for *Kvali*.

In May 1899, Stalin's antagonistic relationship with the priest he'd nicknamed The Black Spot caught up with him. He was expelled from the seminary and would never return. The reason for his expulsion is unclear. It could have been because of his revolutionary behavior or simply that he had missed several exams. Stalin later claimed that the seminary increased the cost of tuition and he had refused to pay it. In any event, the seminary did not put Stalin on a path to God, but it did arm him with a valuable, classical education that helped him become a skilled communicator of both the written and spoken word.

No longer a student, Stalin went to work. His first job was to be a weatherman, a meteorologist at the Tiflis Meteorological Observatory.* In his time away from the observatory, his primary occupation was to

---

* There is no connection between Stalin's first job as a weatherman and the militant Marxist/Communist group the Weather Underground (originally known as the Weathermen). The Weathermen's founding documents were based on Lenin's theory of imperialism; however, the group took its name from Bob Dylan's "Subterranean Homesick Blues," which includes the lyric "You don't need a weatherman to know which way the wind blows."

foment unrest. Only months after his seminary expulsion, Stalin and his cohorts organized their first strike. The city tram workers walked off the job, which brought the Georgian capital of Tiflis to a standstill for a day. The success of the strike earned Stalin his first arrest. The Tsar's secret police were able to pressure a tram worker into informing on the strike organizer. After a brief incarceration, Stalin returned to the Tiflis streets. He appeared each day in his signature black satin shirt, red tie, and scruffy beard with long hair and scuffed shoes. With the belief that sometimes looking the part can get you the part, he was a poster boy for revolution. His fervent, persuasive, well-constructed, and sometimes impromptu discourses on Marxist theory earned him yet another nickname. Stalin's semiliterate audience began to refer to him as "the Priest."

The secret police photographed Stalin and kept him under surveillance. Files in the police archive reported, "Jughashvili is a Social Democrat and conducts meetings with workers. Surveillance has established that he behaves in a highly cautious manner, always looking back while walking."

With the police so closely monitoring his activity, the Priest decided it was time to go underground. He was twenty-one years old. As the calendar turned to the twentieth century, Stalin fled Tiflis and took the road to the oil fields of the increasingly vital city of Baku.

Emanuel's half sister Marta was about the same age as Stalin. As the new century saw Stalin move to Baku, Marta in Saint Petersburg was determined to go to medical school.

For a woman at that time, a higher education of any kind, let alone in medicine, was nearly unheard-of, and Marta found little support for her plans from her mother and siblings. Marta was an exceptional student, and in 1901, at age twenty, against her mother's wishes, she applied to Saint Petersburg's Medical Institute for Women. The institute had been founded only four years earlier by Nicholas II's private physician, and it was the first medical school for women anywhere in Europe.

To Marta's great disappointment, the school rejected her application. She appealed to Emanuel, now forty-two, who was also her guardian. Emanuel supported his determined half sister, and in 1902 Marta applied again, this time including a letter from Emanuel that recommended her admittance. In the autumn of 1902, Marta began her studies.*

These years saw the firm's oil production rise to new heights under Emanuel's leadership. The operational efficiencies of Nobel Brothers combined with the entry of the Rothschilds and Shell meant that oil producers were extracting the abundant reserves of the Caucasus at a record pace and were shipping unprecedented quantities to international markets.

These years also saw a shift in the demand for petroleum. A reliable source of illumination was critical for human comfort and productivity, and therefore nations considered access to kerosene, the most efficient fuel for illumination, to be of strategic value. But by the turn of the century, the advent of electric lighting—a cleaner, safer, and all-around better source of illumination—began to replace kerosene-burning lamps and reduce global demand for kerosene fuel. The remaining market demand would be mostly for industrial lubricants.

This was a potentially catastrophic development for Rockefeller, Rothschild, Nobel, and the entire petroleum industry. Electricity might do to petroleum what petroleum had done to the whaling industry. But just as the demand for petroleum-fueled illumination waned, a new source of demand for petroleum appeared: the combustion engine. The demand came in two primary forms.

The external combustion engine had been in wide industrial use since the days of James Watt in the late eighteenth century. Burning wood or coal to produce steam, the external combustion engine pow-

---

* Marta earned her degree in January 1909 with high marks. She became a major benefactor of the school and paid for the construction of several new buildings. In her medical practice, she concentrated on radiology and skeletal damage, and she made enormous contributions to the medical care of wounded Russian soldiers during the Great War.

ered ships and trains, as well as inland factories. By the late nineteenth century, engineers had developed a new steam engine that burned fuel oil rather than coal. Installed in ships, these updated engines performed remarkably better than the steam engines of the previous century. Great Britain, which boasted the world's greatest navy as well as the greatest merchant marine fleet, led the way in upgrading the old coal burners to engines that burned fuel oil. Every new ship built around the world needed the more efficient, fuel-oil-burning steam engines. The engine conversion of ships represented an important new form of demand for petroleum.

Even more demand for oil was driven by the arrival of the internal combustion engine for commercial use. It was never practical for a motorbike or automobile to use an *external* combustion engine—what with its large coal-burning furnace that heated the water inside a large boiler to steam that moved the heavy gears of an engine. Only a massive ship, train, or factory floor could support such a behemoth. For a motorbike, there needed to be a much lighter and more compact power source.

The *internal* combustion engine didn't require a furnace or a boiler filled with water. It didn't require a chimney stack or need to burn coal or wood as its fuel. The compact internal combustion engine, developed by Nicolaus Otto and others in the late 1800s, burned a gaseous or liquid fuel directly inside the cylinder of the engine. But the engines of these decades were puny and provided little horsepower. As the 1900s progressed, the power and efficiency of the internal combustion progressed. Men like Karl Benz, Wilhelm Maybach, Ferdinand Porsche, and Henry Ford began to install internal combustion engines in their automobiles. The preferred fuel for the engines was gasoline, a distillate of petroleum. Gasoline was a product that refineries already knew how to make because, in a comic twist, refining petroleum to kerosene also produced gasoline, which, until the time of the internal combustion engine, was treated as a nuisance by-product and thrown away.*

---

* Global demand for gasoline surpassed demand for kerosene in 1919.

Though America had been the world's primary source of fuel for decades, the turn of the century saw a previously unimaginable milestone. In 1891, Standard Oil by itself had accounted for seventy-seven percent of the world's refined oil, but in 1901 Russia produced more than America. Baku produced 11.8 million tons of oil, while the United States produced 9.2 million—the rest of the world's producers combined accounted for only 1.7 million tons. America was no longer number one. A dozen years into the role of chief executive, Emanuel accomplished what had been only a dream for Ludvig and Robert.

Nobel Brothers and the Rothschilds began to work more cooperatively to bring the growing quantity of oil to markets in a profitable way. For the German market, they signed a joint distribution agreement to coordinate sales. In England, the two Russian-based firms organized a new company to act as the joint sales agent for the territory. For lubricating oils (as opposed to those for illumination), over the course of several meetings in Paris led by Emanuel, he and the Rothschilds organized the Société Anonyme d'Armement, d'Industrie et de Commerce (SAIC), with headquarters in Antwerp, Belgium, to manage all European sales of lubricating oils. Nobel Brothers was the largest shareholder, and its share combined with the Rothschilds' was a majority.

The sales collaborations had immediate effect. In 1900, Nobel Brothers paid a record-breaking twenty percent dividend, three times better than what the company considered to be a good year only ten years before. The momentum in Baku reignited the stalled discussions with Standard Oil for a union of companies to organize the global market. The primary players in the renewed conversations were Standard Oil and Nobel Brothers. Rothschild was a significant company, but Nobel was the dominant force in Europe and all parties knew it. James MacDonald represented Standard and Hans Olsen represented Nobel Brothers. The two men began to sketch an idea to bring the two giants together.

In January 1903, MacDonald and Olsen reported to their respective headquarters with a plan to form a new corporation through an exchange of shares. MacDonald got a thumbs-up from 26 Broadway. Olsen got a thumbs-up from Emanuel.

In February, Nobel joined Olsen in Berlin for a critical meeting with MacDonald and his colleague William H. Libby. A merger of the top two global petroleum firms would be epoch-making. Standard's bookkeepers dug into the asset values and balance sheet of the Nobel holdings. The parties had to agree on the value of the Nobel shares for the exchange. Emanuel agreed to an audit of his company's assets, then the parties would reconvene in Berlin.

The audit concluded in July. The result was a pleasant surprise for Emanuel and an outright shock to Libby and Standard. The auditors determined that the value of the Nobel shares was nearly ten times the current market value on the public exchange. While Emanuel would agree to a share exchange at the audited price, the level was far above what Standard had expected to pay. Libby did not counter-propose, nor did Emanuel budge. Nobel Brothers was thriving, and—given Emanuel's cozy relationship with Count Witte, Russia's finance minister—he felt that his connections within Russia gave him sufficient advantage.

Just as the new century saw Nobel Brothers bring Russia's petroleum industry to a world-leading position, the Nobel factory in Saint Petersburg helped bring forth Russia's modern industrial era. Emanuel's primary office and residence were in Saint Petersburg, and he had continued to oversee the operations of the factory since the death of his younger brother Carl. In those years he'd made remarkable technical advances, especially with the Diesel engine, a revolutionary internal combustion engine developed by the German inventor Rudolf Diesel.

As the ice thawed on the Volga River in the spring of 1903, Nobel Brothers launched the world's first Diesel-powered tanker. Called *Vandal*, this barge could travel in water as shallow as eight feet. Though it was not an oceangoing vessel, it was perfect for lakes and the river systems of Russia. The ship held seven hundred fifty tons of kerosene and led the way for a transformation not only of the distribution of petroleum products, but of the entirety of merchant shipping. The world's fleet of cargo ships had used steam power for decades, but even for those converted to fuel oil, the engine efficiency was poor, and therefore the ships required frequent stops to acquire more fuel, and the engines themselves required frequent maintenance and refitting of the pipes that conducted the steam pressure.

The Diesel engine was compact in size—without furnace, boiler, or chimney—and the fuel efficiency was a multiple better than steam, such that a Diesel-powered cargo vessel of the early twentieth century could circumnavigate the globe without a stop for fuel. The engine maintenance record was perhaps the best perk of all—Diesel ships often traveled hundreds of thousands of miles without the need for repair.

Diesel engines seem the obvious choice in retrospect, but there were few early supporters of the technology. It would be remarkable enough for Nobel Brothers to have been the first of the petroleum companies to make the bold move to Diesel power for its fleet, but Emanuel did much more than that. He was the Diesel pioneer across all industry—marine and inland use—and for all Russia and beyond. Emanuel had a lifetime of education in entrepreneurship. Initially by his father's side, then alone, he had learned to evaluate opportunity and risk, to make the investments that would keep him ahead of the market.

Six years earlier, Emanuel had never heard of Diesel engines, or Rudolf Diesel. But he had sent one of his talented engineers, Anton Carlsund, on a trip to France and Germany to study new engine technologies, in particular those that could use oil as fuel. In Kassel, Germany, Carlsund attended a lecture by Rudolf Diesel about his remarkable new engine.

Six months later, Nobel and Diesel scheduled an afternoon session to discuss a partnership. Diesel remarked that Emanuel was "a considerate and noble-minded man of imposing, important appearance, with a face framed by a short, grey beard." Though Diesel found Nobel to be a man of deep thoughts and few words, he gleaned that Emanuel recognized the tremendous value of the new engine technology for his petroleum business, for his factory in Saint Petersburg, and to the advancement of Russian industry as a whole. Nobel paid 800,000 marks for the exclusive rights to the Diesel patent in Russia.

One of Emanuel's first Diesel installations pumped oil through a pipeline connecting the Caspian Sea with the Black Sea. He also built Diesels for textile plants in Tsaritsyn, factories in Saint Petersburg, and power plants in Astrakhan, Cherson, Korno, Kozlov, Livadia, and Moscow. Smaller Diesels powered flour mills around the Russian countryside. Even more impressive were the achievements of Nobel's factory with Diesel power for marine use. Nobel's engines soon powered the Tsar's warships as well as a new fleet of merchant ships for Nobel Brothers that was second in size only to the Imperial Russian Navy.*

The Nobel businesses continued to expand rapidly. Count Witte, and therefore Nicholas II, proudly pointed to this Russian-owned superpower as an example of a domestic firm that could not only compete on the world stage but could best the most famous corporations from Europe and America. But a stable political environment is important for success in business, and the winds of dissent were beginning to blow harder in Russia. As Ludvig had predicted decades before, the greatest risk to Nobel Brothers would be political unrest that had little to do with any decisions that Emanuel might make in the boardrooms of Baku or Saint Petersburg.

The unrest was particularly intense in the Caucasus, where Nobel Brothers operated. This was largely due to the machinations of one

* Emanuel Nobel acquired the exclusive rights to the Diesel engine in February 1898. By 1910, Russia was the most "Dieselized" country in the world, behind only Germany. This was due entirely to Emanuel's pioneering efforts and the expertise in his Saint Petersburg factory. Emanuel also owned one of the world's only Diesel-powered yachts, the *Gryadoustiy* (the *Future One*), one hundred feet long, with the design of a small destroyer and two 450-horsepower Diesels. Emanuel sometimes used the yacht, which could reach thirty miles per hour, to impress naval officials who were potential customers.

man who had made the Caucasus his base of operations, who understood the oil business, and who understood that the ships and trains of the vast distribution network for petroleum products could be co-opted and used surreptitiously to disseminate his message.*

By November 1901, as Baku became the world's leading oil producer, Stalin had joined the newly formed Tiflis Committee of the Russian Social Democratic Workers' Party, and the committee dispatched him to the Georgian city of Batum on the Black Sea with the mission to agitate worker dissent.

In December he entered the small apartment he shared with his fellow revolutionary Constantine Kandelaki. According to the roommate's letters, Stalin said, "Guess why I got up so early this morning?" When Kandelaki shrugged, Stalin replied that he had taken a job with the Rothschilds. He would work for the hated oil magnates in one of their petroleum refinery storehouses by the port in Batum.

Days later, on January 2, 1902, the storehouse where Stalin worked went up in flames. A black plume of oily smoke stained the sky and darkened the entire city. The fire raged while the Rothschilds' workers fought to contain it. Eventually they put out the fire, and though the storehouse was a ruin, the fire had not spread to other buildings. As a company policy, the Rothschild firm owed a bonus to the workers who fought the fire, yet the Rothschilds' French manager was certain that the fire was a result of arson, likely set by some of the very same people who put it out, and he refused to pay the bonus. Of course, this was just the response Stalin had wanted all along.

He immediately went about organizing an oil workers' strike. He took the eleven-hour train ride back to Tiflis to acquire a printing

---

* Stalin's protégé Akaki Mgeladze wrote that Stalin had "great knowledge of the oil industry" and that he understood the importance of Baku. In 1942, as Hitler recognized he needed oil or he'd lose the war, he sent his armies toward southern Russia. The Germans needed to pass Stalingrad (Tsaritsyn before 1925). As historian Simon Montefiore remarks, "The result was the Battle of Stalingrad, which in effect was the battle for Baku." Fearing the Nazis would break through to Baku, Stalin told his deputy oil commissioner, "Hitler wants the oil of the Caucasus. On pain of losing your head, you're responsible for ensuring no oil is left behind."

press so that he could print illegal leaflets in both Georgian and Armenian that he would use to expand the reach of his message. With a small band of assistants including Kandelaki, Suren Spandaryan, and a childhood friend known as Kamo, Stalin managed to bring Batum to a boil and force not only the Rothschilds but also Nobel to the negotiating table as the strike quickly affected more than one firm. On February 17, the Rothschilds and Nobel agreed to several demands, including a thirty percent pay raise. The strike was an enormous victory for the young revolutionary, but Stalin was only getting started.

Dressed in disguise, he and his partners continuously moved the printing press to new secret locations, sometimes the apartment of a sympathetic worker, sometimes an abandoned shack miles from the city, sometimes a cemetery, but always the press whirred with new messages urging workers to revolt. Stalin used the world-class distribution of the industrial giants against them, having workers carry bundles of leaflets onto the oil companies' trains and ships to disseminate them to the major cities of the empire. This distribution tactic confounded the Tsar's secret police, who couldn't understand how the same Marxist propaganda magically appeared across borders. At the time Stalin was spreading his writings, another illegal press that the socialists had code-named "Nina" propagated the Marxist writings of another revolutionary who had gained recognition. Vladimir Ulyanov, who had witnessed the execution of his older brother for plotting against Alexander III, was now thirty-two and for about a year had been using the name Vladimir Lenin. His charisma, his impassioned devotion to Marxist ideals, and his fiery speeches had made him a key figure in the Russian socialist movement.

Lenin and the Social Democrats ordered that the Nina printing operation be hidden in the Muslim quarter of Baku. It quickly became the largest underground printing press in the entire empire. Lenin's early teachings rolled off this press and into the hands of young Stalin and thousands of other eager revolutionaries.

The Rothschilds felt the sting of Stalin's success in Batum and responded six weeks after the arson. On February 26, they fired 389 workers deemed to be troublemakers. In reaction to the firings, the workers determined to strike and sent word for "Comrade Soso," the Priest.

Stalin arrived the following day from Tiflis and immediately organized demonstrations against the Rothschilds' BNITO. General Smagin, governor of the province, rushed to Batum with dozens of troops to quash the protests and on March 7 arrested several of the strike leaders, including Stalin's bodyguard. The general delivered the uncompromising message, "Back to work or Siberia."

Stalin was uncowed, and the following day he organized a protest outside the prison that held his comrades. The governor finally offered to meet with the demonstrators. Another of the strike leaders proposed that the workers should accept the offer of negotiation, but Stalin refused, adding, "You'll never be a revolutionary." Stalin had a much larger goal than a few workers' demands or lost jobs. He wasn't interested in small gains but in creating a larger conflict that could spread and increase the ranks of revolutionaries.

Several dozen Cossack troops* with bayoneted rifles guarded the prison. Stalin confronted them, flanked by his top lieutenants, and led a mob of hundreds of workers to the prison. Stalin called for his followers not to fear the rifles and bayonets and to storm the prison. He yelled, "Let's free our comrades!"

The crowd of striking employees from the Rothschild and Nobel firms moved in, their bravery fueled by their sheer numbers. The Cossack soldiers on horseback gripped their rifles and braced for a fight. Suddenly there was a loud disturbance from the prison. The prisoners had taken up the fight, and several had overcome the guards inside. The prison gate opened and several prisoners quickly escaped. The demonstrators raged and the Cossacks galloped into them. The mob grabbed at the passing horsemen and hurled rocks, pelting the soldiers and hitting the Cossack captain in charge. The soldiers shot into the

---

* Cossacks were semi-nomadic warrior tribes descended from the peoples of Ukraine and southern Russia, predominantly East Slavic Christians, who were generally loyal to the tsar.

air, hoping to check the frenzy. The galloping soldiers then retreated to re-form a line in front of the prison.

Stalin's voice again rose above the din, ordering the mob forward to free the remaining prisoners. The mob surged toward the troops. The Cossack captain gave the order. The rifles were unleashed. The repeating sound of gunfire mixed with panicked screams and the crying out of the wounded.

Stalin assisted one of the wounded, then escaped back to his apartment, avoiding capture. There he regrouped with his lieutenants, who reported thirteen dead and fifty-four wounded. All were distraught at the deaths of their friends and coworkers. All except Stalin, who was thrilled with what he saw as an important battle in the bigger picture. He told a comrade, "Today we advanced several years. We lost comrades but we won. The whiplash and sabre render us a great service, hastening to revolutionize any innocent bystanders."

Leon Trotsky, already a national figure of the social democratic movement with far greater fame than Stalin, had read some of Stalin's writings, and Stalin had read Trotsky's. Far in the north of Russia, Trotsky received word of the Batum Massacre of 1902 and remarked, "It stirred the whole country."

Stalin was quickly becoming Lenin's key man in southern Russia, though they had not met face-to-face. Stalin knew the Caucasus region, understood the mindset of the multitude of oppressed workers there, and had firsthand knowledge of the petroleum industry that was increasingly important to the Tsar and to all nations.

The secret police identified the Priest as the chief provocateur behind the Batum riots. Stalin went underground, and his hidden printing press worked more feverishly than ever. He operated the press in a friend's home, four miles outside Batum.

His host, Hashimi Smirba, remarked that the press had been running almost nonstop for days. Stalin took a leaflet from the top of a stack. He handed it to Smirba and said, "We're going to overthrow the Tsar, the Rothschilds and the Nobels." It must have sounded like unhinged thinking.

PART II

A WAR WOULD BE A VERY USEFUL THING

1904–1916

A war between Russia and Austria would be a very useful thing for the revolution, but it is not likely that Franz Joseph and Nicholas will give us that pleasure.
—Vladimir Lenin, 1913

CHAPTER 9

The Danger Is from Within

FORTY YEARS AFTER the Tsar Liberator's emancipation of the serfs, millions of unskilled and semiliterate Russians had moved to the cities. This created a bulging labor class that was, in general, either underemployed or cruelly employed. Across the empire, there was no more extreme example of these conditions than in Baku.

The oil boom in Baku was only thirty years old, coming just on the heels of emancipation, and hundreds of thousands of peasants had joined the rush to Baku for jobs in the refineries or on the thousands of derricks in the desert sands of the city outskirts. These jobs had grueling hours, low pay, and high death rates. Living conditions were ramshackle—groups of men sharing hastily built huts with dirt floors. The earth, air, and water were polluted with oil. Bribery, theft, and murder were rampant. In the pre-boom era of 1850, the population of the city was 7,500. By 1897, the population had ballooned to 112,253. Over the next three years, the population grew sixty percent to 179,133 and continued to soar in the new century.

The historian Simon Montefiore describes Baku at this time as equal parts Dodge City and medieval Baghdad, noting that "it was said there were only ten honest men in the entire city: a Swede—Mr. Nobel, of course—an Armenian and eight Tartars."*

Emanuel went to great lengths to develop a workforce that was content and productive within a region that was otherwise a hotbed of discontent. Unfortunately for him, even as he offered better terms of employment, there was no way to buffer the workers of Nobel Brothers from the disquiet among the rest of the community. Karl Hagelin, who oversaw Emanuel's Baku operations in the first years of the twentieth century, reported to Saint Petersburg headquarters that the Nobel employees were not inclined to strike, but after they and their families were threatened by professional agitators, they tended to go along.

When contending with foreign rivals Rockefeller and Rothschild, Emanuel had managed to turn competition into cooperation when possible. When cooperation was not possible, he made sure he had the upper hand both operationally and politically. But this was a different kind of risk to the Nobel empire. Emanuel's observation of Russia at this time was similar to Abraham Lincoln's observation of America decades before: "At what point then is the approach of danger to be expected? I answer, if it ever reach us, it must spring up amongst us. It cannot come from abroad. . . . [W]e must live through all time, or die by suicide." As with Lincoln's America, the only thing that could kill Russia was itself.

The death and rebirth of Russia were exactly what Stalin and Lenin intended. Weeks after the Batum riots, on April 5, 1902, the police caught up with Stalin, arresting him for the second time. The charge this time was "deliberate incitement to disorder and insubordination against higher authority."

Stalin simmered in a Baku prison cell for more than a year. Then, on July 7, 1903, the Tsar signed off on the police recommendation to sentence Stalin to an additional three years in Siberian exile.† Yet,

* Tartars were predominantly Sunni Muslims.

† In Trotsky's words, "The exile system was a sieve." From 1901 to 1916, Stalin would be arrested a total of nine times, exiled seven times, and escape custody eight times.

even with Stalin in custody, his disciples remained active, and that same month the Baku oil workers called another strike. Leaflets and word of mouth spread the movement like a virus throughout the Caucasus, and within days workers in Batum, Tiflis, Kiev, Ekaterinoslav, and Odessa put down their tools. It was the first general strike—meaning a strike across multiple industries—in the history of the Russian Empire.

The government spiraled into crisis. Nicholas removed Count Witte as his finance minister. The loss of this talented minister increased Russia's instability, a condition made even worse by the person Nicholas chose to replace him. Vyacheslav von Plehve, formerly the head of the Okhrana, the tsarist secret police, was a heavy-handed, aggressive nationalist and ardent supporter of the autocracy. Under his watch, the government hatched two disastrous schemes to combat the socialist revolutionary threat.

First, in February 1904, Russia went to war against Japan. Russia's presence in Manchuria and Korea had rubbed against the imperial interests of Japan for decades. The Tsar and Plehve felt a quick military victory over Japan would secure valuable territory and, more importantly, rally a sense of national pride that would distract his subjects from the domestic turmoil. However, this little war against what was thought to be a much weaker opponent turned out to be something far different from what Plehve and Nicholas II expected. A Japanese surprise attack on Port Arthur, a coastal Russian stronghold near the Korean Peninsula, resulted in the destruction of several of the Russian navy's most valuable ships. The Japanese followed up with a series of astonishing land and sea victories.

Emanuel, who was supplying the Russian military with munitions and Diesel engines, followed the news of these losses with trepidation. The last time the empire lost a major war, his family went bankrupt.

But Russia had massive scale and could absorb an enormous amount of punishment. Japan recognized that a prolonged war favored no one. Ultimately, a peace settlement was reached through negotiations hosted by the United States in New Hampshire, moderated by President Theodore Roosevelt.* The terms of the truce were relatively painless for Russia, thanks to the skilled diplomacy of Witte, whom the Tsar had wisely called back to service. Russia paid no monetary reparations, the Tsar's treasury was spared, and the government honored and paid contracts with Emanuel.

However, the international humiliation of the Russian military was resounding and served to worsen domestic disaffection. Plehve would not live to see the peace that resolved his botched war plans. After three failed attempts on his life, a fourth attempt killed him in July 1904 when a member of the Socialist Revolutionary Party threw a bomb inside the minister's horse-drawn carriage as he was traveling to meet the Tsar in Saint Petersburg.

This string of attacks on Plehve had been in part due to his authorship of the second ruinous scheme that he'd designed to curb domestic strife. Plehve wanted a scapegoat for the misery felt by the Russian people, and he used an apparatus of agitators who were as ruthless as the most extreme of the socialists. The Black Hundreds was an ultra-nationalist group that supported the House of Romanov. Their motto was "Orthodoxy, Autocracy, Nationality." Plehve had encouraged the Black Hundreds to subdue socialist agitators with violence. This fanatical group incited racially motivated attacks between Muslim Tartars and Armenians, conducted raids on socialist revolutionaries, and with fervent antisemitism carried out horrific pogroms against Jewish populations. There seemed to be a complete absence of a political center, as though the centrifugal force of a dizzying spin had forced ideologies to their edges, creating violent extremist groups on both the left and the right, a hallmark of political turmoil that echoes to the present day.

Stalin desperately wanted to be back in the Caucasus. In August 1903, during his Siberian incarceration, the Second Party Congress of

* In 1906, the year following the Treaty of Portsmouth that ended the war between Russia and Japan, Roosevelt won the Nobel Peace Prize for his mediation efforts, only the fifth year of the Nobel Prizes.

the Social Democratic Labour Party took place in London. Vladimir Lenin led the revolutionary faction in attendance, and Julius Martov led the rival, reform-minded group. These meetings, illegal in Russia, took place in cities throughout Europe where organizers felt they could safely convene. In London, the two powerful leaders disagreed on policy, and the result of the meeting was a formal split in the Social Democratic Labour Party that would define the order of socialism in Russia for years to come. Lenin and his followers formed the revolutionary Bolshevik Party, which translates to "members of the majority," and Martov formed the Menshevik Party, which translates to "members of the minority." The naming is ironic as the Mensheviks overall were greater in number, but at this particular meeting, Lenin's followers were in the majority and seized on the name.

Lenin worked to shore up his constituency.* In December 1903, Stalin received his first-ever direct contact from Lenin through the Siberian post. Motivated by his mentor, Stalin promptly escaped his Siberian prison and rode the Trans-Siberian Railway back to Tiflis in January 1904. Now an escapee constantly on the run from the Tsar's secret police, he used unconventional tactics to avoid detection. He found that the safest place to hide was a brothel, and when not in one of those, his usual method of finding housing was to exploit his charms to seduce a woman who would then be willing to take him in.

Moving from hideout to hideout, Stalin was back in Baku by the end of the year, where he led the region's next significant labor strike in December 1904. He roused an astounding forty thousand workers to strike, nearly all from forty factories in Baku, including those of Nobel and Rothschild. The strike extended from Baku to the nearby oil fields, where production was shut down and more than a hundred wells were set on fire.

---

* The Russian Empire sentenced Lenin in 1897 to three years exile in Siberia. In July 1900, Lenin left Russia for Western Europe, where he launched his newspaper *Iskra* (*The Spark*). He lived variously in Zurich, Munich, Paris, London, Krakow, Prague, and Copenhagen. Though his writings reached across Russia, aside from a trip to Saint Petersburg in 1905, from 1900 to 1917, Lenin spent hardly a day on Russian soil.

The strike was otherwise mostly peaceful, considering the size of the protests. Two weeks of negotiations between representatives of the oil producers and the workers led to what came to be called the Mazut Constitution, Russia's first-ever collective agreement. This bargain ensured a nine-hour workday (eight hours for those working the drilling rigs), an increase in pay, and four paid days off per month.

It was a peaceful solution in Baku, but the peace was incredibly short-lived. Almost simultaneously, in Saint Petersburg, on Sunday, January 9, 1905, a revolutionary-minded priest named Father Georgy Gapon led a procession of 150,000 workers toward the Tsar's Winter Palace. Intimidating in the sheer scale of the demonstration, the workers were otherwise nonviolent, singing hymns as they walked with Father Gapon to deliver a "Humble and Loyal Petition" to Nicholas II for changes in working conditions. This nonviolent entreaty would quickly become one of the most consequential events in the history of the empire.

As the enormous parade of workers approached the palace, Cossack troops blocked the way. Confronted by such massive numbers, the troops were anxious. They fired two warning salvos into the air, hoping to halt the march of the demonstrators. The rifle blasts gave pause to the front rows of protestors, but pressing behind them were enough people to populate two midsize cities, and the momentum of the crowd pushed them forward.

The rifle blasts seemed only to raise the stakes and anxiety of the moment. When the workers continued to advance on the greatly outnumbered Cossacks, the troops fired directly into the crowd, then charged forward, scattering the protestors. The hymn singing stopped as the unarmed protestors were cut down in the streets. Bullets and smoke added to the frenzy, and the smell of exploded gunpowder crept through windows around the city.

Revolutionaries named the day Bloody Sunday. In the course of events, the Tsar's troops killed two hundred peaceful protestors and injured hundreds more. It was another of the moments that Stalin hoped for. Word of the travesty spread quickly to the Caucasus, where

Stalin published en masse to his followers, "Workers of the Caucasus! The hour of vengeance is now!"

Unrest metastasized throughout the empire, including factions of the army and navy that were already aggrieved due to the disastrous outcome of the war against Japan. The Tsar's prestige was increasingly diminished. 1905 blossomed into a year of revolution. Strikes and demonstrations flared up in cities and towns throughout Russia; mobs stormed manor houses and burned palaces.

In Baku, the damage was catastrophic. Rioters destroyed more than a thousand oil wells. Infrastructure in the ports and refineries was devastated. In a matter of only weeks, the region's petroleum industry was crippled, decades of work leveled to the ground. Fortunately for Emanuel, Nobel Brothers suffered the least damage of the major oil producers, having been on good terms with both the Armenian and Turkish workers. Attacks on facilities owned by the Rothschilds were far more severe.*

Ethnic killing was unrestrained, with all attendant horrors. Armenians, many of whom had become economically successful in Baku's boom years, were a particular target. Roving hordes looked for Armenians and murdered them in cold blood. Thousands of armed Tartars controlled the streets and laid siege to the homes of Armenians, who locked themselves inside with their children. Within hours, or days, if need be, the Tartars would force them out and butcher them all, sadistically mutilating the corpses, then continue to hunt other Armenians in hiding.

Sergei Alliluyev, who would later become Stalin's father-in-law, wrote that it was the Black Hundreds who incited the ethnic violence, "stirring feuds by all sorts of tricks . . . [C]orpses lay about on roads . . . [S]oldiers and policemen stood about and watched the slaughter. The Black Hundreds then set fire to the oil wells and spread wild rumors that this had been done by the strikers . . . [T]he fires in the oil works

* Russia would never again lead the world in oil production, and nearly twenty years would pass before Baku reached its pre-1905 production levels.

became awe-inspiring, savage and untamable." Jews were also marked for particularly violent attacks, both by the revolutionaries and the counter-revolutionary Black Hundreds.

Stalin was in the thick of the carnage. At twenty-six, he led armed men for the first time, having formed a gang of Muslim warriors who killed and looted. He issued orders to steal printing equipment wherever possible.

Within months, even the slow-witted Nicholas II recognized that concessions needed to be made to restore peace and stability to his empire. On October 17, 1905, the Tsar reluctantly took the massive step of issuing the October Manifesto, which guaranteed to all Russians the civil liberties of freedom of speech, freedom of the press, and freedom of assembly. Importantly, the manifesto also established a legislative body to be popularly elected, called the Duma. The enactment of all future legislation required the approval of the Duma. This document marked the end of unlimited autocracy in Russia.

The manifesto satisfied the more moderate factions of the revolutionary movement. Violence abated and calm was restored. The Tsar had managed to blunt the efforts to topple him for the moment. Lenin traveled from Switzerland to Saint Petersburg late in 1905 to catalyze the movement with his furious charm, but he was too late. He had underestimated the value of a moment and how quickly it can pass. He and his lieutenants regretted the lack of a centrally planned and directed uprising. Lenin and Trotsky would come to refer to the 1905 revolution as a dress rehearsal. They did not intend to make the same mistake again. Given another opportunity, they resolved to be far more decisive and organized.

Though the streets of Russia's cities slowly returned to normal, the spirit of revolution was not dead. As with his grandfather Alexander II's initial reforms, Nicholas's concessions had put him on a difficult middle ground. The terms of the manifesto were too half-hearted to satisfy the most ardent socialist factions, yet they were clearly a sign of weakness that outraged the most conservative members of the empire, who felt that to liberalize the autocracy was to violate the will of God.

Lenin, Trotsky, Stalin, and their fellow Bolsheviks smelled blood in the water. For his part, Stalin advocated a boycott of the Duma election, claiming it to be a sham and a diversion from the revolution. He wrote, "Only on the bones of the oppressors can the people's freedom be founded—only the blood of the oppressors can fertilize the soil for the people's self-rule."

Lenin (the son of nobility) and Trotsky (born Lev Bronstein, the son of a wealthy Jewish businessman) tended to avoid such barbaric language. But for Stalin, the son of former serfs, barbarism was part of his cultivated image. As a policy matter, Stalin and Lenin were aligned on the principle of revolution, and Stalin led the ideological attack on the moderate Mensheviks, whose participation in the Duma process undermined the Bolshevik goal to end the monarchy altogether.

Revolutionary discourse remained illegal, but with the manifesto's decree for freedom of assembly came the legalization of political parties that refrained from revolutionary principles. The two most prominent legal parties to form in the wake of the manifesto were the Constitutional Democratic Party and the Union of October 17 (called the Octobrists). In general, these parties advocated for a system similar to what Alexander II had envisioned decades before: a market-driven business environment and a constitutional monarchy in which the Tsar could work in concert with an elected government body.

As the empire's most successful business owner, and apparently one of Baku's only honest men, Emanuel Nobel assisted with the founding of the Octobrist Party, became a member of the party's central committee, and served as treasurer. The mission was to work in collaboration with a reform-minded monarchy. Still friendly with the Tsar's ministers, Emanuel was more firmly than ever in the seat of Russian power. Yet Stalin's power was also growing, and the epicenter of power for both Stalin and Nobel was the volatile city of Baku. A collision between these two men was inevitable.

CHAPTER 10

The Second Baptism of Fire

Alphonse de Rothschild died in May 1905 in Paris. The French branch of the Rothschilds had pioneered the family investments in petroleum, and with the death of the patriarch their investments in Russia looked uncertain, particularly with the Tsar facing a possible revolution and Baku quite literally on fire.*

Additionally, while nearly all of Europe was hostile to Jews, Imperial Russia seemed to be especially antisemitic. The Rothschilds' financial might was frequently able to steamroll deeply felt prejudices against them, and often the Rothschilds were able to link their issuance of immense sovereign loans with a government's guarantee to repeal legislation that persecuted Jewish people. But operating a business was an uphill battle for Jewish owners in Russia. The Rothschilds' Russian assets were more susceptible to theft, sabotage, and a workforce that at

* The various branches of the Rothschild family often intermingled. Alphonse's father, James, had established the family's French branch and married his niece, Betty von Rothschild, who was the daughter of his older brother Salomon, founder of the family's Austrian branch. Alphonse followed in his father's footsteps by marrying his cousin Leonora de Rothschild, of the family's English branch.

times was all but uncontrollable. Against competition as capable as the Nobels, this was a formidable disadvantage.

Edmond de Rothschild, younger brother of Alphonse, now held the reins for the French branch of the family. Even though the Rothschilds had managed areas of collaboration with Emanuel Nobel, the gorilla of the Russian oil industry, Edmond was worried about other competition emerging. British petroleum firms were making an increased commitment to the Caucasus, and relations between the governments of Russia and Great Britain were warming, in part due to a mutual fear of Germany. The improved relationship eased the way for these British firms to compete in Russia's oil region. There was also the ever-present threat of Standard Oil, combined with the fact that exploration and drilling were getting more expensive because the easiest wells to reach had already been tapped. As the Rothschilds' old wells slowed in production, they needed to find new ones, and when they did, they found they needed to dig deeper to get the oil.*

Lending out the Rothschild box at the Paris opera to Russian ministers as well as paying cash bribes could not fully overcome endemic antisemitism. In late 1905 Edmond waved the white flag. He instructed Jules Aron, still in place as the Rothschild agent in the Caucasus, to approach Nobel Brothers with an offer to sell. Edmond believed it would be best to fold his interests into a firm that was better positioned to win and grow, so he structured the payment for the assets mainly in shares of the proposed new Nobel firm. Emanuel considered the offer but declined.

Emanuel believed that absorbing the assets would gain him nothing new. He already had market and trade agreements in place with competing firms, and to bring in the Rothschild infrastructure would create only duplication and confusion for his existing business. Though Edmund could not reach a deal with Nobel Brothers, late 1905 marked the beginning of the Rothschilds looking for an exit. Once again,

* From 1904 to 1907 the cost of drilling in Baku increased sixty-four percent.

Emanuel had rejected the offer of a rival to merge, believing in the future of the business he and his father had built.

Meanwhile, Stalin roamed the Caucasus, a bandit with a higher cause. Accounts of priests and merchants who met him, as well as the henchmen who rode with him in these years, give a sense of his movements. He smuggled stolen guns and cash to raise funds for the Bolshevik cause while also constantly relocating his illegal printing press to maintain the flow of revolutionary Marxist propaganda.

Stalin's work in the Caucasus gained him some reputation nationally, and in 1905 he received an invitation to attend the national meeting of the fractured Social Democratic Labour Party (now comprising the distinct factions of Bolsheviks and Mensheviks) as the Bolshevik representative for the Caucasus.

The meeting was set for December in Saint Petersburg. Details were kept secret to avoid interference by the Tsar's police. Leon Trotsky planned to attend. While Stalin operated mainly in the south, Trotsky, an even higher-profile figure within the party, operated mainly in the north. Trotsky was still a Menshevik at this time, and throughout Russia his oratory had made him the public face of socialism, perhaps even more so than Lenin. While many noted Stalin to be personally charming, with a beautiful singing voice and seductive ways, Trotsky was an international figure and had charisma on a far grander scale.

Stalin rode the train north to Saint Petersburg. Lenin also planned to travel to the capital for the meeting, and the two men would meet for the first time, but while they were en route the Tsar went on the offensive. Nicholas II had allowed greater freedoms regarding the press and public assembly, but this did not extend to revolutionary socialists. When Stalin disembarked in the capital, he was in for a surprise. Secret police had arrested Trotsky hours before and rounded up many of the senior members of both socialist parties. Stalin went, as instructed, to the offices of the Social Democrat newspaper *Novaya Zhizn* (*New Life*), but the police had already raided the building. The remaining revolutionaries had scattered throughout Saint Petersburg.

It took Lenin's wife two days to contact Stalin and provide him with cash, a code name, and a rail ticket to the new location for the party meeting, across the border in Finland. At that time, Finland was a semiautonomous duchy of the Russian Empire and was less under the thumb of the secret police, the Okhrana. Disguised as a teacher on a field trip, Stalin arrived in Tammerfors, Finland (now Tampere), on December 24. Stalin, then twenty-seven, would finally meet his mentor, who was still a young thirty-five.

Like the Scottish Highlanders disappointed to discover that William Wallace was not a colossus of a man, Stalin was initially disheartened to behold the small, stocky, balding leader of the Bolsheviks. But when Lenin took to the podium, he dominated the room. Along with the others, Stalin was captivated by Lenin's intellect, fierce pragmatism, and iron will. Stalin wrote that Lenin "thoroughly overpowered his audience, gradually electrified it and then carried it completely."

The participants still buzzed with the excitement of the uprisings back in January, and the forced concession of the Tsar to form a Duma. Before 1905, there had been only three countries in Europe that lacked a parliament: Russia, Montenegro, and the Ottoman Empire. Now there was a crack in the Russian autocracy and the socialists were split on how to press their gains. Stalin remained firmly of the opinion that negotiation and reform were antithetical to the movement.

Stalin was enthralled with Lenin, but not so much that he didn't voice disagreement on points of policy. When the congress raised the possibility of reuniting the Bolsheviks and Mensheviks to form a broader and stronger Social Democrat Labour Party, Lenin was open-minded and Stalin vocally opposed. When the congress raised the issue of participating in the Duma elections, again Lenin was open-minded and Stalin opposed. Stalin was not interested in compromise and stability. He wanted war and the annihilation of the autocracy.

Firing a direct shot at Stalin's theft and smuggling operations in the Caucasus, the congress voted to condemn the raiding of government arsenals as well as the robbing of banks and treasury transports. Such a resolution would never have happened if the prevailing sentiment was that the revolution was still on the upswing and that the Tsar could be deposed. Only Stalin and a minority continued to believe that a violent overthrow of the Tsar was possible. The majority looked only to solidify the gains already made. In the end, Stalin viewed the congress as a failure, that Menshevik moderation had prevailed. Some socialists appreciated his zealotry, but many began to fear it.

Stalin returned to Tiflis. Despite having failed to bring the leadership around to his point of view, his stature within the Bolshevik Party was on the rise. Then, only months after returning from his meeting with Lenin, his life added a surprising new dimension: he fell in love. For a man utterly dedicated to revolution and whose sexual encounters were typically ploys in the service of remaining hidden from the Tsar's police, a true romance was an unlikely occurrence.

The idea of Stalin having romantic feelings seems incongruous with his demonstrated ease with violence and death, but by all contemporary accounts he did fall deeply in love. On July 15, 1906, Stalin married his already-pregnant lover, Kato Svanidze. Because Stalin was still on the run as an escaped exile, the two married in secret in the middle of the night.

Kato was beautiful and educated. She worked as a seamstress. Her brother Alexander* was a Georgian Bolshevik and friend of Stalin's, and Alexander introduced the pair. Unlike the women Stalin met in his trysts in brothels or when he needed a roof over his head, Kato became a true companion. Stalin and Kato never legally recorded the marriage, but the police came to know of it nonetheless. Stalin continued his work in the revolutionary underground, but Kato was living out in the open. Four months after the marriage, the police arrested her on the charge of harboring a revolutionary.

Visibly pregnant, Kato spent six weeks in a cell, then the police

---

* Stalin ordered the arrest of Alexander Svanidze during the Great Purge of 1937, then had him shot in prison in 1941. Bizarrely, Alexander's son, Ivan, married Stalin's daughter, Svetlana, in 1962.

transferred her to a residence outside the prison, where she gave birth to a boy, Yakov, in March. By June, with mother and child out of police custody, Stalin relocated them just outside the Baku city limits in a small apartment he'd rented from a Turkish owner. Here Stalin got back to work, hoping to keep the fires of revolution burning.

By 1907, the tides of a political countermovement against revolutionary zeal had begun to settle in. The Tsar was back on firmer footing with the public. He had convened, dissolved, and reconvened the Duma. The reform-minded faction of the Social Democrats was prevailing over the extremist voices who were calling to burn it all down. The workers were largely back on the job, and the secret police under Prime Minister Pyotr Stolypin had the revolutionaries either on the run or so far underground that they were impotent. Lenin continued to write and preach from foreign cities. He argued fiercely against the labor unions forming in Germany. Though the new unions promoted benefits for the working class, Lenin aimed to eradicate capitalism, not evolve it. Working from distant Western Europe meant the Okhrana couldn't reach him, but also that he could not effectively reach the Russian people. He could not unleash his oratory skill to stir the crowds.

Only in Baku was there a bit of revolutionary heat still on the pan. The enormous disparity in wealth between the oil owners living in extravagant mansions and the densely packed workers who kept the wells drilling and the refineries pumping was stark, particularly in a city rife with crime that had a corrupt local police force and a population bursting out of insufficient infrastructure. Only in Baku did the revolutionary Bolsheviks outnumber the Mensheviks.

This was partly due to Stalin, who by 1907 was back on the Rothschild payroll, working in their refineries yet also robbing banks and payroll trucks as well as operating extortion and protection schemes to raise money for Lenin. But in the grand scheme of the socialist movement, this was small work done by a lone wolf.

From exile in Europe, Lenin felt dismay. He recognized that he'd missed the moment of the revolution, and he observed the work of

Stalin and his colleagues in Baku with only a glimmer of hope. He wrote of these men, "These are our last Mohicans of the political mass strike."

Stalin remained undaunted. He knew that just a few years before it was the strikes in Baku that had preceded the events of Bloody Sunday in Saint Petersburg. He felt he could again be the spark of revolution. Stalin wrote that this time in Baku "would be my second Baptism of fire."

In June, Stalin led a bank heist reminiscent of Billy the Kid and the Regulators. The Russian State Bank dispatched two mail coaches stuffed with cash for deposit at its Tiflis branch. Cossack guards on horseback surrounded the coaches, two in front, two in back, one on either side. Inside the coaches were two representatives of the bank along with a detachment of guards armed with rifles. Attempted robberies were common, especially in the Caucasus. The coaches carried 250,000 roubles in oil money.

Though Tiflis was the capital of Georgia, the city proper was quite tiny. One could walk from Stalin's childhood home to the seminary where he studied, over to the Viceroy's Palace, then to the bank in the center of town all in a few minutes. The roar of the horses' hooves announced the arrival of the cash. Dust kicked up by the horses drifted across the open town square as the two coaches slowed in front of the bank on Sololaki Street.

One of Stalin's henchmen, positioned out in the square, lowered his newspaper and tossed it to the side. The signal. The team of gangsters converged at once. From their coats they pulled "apples"—grenades that Stalin had smuggled into Tiflis. Four of these exploded underneath the coaches and tore into men and horses. Amid the deafening concussions and smoke, the gangsters stalked forward with pistols drawn and fired at the stunned Cossacks.

Passersby fled in a screaming panic, windowpanes around the square had shattered from the force of the bombs, more earthshaking blasts continued the delirium—in all more than ten bombs exploded. The square became more battle scene than bank heist. Stalin's men made off with the cash, leaving behind nearly forty dead and more than twenty wounded. Within days the cash had traveled the rails north to Lenin in Finland.*

While Stalin's ambition was to tear down, Emanuel's was to build. In Saint Petersburg, Emanuel was busy constructing "workers' suburbs" for his employees. Similar to Villa Petrolea that the Nobels had built in Baku, Emanuel developed a fifty-nine-thousand-square-meter site with thirteen residential structures as an extension of his machine factory in the capital. The workers came to call this Nobeltown. Emanuel opened a five-year school on Nystad Street (now Lesnoy Prospekt) for two hundred students, equally divided between boys and girls.

Stalin and Nobel were working toward diametrically opposed visions for Russia's future. As Stalin's men acted on behalf of the Bolsheviks to sabotage industrial property such as refineries in Baku, the Tsar's government appointed Emanuel to be the chairman of the Committee for the Protection of Industrial Property. Nobel now had a formal government title that put him in direct opposition to Stalin's looting and demolition.

The 1907 Tiflis heist was Stalin's most grievous act to this point. Mensheviks and other Social Democrats suspected that he had led the attack but could not confirm his involvement.† However, they felt certain enough that, as the most powerful Bolshevik in the region, Stalin had played some role, and they denounced him, hoping to hobble his political influence. This condemnation seemed to undermine Stalin's

---

* Under constant threat of banditry, the State Bank of the Russian Empire had marked the serial numbers of the five-hundred-rouble notes and sent the numbers to financial institutions around Europe. It is possible that Lenin was unable to use the cash. Trotsky later claimed that Stalin's heist "brought no good," though this might have been a reference to the political fallout from Stalin's aggressive act.

† After Gorbachev's perestroika, many archives in countries of the former USSR opened their doors, at which point researchers discovered new details of Stalin's early years that he had kept from the official histories of Communist Russia, including accounts of his involvement in the Tiflis heist. Stalin often dressed in women's clothing to escape manhunts, which, as the leader of all Russia decades later, was a past he surely hoped to erase.

national appeal and tarred him as a mere thug. But Stalin was content knowing that Lenin was pleased with his work.

In October 1907, with growing popularity among the Social Democrats of the Caucasus, and with Lenin's support, Stalin was elected to the Baku Committee. He also began the publication of the *Baku Proletarian*, writing his first articles using the Russian language rather than Georgian. There were likely two reasons for this shift. First, there were very few Georgian speakers in Baku, and of the many languages spoken in the eclectic city, Russian was the unifying one. Second, publishing in Russian was an effort by Stalin to assimilate with the leading revolutionaries. He hoped eventually to be considered in the same league as the dazzling and nationally esteemed Trotsky (still a Menshevik in the Social Democratic movement), rather than just a backwater Georgian who specialized in dirty work.

Amid these ambitions, Stalin faced a personal tragedy that further hardened him. Stalin's young wife, Kato, who had been frail, fell sick in Baku. In the toxic environment of the oil city, her health quickly worsened. By the time Stalin reached her bedside, she was hemorrhaging blood from her bowels. It was a gruesome and swift death. She died on November 22, 1907, at the age of only twenty-two.

Stalin was so distraught over the loss that his friends became alarmed by his behavior. Days later at the funeral service, a small group of comrades gathered by Kato's open grave. Stalin was beside himself, unsteady on his feet and openly weeping. Suddenly, he shed the embrace of his comrades, pushed them aside, and made for the casket. The group looked on in horror and dared not intervene as Stalin climbed inside the open grave and lay on the casket, crying out for his dead wife.

Friends eyed him nervously, more preoccupied with his state of mind than with the loss of Kato. In the days after her death, Stalin appeared so morose and capable of self-harm that his friends kept his guns hidden and wouldn't let him spend time alone. Stalin blamed himself for not having been by Kato's side in life, for not having taken better care of her, and for bringing her to the miserable heat and polluted air of Baku, which likely contributed to her poor health.

Stalin abandoned his eight-month-old son Yakov to be raised by Kato's family, and for about two months he went quiet and disappeared from the world. It was a rare inactive period. When he reemerged, his heart was perhaps stonier than before. After his time of mourning, he threw himself back into his revolutionary work with even greater zeal. He organized kidnappings and protection rackets in which he forced the managers of the oil fields to pay up if they wished to see their children make it home safely from school or ensure that their oil wells wouldn't catch fire. Stalin's criminal organization became more profitable than ever.

Via these sorts of protection schemes, it was the Nobels and Rothschilds who largely funded the Bolsheviks in Baku. The files of the Okhrana noted the details of Stalin's extortion of the oil tycoons, recording that he "concentrated on collecting donations and got money from Landau [managing director in Baku] of the Rothschilds."

Stalin planned several more heists in 1908, including robbing the steamship *Nicholas I* while she was at rest in Baku harbor, and traveled to Switzerland to meet Lenin to deliver news and cash. Some of the cash from successful heists he'd keep and spend on parties with his gangster friends. Eventually his celebrations drew some unwelcome police attention, and after four years of shadowy work while on the lam from the Tsar's police the Okhrana caught up with him.

On March 25, 1908, police in Baku arrested Stalin and took him to Bailov Prison, a two-story stone building in Baku, where other prisoners immediately recognized him. They feared him more than they feared the police. Stalin was placed in Cell 3 with the other Bolshevik prisoners and was atop the power hierarchy. Mensheviks were in Cell 7, and Stalin used his time in jail to network with other revolutionaries. He spent nearly eight months in the Baku prison awaiting exile orders. In November the order came down for a two-year sentence in a Siberian prison in Solvychegodsk. By February 1909 he had arrived in the barren wasteland.

Yet exile in the time of the tsars was typically not unbearable or a death sentence. It was nothing like the brutal gulags Stalin would create once he came to power decades later. Perhaps Stalin imposed a more murderous brand of exile because he recognized the dangers of the lighter touch under the tsars. Stalin's own period in exile, though incredibly boring and at times frigid, was otherwise not cruel. His fellow exiles were often university intellectuals or noblemen who were linked to sedition, and small groups would gather to read (often books smuggled in through bribed guards) and discuss revolutionary ideas. Stalin also enjoyed the company of multiple mistresses and fathered children while in Siberia. The Tsar even paid a stipend to the prisoners: twelve roubles for a nobleman (such as Lenin), eleven roubles for a university graduate, and eight roubles for a peasant (such as Stalin) to pay for clothes and food.

Stalin wouldn't stay comfortable in Siberia for long, however. He wanted to be home, and distance seemed only to fuel his wrath against the autocracy and the capitalists who thrived under it. He yearned for a time when he would no longer be a furtive, anonymous employee of oil tycoons like the Nobels and Rothschilds but could openly lead a force against them.

Russian newspapers published cartoons such as this poster from 1914 that mocked Rasputin's apparent dominion over Nicholas and Alexandra. These parodies contributed to the public's fear of the strange monk and general discontent with the Emperor and Empress.

CHAPTER 11

Rasputin

As THE FIRST decade of the century came to a close, Emanuel's primary business concern was the political instability of the Russian Empire. In his new role overseeing the protection of industrial property, he witnessed the constant harassment and sabotage of industry that was wrought by socialist agitators whose aim was to subvert the Tsar.

Emanuel was in good stead with the monarchy. Nicholas II remembered his visit to Baku as a teenager in 1888, when Emanuel had led the royal family on a tour of the city. In the years since, Emanuel had maintained a regular and friendly correspondence with Nicholas II's mother and widow of Alexander III, the Dowager Empress Maria Feodorovna. Emanuel knew that a stable monarchy, modestly reformed, would be good for business in Russia. But Nicholas II was not a strong monarch. As Nicholas's hold on power seemed at its weakest, one of the most peculiar figures in history appeared and would further unsettle the Tsar.

Stalin was not the only descendant of serfs educated by the clergy who would become an agent of chaos. From the vastness of Siberia came Rasputin, an oddball charlatan who would somehow walk the halls of the Winter Palace, to issue directives to senior ministers, to become close with the royal children and strangely intimate with the Empress.*

Future prime minister Alexander Kerensky later declared that without Rasputin there could have been no Lenin. Kerensky meant there could have been no revolution had the virulent monk not been let inside the royal household to disable it. Lenin himself later declared that the reason the nations of Western Europe were more resistant to revolution than Russia was because they had no one so unsuited for leadership as Nicholas II and Rasputin.

Grigori Rasputin was born to a peasant family in a small Siberian village in 1869. His father was a farmer and church elder. By his teenage years, he had a very athletic build, a handsome face, and a mane of thick black hair. His most remarked-upon features were his sparkling blue-gray eyes, which were frequently described as hypnotic.

Like nearly all Siberian peasants, he had little formal education. Yet from an early age Rasputin displayed a zest for exploration and storytelling. In his youth he made several short pilgrimages to neighboring communities, and his early commitment to religion seems to have been sincere. Through these journeys he acquired a small following as he enraptured audiences with sermons, refining his oratory skills to augment his natural charisma and arresting appearance. He was not altogether pious, however. Rasputin interspersed his pilgrimages with bouts of heavy drinking, petty theft, and an overactive sex life.

He married at eighteen and fathered seven children with his wife (only three survived to adulthood). Through the 1890s, Rasputin became fully committed to the life of a pilgrim, leaving his family behind for months or even years at a time as he traveled hundreds of miles on foot, building a reputation for himself as a *strannik* (holy wanderer). Around 1905, Rasputin arrived in Saint Petersburg, and by this time his *strannik* persona was fully developed.

---

* Most historians believe that the widespread rumors of a sexual relationship between Rasputin and the Empress were unfounded.

His hair was long, greasy, and unkempt. His robes were filthy, his body unbathed and foul smelling. Despite his off-putting looks and scent, he projected a rehearsed and dramatic veneer of profundity. Somehow, his repulsive appearance and holy bearing managed to confirm each other. In one of Rasputin's greatest feats of magic, he convinced the Russian aristocracy that smelling like a goat was part of his charm.

Perhaps this ruse was possible only in Russia, which was shrouded in paranoid mysticism, rumormongering, and religious conspiracy theories. In this context, the aristocracy of Saint Petersburg—especially those most pampered and bored—took up Rasputin and showed him off in their gilded salons as a sort of fascinating grotesque.

Rasputin quickly gained friends and followers in Saint Petersburg, mostly female, including two princesses who had married cousins of Nicholas II. These two, nicknamed "the Black Princesses" due to their interest in the occult, decided to introduce Rasputin to a besieged and vulnerable Tsar, who, in the autumn of 1905, was fresh from worker strikes and the humiliating defeat in Russia's war with Japan.

After the slaughter of Bloody Sunday and the agreement of concessions to Japan, both of which the public largely blamed on the Tsar, Nicholas decided he needed greater personal security. He moved his permanent residence from the Winter Palace to his palace in the beautiful surroundings of Tsarskoye Selo fifteen miles south because it was at a safe distance from the urban mob and more easily defended. Tsarskoye Selo was an isolated town founded by Peter the Great and augmented by his heirs, designed to be a fantastical world in miniature for the reigning monarch. It was full of monuments, triumphal arches, parks, a great lawn, an artificial lake large enough for sailing, mansions for the nobility, and the magnificent Alexander Palace.

Almost seventy years earlier, during the time of Nicholas I, the Romanovs connected this royal enclave to Saint Petersburg by the first railway ever built in the Russian Empire. On this rail, Rasputin first came to Tsarskoye Selo on November 1, 1905. When Nicholas II met Rasputin, he wrote in his diary that evening that he had met "a man of God."

Nicholas and his wife, Alexandra, were in need of such a man. After four daughters, Alexandra had finally delivered the critical male heir to the Romanov throne in 1904, but there was a terrible problem—a problem shared by several of the monarchies of Europe at that time. Many royal families could trace lineage back to Queen Victoria, who was called the "Grandmother of Europe." Russia was no exception, as the Empress Alexandra was Victoria's granddaughter. Many of Victoria's descendants inherited the gene for hemophilia, a condition that prevents the blood from clotting. A minor cut can cause a hemophiliac to bleed to death. A simple bruise can cause unchecked internal bleeding that leads to excruciating swelling and even death. The life expectancy of a hemophiliac in the early twentieth century was about thirteen years. The infant Tsarevich Alexei had inherited the disease.

After Rasputin's first visit to the palace in November 1905 or his second in July 1906, Nicholas and Alexandra came to think of Rasputin as a healer who could save their boy. Rasputin certainly promised that he could do it, and by all appearances he did.

After a fall and minor bruising, the poor child lay writhing in bed, tended by doctors who could do nothing to relieve his pain or improve his swollen condition. The Tsar summoned the healer Rasputin. The pilgrim came to the boy's bedside, held his hand, and calmly looked into the boy's eyes with a hypnotic blue gaze. Rasputin asked for God's help, then informed all that God would quickly heal the boy and the Tsarevich would be well.

The following day Alexei was fine. It might have been only fortunate timing on Rasputin's part, or a placebo effect (medical research leaves room for the idea that inducing calm for the boy might have lowered his heart rate and blood pressure, which would help clotting), but in the eyes of Nicholas and Alexandra their new friend had performed a miracle. This bizarre figure was now burrowed into the royal house, and his influence would extend to political, economic, and social issues. As Russia already brimmed with chaos, Rasputin brought yet another dimension of mayhem to Saint Petersburg.

Those in the orbit of government power came to fear Rasputin's rising influence within the autocracy. He seemed to know just how to play his hand, which was primarily to be a salve to the Tsar's insecurities. Conservative by nature and of peasant origin, Rasputin repeatedly told Nicholas that the Russian people loved the Tsar and hated the politicians. He told Nicholas that the people thought of the Tsar as their father. Rasputin even took to addressing Nicholas and Alexandra informally as Papa and Mama. And as Rasputin had established himself in the minds of the monarchs as a trusted man of God, Nicholas began to trust Rasputin's counsel on all matters.

Rasputin soon earned a range of rivals and enemies who resented the pilgrim's expanding sphere of influence, which encroached on their purview. Those loyal to the monarchy came to hate Rasputin for weakening the Tsar's reputation, and the revolutionaries opposed to the monarchy hated Rasputin too. The clergy hated him, and so did the military and all ministers. Nearly overnight Rasputin became the most despised person in all Russia, universally abhorred, except for Nicholas and Alexandra (and several wealthy women), who loved and trusted him.

Though Stalin had acquired political and economic power through cunning and viciousness, and though Emanuel Nobel had built political and economic power through industriousness and business acumen, within the autocracy their positions could be fleeting. Everyone's freedom was at the pleasure of the Tsar. The Duma was weak, and the true power in Russia still flowed through Nicholas II. Yet many in Saint Petersburg began to wonder if the Tsar was bewitched. In short order, through a run of good luck and parlor games, Rasputin had become possibly the second most powerful person in Russia, behind only his "Papa."

He was another unstable ingredient in Russia's political stew. In the three-way struggle for Russia's future among the revolutionary Social Democrats, the ultraconservative monarchists, and the industrialists like Nobel who urged the advance of moderate reforms that would spur economic growth, it was Rasputin who had enchanted the monarch. But neither Emanuel and reform-minded industrialists in Saint Petersburg nor Stalin and fellow revolutionaries in Baku and elsewhere could know to whose benefit the enchantment would inure. What was becoming clear to the ministers closest to the royal house was that an already weak ruler was starting down a ruinous path.

CHAPTER 12

The Best Customer of Fabergé

IN 1909, EMANUEL Nobel turned fifty and his petroleum company celebrated thirty years in business. Emerging from the wreckage of Bloody Sunday, each new year seemed to bring greater profitability and record-high dividends paid to shareholders of both the Ludvig Nobel Machine Factory and the Nobel Brothers Petroleum Company.

Independently, the businesses were of enormous value. Indeed, in 1910 Nobel Brothers was the most valuable listing on the Russian stock exchange, with a market value of 150 million roubles. (Again, a simple inflation adjustment to present day undervalues the company at US$1.5 billion. Other methods that better capture the true contemporary value are closer to US$35 billion.) In combination, the two companies were even more valuable, and by 1910 Emanuel began to make the most of the synergies within his business empire.

Nobel's engineers in Saint Petersburg had developed elite expertise with the Diesel engine. From 1910 to 1912, a full eighty percent of the plant's revenue came from the sale of Diesels, and by some accounts Nobel's manufacturing plant was delivering more Diesel engines than any other company in the world.

Synergistically, Nobel Brothers was the natural supplier of fuel for these Nobel-made Diesel engines, which burned a heavy fuel refined from crude. In addition to the Diesel combustion engine as a demand driver, many of the large surface ships—both military and commercial—were updating their steam engines to burn fuel oil or installing Diesels. Military and merchant fleets around the world scrambled to refit fleets to stay competitive on the seas.

Demand for petroleum created by the combustion engine came to exceed the demand created by the market for illumination. In 1890, driven mainly by the demand for illumination, the world consumed 10 million tons of petroleum. In 1910, even as the use of kerosene lamps had declined, the world consumed more than fifty million tons of oil.* Emanuel continued his father's tradition of visionary application of new technologies. He launched the world's first oceangoing Diesel-powered oil tanker in 1908, the *Dyelo.* From the founding of the company, the Nobels had observed the old Russian saying that "the Volga is a good horse," but Emanuel needed distribution across more than just the Volga—he needed the oceans to carry his product as well. The oil tanker with Diesel engines ushered in a new era in commercial shipping. In the same year, Emanuel's factory delivered the first Diesels for a Russian navy gunboat. In October 1908, Nobel delivered a pair of 120-horsepower engines for Russia's first-ever Diesel submarine, the *Minoga.* The sub was 107 feet long, with two forward-facing torpedo tubes, and cruised at eleven knots.

The following year, Nobel delivered the *Akula*, with four torpedo tubes and three 300-horsepower Nobel engines. The *Akula* became the standard for submarine construction to follow.†

---

* Also in 1910, the world consumed the equivalent of 731 million tons of coal. However, demand for oil would spike throughout the century. By 1920, annual demand was 91 million tons and by 1930 it was 207 million tons. In the 1960s, demand for oil outstripped demand for coal. By 1970, annual demand for oil was 2,237 million tons and 1,387 for coal.

† Tom Clancy fans will recognize the name *Akula*, as the Russian navy (much later) borrowed it for the designation of the class of nuclear submarines that appear in the book and film *The Hunt for Red October.*

The Russian Imperial Navy recognized the quality of these ships, and also that the state-owned Neva Works in Saint Petersburg and Baltic Works in Reval could not deliver the same quality in the required time frame, so the government turned to private machine shops to carry more of the load. Encouragement from the state led to a joint venture between two of the leading privately owned Russian manufacturers; one of course was Nobel. The other was G. A. Lessner Ltd., founded by a German, Gustav Lessner. Lessner's four sons, all German citizens, now managed the firm, which also had a manufacturing plant in Saint Petersburg. One of these sons, Arthur, had worked for decades for Emanuel as a technical director in the Baku oil fields.

The two companies were a natural fit. The newly formed venture was incorporated in 1912 and took the name Nobelessner. Lessner built mostly military products and was the empire's leading manufacturer of torpedoes, while Nobel built the Diesel engines. The combination proved to be another powerful example of industrial achievement in tsarist Russia.

The Ministry of Trade required that the company chairman be Russian. This stipulation for citizenship demonstrated again the advantage Emanuel had over foreigners doing business in Russia. The Tsar's government had embraced Emanuel and granted him citizenship, which came with massive economic value. And as a further reflection of the Nobel advantage over the Rothschilds, the ministry went a step further in revising the draft of the Nobelessner charter, directing that all board members must be "Russian subjects of non-Jewish faith."

Right away the new firm received a government order for four submarines, then twelve more the following year. This added a third major enterprise to Emanuel's portfolio to manage. And unlike his father, Ludvig, Emanuel had no siblings with whom to share responsibility. In this family-run business, he was the only executive of Nobel blood. His half brothers were decades younger, and only the youngest, Gösta, who was twenty-seven years younger, seemed to be on the leadership track. Emanuel nurtured Gösta's development, but he could not yet be a peer. Of this huge and expanding conglomeration that was critical to the future of Russia's commerce and military, Emanuel was the unquestioned king.

Emanuel was also widely respected internationally. Among his admirers was the famous German inventor Hugo Junkers, considered the father of modern aviation, who had also been a high school classmate of Emanuel's in Barmen, Germany. In 1910, Junkers had patented a breakthrough design for fixed-wing aircraft and built the world's first metal airplane, a feat most aviation engineers thought to be impossible during an era in which planes were made of wood and cotton fabric. After a visit with the Nobel family soon after his patent, Junkers wrote a letter in 1911 to Edla Nobel describing her stepson Emanuel. Junkers wrote of his admiration for Emanuel's "broad-minded and far-sighted love" and that "[Emanuel is] a true Christian, an unordained but genuine priest, a priest who is not content with promising his fellow human beings heaven after their death, but who, with his infinite love, brings them heaven on earth, as Christ did and willed."

As the Nobel businesses thrived, the Rothschilds were reaching their breaking point. Having looked for a buyer for years, in 1911 they found a suitor in Royal Dutch Shell Group, led by Henri Deterding. Deterding had been born in Amsterdam and began his career in banking before entering the oil business. In 1907 he led the merger between Royal Dutch Petroleum Company and the United Kingdom's Shell Transport and Trading Company. Deterding then edged out Marcus Samuel, who had led Shell prior to the merger, to lead the combined company called Royal Dutch Shell. Deterding was now a global player in the oil business, feared and respected by rivals, who had given him the nickname "the Napoleon of Oil."

While Nobel had passed on the opportunity to buy out the Rothschilds, feeling their assets were redundant to his own, the opportunity fit Deterding's expansionist plans. The Dutchman entered negotiations and soon agreed to a purchase price of 27.5 million roubles for "a fleet of ten tankers, forty barges, eight hundred thousand tons of storage capacity, an annual production of four hundred thirty-six thousand tons of crude, and three hundred thirty-eight thousand tons of refined." All this was less than half the scale of Nobel's petroleum operation but was an important foothold for Deterding inside Russia.

The Rothschild deal was for stock in Deterding's business. As such, the Rothschilds managed to transfer their assets out of deeply antisemitic Russia and into the shares of a Western company with shrewd leadership. After twenty-seven years in the Russian oil business, the Rothschilds were glad to be out.

Emanuel viewed the change warily. He had previously established with the Rothschilds a cooperative approach to market in which Emanuel was clearly the stronger player. He did not yet know what to expect from the new ownership, but given Deterding's reputation for sharp elbows, he anticipated conflict. And as the governments of Russia and Great Britain grew more friendly, Deterding was likely to receive far better treatment inside Russia than the Rothschilds had.

But, for the moment, Emanuel was the captain of the industry. Nearly everything he attempted turned wildly profitable given his combination of ingenuity, his access to capital, and his warm relations with Russian authorities. His Midas touch extended even to agriculture. In his Saint Petersburg machine shop, one of his product lines was dairy separators (which use centrifugal force to separate cow's milk into cream and skimmed milk—another form of mechanical distillation!). As the Russian agricultural industry expanded in Siberia, growing at an astonishing rate beyond anywhere else in Europe (only America was comparable), demand for dairy separators exploded. With a Swedish partner, Emanuel formed a new Russian venture called Alfa-Nobel to meet the market demand. In 1912 he sold more than twenty thousand separators—up from only a few hundred annually a decade earlier.

Alfa-Nobel made the fourth major company in the Nobel empire along with Nobel Brothers Petroleum Company, Ludvig Nobel Manufacturing Company, and Nobelessner. All four were world-class, capable of winning international markets. Emanuel was the dominant industrialist in all of Russia and soon had a title of sorts to match.

Immediately after Bloody Sunday, many organizations and unions had sprung up to advocate for the rights of the peasants and the proletariat. But there was no such broad association to promote the varied interests of entrepreneurs and business owners. Ultimately this function took the form of the Saint Petersburg Association of Factory Owners and Manufacturers, founded in 1906 (one year after the publication of the October Manifesto), at which time Emanuel was offered honorary membership. Now, in 1912, the business owners of Russia elected Emanuel to be their chairman.

The bachelor Nobel worked hard but also enjoyed his wealth and position. He frequented the theater, hosted grand parties for Russian and foreign dignitaries, and traveled extensively for business and pleasure. He was extremely generous with friends, and his female guests at dinner parties typically received lavish gifts. A Russian jeweler of the time remarked, "For Dr. Nobel, a dinner party was no dinner at all unless the ladies were suitably rewarded." Emanuel commissioned his most extravagant gifts of all from the House of Fabergé, where he was the best customer (with the possible exception of the Tsar) of master craftsman Peter Carl Fabergé.

Business had been going so well for Emanuel that he had planned an enormous banquet for his best international customers and business partners. For the wife of each of the forty men in attendance he planned to hide a jeweled surprise in their dinner napkin. He visited the Fabergé workshop in the bitter cold of a Saint Petersburg winter morning, where he met with the firm's rising star designer, the twenty-three-year-old female prodigy Alma Pihl. He told Pihl that guests were coming to his home for a reception and that he wanted to gift them each a Fabergé brooch. What the brooch should look like, he left to the genius of Fabergé and Pihl.

Emanuel returned to his headquarters while Alma laid out her sketch pad at her drafting table beneath a large window. It was January, the coldest month in Saint Petersburg. The window was frosted over. Alma sat with her empty sketch pad as the sun rose. When she returned her gaze to the window, the slightly altered angle of the sun's rays had brilliantly lit the ice crystals on the glass pane. The window transformed into a magical glow, a floral pattern that was a dazzling refection of nature's design. She began to sketch.

Following Alma's design, the jewelers used platinum, silver, and tiny rose-cut diamonds to make the winter-motif brooches, which they named "snowflakes." Nobel was thrilled with the brooches. The dignitaries that came to visit each took home this symbol of the Russian winter.

Fabergé's head craftsman, Franz Birbaum, wrote that Emanuel Nobel "was so generous in his presents that at times it seemed that this was his chief occupation and delight. Orders were constantly being made for him in the workshops and from time to time he came to have a look at them. Often he decided for whom the present should be only when the work was finished."

Emanuel had the exclusive rights to the winter theme with Fabergé. He commissioned more snowflake brooches for friends, family, and bridesmaids. The motif extended to vases, jeweled eggs and boxes, medals and commemorative plaques, and became an important chapter in the history of the House of Fabergé, considered by many to be the zenith of Western decorative arts. Emanuel made one exception to his exclusivity to accommodate Tsar Nicholas II, who had asked to use the winter motif with Fabergé for an Imperial Easter Egg that was a gift for the Dowager Empress.*

Fabergé historian Ulla Tillander writes of the dozens of jeweled eggs, brooches, elegant timepieces, and other treasures Emanuel gave to family, many of which survive to this day in the collections of Nobel descendants. To his younger sister Marta, who was at the time a physician, he gave a white enameled egg decorated with a red cross made of rubies. This was one of several dozen eggs he gave to Marta alone. Nieces and nephews recalled childhood days playing with precious

* Nicholas II presented it to her on Easter morning 1913. The young and talented Alma Pihl also designed this Imperial egg.

stones that were presents from Uncle Emanuel.* "For Christmas and Easter, he stocked up on gifts in earnest—at Easter with jeweled miniature eggs galore. Fabergé delivered them in small silk pouches tied at the top with an elegant silk cord."

Gone were the days of Emanuel's father when the capital requirements of the petroleum company pushed the family to the brink of bankruptcy, when suicidal price wars against a chaotic throng of new competition threatened to ruin the family business prospects altogether. Emanuel had tamed the competition, perfected his business model, and secured his advantageous relationship with government ministers. Likewise, the Tsar had managed to establish a period of relative calm, and Russian industry was growing at a faster pace than anywhere in Europe.

Yet this prosperity did not ease Emanuel's sense of foreboding. With operations in Baku, he knew better than most that the revolutionary forces that had come so close only to fail in 1905 were not gone but merely dormant. The leaders and agitators were working in the shadows, waiting for a chance. Revolutionary zeal could return to full bloom with only a minor catalyst. Much like his friend and colleague Rudolf Diesel, whom he had hosted in Saint Petersburg in 1910, he felt that a rising tide of nationalism threatened peace in Europe and the stability of all governments. Emanuel declared to his friends, "*Nationalism* is a pretty word for the meanest of actions."

The October Manifesto seemed to quiet urban unrest in Russia for a brief few years, but the economic conditions that make fertile ground for uprisings continued. Russian industry was growing by leaps and bounds, as was the wealth disparity between classes. In Baku all oil producers, not only the Nobels, were enjoying record profits and divi-

* Emanuel never married and had no children of his own. There is no account of a romantic relationship, which has led some historians to speculate privately that he might have been gay.

dends during the prewar years. At the same time, with the exception of Nobel Brothers employees, conditions for the Baku proletariat were as brutal as ever. Pollution, abysmal housing, poverty, and violent crime continued to plague the lower classes.

Maja Huss, a Baku hospital nurse, wrote in 1910 that "there is no end of the poverty and misery here, and most of it can be blamed on vodka." The violence of the oil city was perhaps best reflected in the rather efficient murder-for-hire market. The services of a bandit-cum-assassin were easy to obtain. The murder of a person deemed less significant cost a mere fifty kopecks (half a rouble). The arranged murder of a doctor, engineer, or government official would run three roubles—about $100 today. For this reason, Emanuel hired armed protection for his bosses in the oil fields. Even so, the murder of one or two of his engineers each year was commonplace.

The potential for broader havoc had also increased. An official of the tsarist police complained that by 1910 the knowledge of bomb-making had become "so widespread that practically any child could produce one and blow up his nanny."

But the aggressive posture of the tsarist police kept a lid on the revolutionary movement. Disruptions were small, uncoordinated, and lacked the leadership to bring national momentum. The Social Democratic Labour Party had peaked in 1907 with more than 150,000 members across the empire. By 1910, membership had fallen below 10,000.

The Tsar's police were effective, and even Lenin's Last Mohicans were silenced. There was no energetic, fearless agitator in Baku to stir the persistently simmering discontent of the local proletariat into something greater. These were Stalin's quiet years. He wasn't even in the Caucasus.

From 1910 through the outbreak of the Great War, as Nobel thrived and enjoyed his banquets, authorities had Stalin mostly tucked away in exile. Several times he relocated between remote villages, often bedding the daughter of his landlord, or even the landlady herself. Archives suggest these trysts resulted in at least one child. Stalin also nurtured his intellectual side with all his free time. During the period of his 107-day exile in Vologda, the Okhrana observed him visit the local library seventeen times.

He was the subject of frequent surprise searches. Yet he eventually was able to slip the rural police, and in September 1911 he pulled off another escape. The Bolshevik party higher-ups wanted Stalin back in the Caucasus, causing his brand of mischief. The party sent fellow Bolshevik Pyotr Chizikov to Vologda to assist Stalin's escape. Using Chizikov's actual legal travel documents, Stalin sneaked away under cover of darkness to the rail station and rode out of Vologda on a train bound for Saint Petersburg.

But while the police presence in rural towns was scant, in the larger cities like Baku and Tiflis, and especially in the capital, the Okhrana was in force. Within three days, Stalin was rearrested.

Stalin's relentless efforts gained him attention, though, and soon a promotion. Lenin's machinations from abroad succeeded in the Bolsheviks taking majority control of the entire Social Democratic Labour Party by late 1911. Then, during a meeting of the Central Committee of the Russian Social Democratic Labour Party in Prague in January 1912, Lenin appointed Stalin as one of twelve top Bolsheviks to the committee.* Stalin was actually not present at the meeting, as he was in exile in Vologda. This appointment would prove to be the breakthrough moment Stalin craved.

Lenin spoke openly to colleagues of his fondness for Stalin, asserting that there was no limit to what Stalin would do for the cause. Lenin declared to his fellow committee members, "This is exactly the kind of person I need!"

During the summer months of 1912, Stalin escaped again, was rearrested, then escaped yet *again* (the leniency of tsarist-era exile seems almost absurd—the future Stalin would certainly have shot such a prisoner), this time carrying the passport of a Persian merchant and traveling by boat to meet Lenin in Krakow in September. During this brief

---

* The post came with a party stipend of fifty roubles per month.

stretch of freedom, he shared with Lenin his most famous piece of writing to date, an article titled "Marxism and the National Question."

Lenin loved the piece and wrote to his friend the author Maxim Gorky, "We have a marvelous Georgian who has sat down to write a big article for *Enlightenment.*" The piece discussed revolution in the context of the multicultural Russian Empire and defined "a nation" by the characteristics of common language, territory, and economic ties.* Significantly, for the first time, he published under the name Stalin (meaning "Man of Steel").

With his new name and ascending rank within the hierarchy, the slightly crippled, undersized, and pockmarked boy from Georgia was no longer a young recruit to the movement who rotated aliases and moved in the shadows. He was willing to challenge those in the party leadership who opposed him, regardless of rank. He embraced the character of the strongman, convincing those around him of this role and, critically, convincing himself. From 1912 forward, he identified only as Stalin and his mask became his face.

Stalin was free and relishing Saint Petersburg at the time of the publication of his article in the March through May 1913 issues of *Enlightenment.* With his greater party status, he was enjoying a fancier lifestyle as well. Finely dressed one spring evening, he attended the fundraising ball for International Women's Day. With a drink in hand and dozens of attractive young women in sight, Stalin stalked the decorated banquet hall. Loyalties among revolutionaries could be fleeting, though, and a low-level Bolshevik had betrayed Stalin's whereabouts to the police. In the midst of an otherwise delightful night out, the Okhrana ambushed him and sent him back into exile yet again.

---

* The effort to unify Russia, whether in a movement for or against the Tsar, has confounded all leaders throughout Russian history given the empire's incomparable diversity. The definition of *nation* for Russia was complex, and the struggle to unify the country prompted Prime Minister Sergei Witte to record in his diary in 1910, "The mistake we have been making for many decades is that we have not admitted to ourselves that since the time of Peter the Great and Catherine the Great there has been no such thing as Russia, there has been only the Russian Empire." The struggle to determine which peoples belong to Russia continues to the present day.

By this time the trajectory of his status within the party was high, but the trajectory of the party as a whole was rather low. There were barely a hundred Bolsheviks left in all of Baku. Stalin had a larger share of a pie that was small and shrinking. In the political context of the empire at large, he was a nobody.

As historian Stephen Kotkin writes, "For a Georgian from small-town Gori—via Tiflis, Chiatura, Baku and Siberian exile—to rise anywhere near the summit of power, and to seek to implement Marxist ideas, the whole world had to be brought crashing down. And it was."

Europe was certainly on edge; militarism and nationalism were on the rise. But Europe was enjoying the longest period without a major war in its history, and most thought diplomacy could continue the peace. The Tsar had been advocating a foreign policy centered on a league of three emperors that would include Russia, Germany, and Austria. Autocrats prefer the company of autocrats. But Nicholas II faced internal opposition to this policy.

The Duma and constitutionalists in Russia wanted closer relations with the more constitutionally minded nations of France and Great Britain instead. These competing interests would play out amid the rapid industrial expansion in Germany and Russia that caused fear in their neighbors. This expansion was contemporaneous with the diminished presence of the weakening Ottoman Empire in the Balkans. The appetizing, potentially available prizes in the Balkans caused the colonial interests of the Great Powers to grind against one another. The complex web of alliances among the European powers was in constant flux.

On the eve of one of the most catastrophic events in world history, two towering figures represented diametrically opposed futures for Russia. On the one side was Stalin, a revolutionary from a broken and abusive home who was educated by an occupying force of Russian priests in his native Georgia. A survivor who had risen to the top rank of a violent band of political extremists by evangelizing Marxist principles, acquiring funds for the movement through plunder, and sabotaging the empire's great industrialists who were the face of capitalism.

In his exalted party position, he earned fifty roubles per month, a sum greater than he had ever earned while working in the petroleum fields of the Rothschilds or Nobels.

On the other side was Emanuel Nobel, born in Sweden and the only member of his family to become a Russian citizen, by invitation of the Tsar himself. A talented financier raised by a father who loved and mentored him and who gave him the mantle of the Russian oil industry. He introduced employment practices that increased the quality of life for workers and gained the Nobel companies international praise while expanding the family empire to be one of the most successful industrial concerns in the world. He was a proponent of liberal reform of the autocratic government and was a beacon for what free markets and industry could create. The circumstances of the two men in the prewar years could not have been more different. Emanuel could spend the Bolshevik stipend of fifty roubles on lunch while on the way to meet his jeweler, Peter Carl Fabergé.

Neither could survive the triumph of the other.

CHAPTER 13

World on Fire

FROM ONE MOMENT to the next, global demand for petroleum skyrocketed. Governments that had previously viewed oil as conceptually important for industrial growth now saw it as an immediate necessity for an increasingly likely war. Oil would determine whether commanders could deploy military assets and execute a battle plan. In this new era of militarism, fuel was more important than food.

Great Britain, an island nation that relied on a dominant navy and a life-sustaining merchant fleet, was the most desperate of the European powers in the race to modernize ships. Coal was out and fuel oil was in. Petroleum was now a matter of national security.

Winston Churchill assumed the post of First Lord of the Admiralty in 1911, leading Britain's Royal Navy just as the Anglo-German naval arms race reached a fever pitch. Churchill's recognition of Britain's dire circumstances was the thrust of a speech to Parliament in 1912 in which he declared that Britain's continued "mastery" of the seas rested upon the nation's ability to upgrade its fleet with engines burning fuel oil coupled with reliable access to petroleum during both peacetime and wartime. The rub was that Britain had plenty of coal in the ground, but no petroleum. Churchill needed to find oil from abroad.

He supported expeditions in Persia (modern-day Iran)* and also looked to Russia. The British founded a holding company in 1912 called the Russian General Oil Corporation (RGO). This extremely well-funded holding company comprising British bankers as well as several banking heads throughout Western Europe began to organize all the large independent Russian petroleum companies outside the Nobels and Royal Dutch Shell. This coordinated collection of suppliers created a third major force in the Russian oil market.

In the two years leading up to 1914, on the Berlin stock exchange, RGO began to buy up shares of Nobel Brothers. The British firm bought large quantities, driving up the price of the stock. By early 1914, RGO had bought more than six million roubles' worth of Nobel Brothers stock and attempted a boardroom coup.

The British holding company was hoping to oust and replace the management of Nobel Brothers. If they could get rid of Emanuel, they would then be able to direct the single-largest supply of oil in the world, and Churchill could rest easy.

But six million roubles were nowhere near a majority holding. RGO needed to lead a broader shareholder revolt for a hostile takeover to work, and the British badly underestimated the extent of the support for Emanuel from those who had benefited from his leadership for three decades. Shareholders firmly stood by Emanuel and his team. In addition, directors of several banks that had worked with both RGO and Nobel, including the Saint Petersburg International Commercial Bank and the Russo-Asiatic Bank, endorsed Emanuel as the more capable leader for the company.

RGO's attempted coup was an utter failure. In further humilia-

* The Anglo-Persian Oil Company was founded in 1909, and Churchill oversaw the government purchase of fifty-one percent of the company in 1914, effectively nationalizing the company to secure price stability for the Royal Navy. In 1954 the company was renamed British Petroleum. The British government sold its last remaining shares in British Petroleum in 1987, which privatized the company.

tion, within months the shareholders of RGO offered to sell their stakes in the British company to Emanuel at bargain prices. A resentful Emanuel initially rebuffed the offers but eventually agreed to acquire RGO stock at advantageous prices. He ultimately purchased twenty million roubles of RGO stock, shy of a majority position but enough that he was by far the single-largest shareholder and most powerful director, effectively making him the leader of the holding company. It was a comprehensive backfire on the part of RGO that greatly increased Emanuel's market influence. As a result, Emanuel controlled more than fifty percent of the entire Russian oil industry. All this in addition to his other three industrial concerns: Nobelessner, Alfa-Nobel, and the Ludvig Nobel Machine Factory.

By 1914, three things were happening at once. First, Emanuel's influence in the global petroleum market reached its highest point.

Second, the global need for petroleum to fuel the apparatus of industry and war also reached a new high, and as Churchill acknowledged, this precious commodity would decide the fate of nations.

Third, all hell broke loose.

Many forces contributed to the start of the Great War, though perhaps the most powerful explanation for Germany's willingness to join with Austria-Hungary against Russia is the theory of a preemptive war, a strategy promoted by many of Germany's generals that posits that a German war against Russia was inevitable and that it was better for Germany to fight sooner rather than later. German strategists recognized this likely meant fighting France as well, but hopefully not Britain.

Germany was large and its population and industrial capacity were growing quickly. Russia was even larger (in terms of population, landmass, and natural resources) and, by the same measures of industrial capacity, was growing even more quickly than Germany. In 1914 the German military was still more powerful than the undisciplined Russian military. But the prevailing belief of the German command was that within as little as five years this would no longer be the case and that Russia's military would become too powerful to defeat. Thus, these German commanders argued for a preemptive war.

The Germanic people and the Slavic people of Russia had been rivals for centuries. Kaiser Wilhelm II and Tsar Nicholas II were cousins and on fairly friendly terms (even penning a series of correspondence that history refers to as the Willy-Nicky Letters), but this ran counter to the ethnic enmity. A large reason for Empress Alexandra's unpopularity in Russia was her German heritage. The Russian people simply did not trust the Germans, and Russians were not viewed any better inside Germany. There was a persistent air of paranoia between the two empires, and a belief among many of the respective military commanders that a war must come.

When Serbian nationalists assassinated Austria's Archduke Franz Ferdinand in Sarajevo on June 28, 1914, which precipitated Austria-Hungary's declaration of war against Serbia and then Russia's commitment to defend her ally Serbia, many in the German military saw these cascading declarations of war as an opportunity.

Germany was well aware that Emanuel Nobel led much of Russia's industrial advance because Nobel had done much of his financing over the years with German banks. Kaiser Wilhelm II considered that perhaps after participating in a swift military victory over Russia and Serbia, Germany could reap war concessions that would even include Baku.

On July 30, 1914, Nicholas II ordered the Russian military to mobilize, his intention being to deter Austria-Hungary from invading Serbia. On August 1, Germany declared war on Russia. This set the table for the Eastern Front of the Great War.

Nicholas had not been eager for a European war, but the insecure Tsar had often felt bullied and patronized by his older cousin Wilhelm and decided that it had come time to show some resolve. Rasputin had not been eager for a war either. Like most peasants, he held an inherent dread of war, knowing that when Russia goes to war, it is the peasants who are offered up to the slaughter.

And it was no different in 1914. The initial battles on the Eastern Front saw Germany's disciplined and better-equipped armies rip through the Russian rabble. As has often been the case throughout history with the Russian army, the men were poorly equipped and the dead were easily replaced. Russian newspapers estimated that twenty-five percent of new recruits reached the front lines unarmed, forced to wait for the death of a nearby compatriot in order to pick up a rifle.

While Russia's military leaders tried to shore up the troops, Russian industry kicked into a higher gear, of course turning to Emanuel and his various businesses to make this happen. Within days of the mobilization order, the military ordered Emanuel to send all possible fuel oil to Saint Petersburg. Germany had sealed the Baltic and blocked any imports to Russia from the west, including the supply of British coal. Karl Hagelin, Emanuel's director in Baku, chartered or bought every ship and barge he could find that was capable of riding the Volga to the Russian capital.

Emanuel's wells and refineries operated around the clock. In 1915, more than seventy percent of Nobel Brothers' petroleum production went to the Russian military. The year earlier had already been a record year that delivered an all-time-high dividend of twenty-five percent. In 1915 the dividend was an astounding thirty percent.

Emanuel's team in Baku solved yet another problem for the Tsar and his war ministers. For years, the Russian military had been reliant on the Krupp factory in Germany for the import of trinitrotoluene, more commonly known as TNT. Due to the Romanovs' paranoid and long-standing ban, there was not a single company inside Russia that produced the chemicals required for manufacture, and this short-sighted blunder created a sudden and severe problem when Germany cut off the supply of explosives needed for the war effort.

In a feat of engineering, aided by the Nobel family's familiarity with dynamite, before the year 1914 was out, Emanuel had a plant up and running in Baku to produce toluol, a gasoline distillation by-product used for the manufacture of TNT.

The machine factory in Saint Petersburg also primarily served the war effort, delivering more than eighty Diesel engines that were critical for the Russian navy's warships and submarine program. But these redirections of resources came at a heavy price. As petroleum went to the war effort rather than industry, as factories built machines for war rather than agricultural production, Russia suffered a food shortage and a severe economic slowdown, compounded by the fact that foreign imports had dwindled, and the empire's internal transportation system over rivers and rails to move food to places that needed it was badly hampered.

The Russian population, initially galvanized by a fight with Germany, was growing weary after a year of war. The empire was in shambles. By the end of the summer of 1915, the Russian army had lost more than four million men, far more than any other combatant. Wartime misery opened the door again for socialism and revolutionary propaganda.

For a period of several days around the New Year 1915–16, the workers at Emanuel's Saint Petersburg factory went on strike, but this was a different kind of strike than any he'd faced before. The workers' leaders who normally represented the demands of employees were not allowed to be present. Instead, according to Emanuel, there were "new people altogether . . . who had been in the workshop for only three days" who turned up at the factory office to lead the strike. Strangely, these strike leaders made no demands. Emanuel realized he was no longer dealing with workers' representatives and trade unions that genuinely sought to improve working and living conditions. Emanuel's offers of cultural and educational improvements for workers or other concessions could have no purpose here. These were professional agitators. They weren't there to negotiate. Their only aim was to overthrow him. In the calamity and suffering of war, these agitators were gaining momentum.

Emanuel had ramped up production in his factories and oil fields, and his businesses thrived during the war years, but he also refitted many of his productive assets for humanitarian purposes.

In November 1914 Emanuel converted the People's House into a hospital dedicated to caring for the wounded. The People's House was the Saint Petersburg equivalent of Villa Petrolea, which the Nobels had built in Baku, only on a far grander scale. Emanuel and his architect designed the complex on a fifty-nine-thousand-square-meter site (almost fifteen acres) that included a library, lecture halls, tennis courts, employee housing, and a school. Nobel's intention was to stimulate education, and the official title of the campus was "Lecture Hall for the People."

Upon the outbreak of war, Emanuel had remade the People's House to provide 180 hospital beds. In the autumn of 1914, he visited the former lecture hall that he'd redesigned. The floors were slippery with blood; the air held the stench of rotting wounds and the sounds of delirious men. Emanuel discreetly touched the shoulder of a physician he'd personally recruited to work in his hospital. He inquired what supplies might be needed, what more he could do. Emanuel, along with his sisters, led by Marta, who was by then a trained physician, and the company directors devoted the bulk of their time in Saint Petersburg to Nobel's new hospital in the People's House. All were daily witnesses to the ghastly results of battle. In the first year of the war more than eight hundred soldiers were treated for their wounds there. A steady stream of butchered men continued to arrive from the front.

Emanuel noted with dismay that the war had brought the ancient ethnic hatred between the Teutonic Germans and the Slavic Russians to a crescendo. In a letter to his Swedish business partner Marcus Wallenberg, Emanuel wrote, "Stories about the way in which Germans are treating Russians who were not fortunate enough to escape in time are causing indignation and despair here in the highest degree." Coming from someone familiar with the horrors of rape and genocide in Baku only a decade before, his observation gives a sense of the scale of the war's brutality.

Nicholas II announced that he was changing the name of the capital to Petrograd because Saint Petersburg sounded too Germanic. The government confiscated German-owned land, shut down German businesses, and deported hundreds of thousands of Germans living within Russia's borders.

Ironically the autocracy itself was not spared from this prejudice. It had been common practice for generations of Romanov men to marry German aristocrats, but with the war on, as well as Alexandra's bizarre and secretive relationship with Rasputin already raising concerns, the Russian press treated the German-born Empress with increasing suspicion and scorn.

The anti-German movement also ensnared Emanuel when the government forced him to remove the German Lessners from their posts at the Nobel businesses. Emanuel adjusted to meet the reality of the times. And as the war raged on, so did Russia's need for petroleum, munitions, machinery, and other goods. Emanuel spurred the Nobel empire to meet the needs of the Romanov empire. From a business standpoint, he'd never been so successful.

Despite his extraordinarily busy professional life, Emanuel still found time to prioritize family. He combined his interest in the arts—especially the art of the goldsmiths at Fabergé—with doting on his expanding brood of nieces and nephews. When his niece Andriette "Andri" Nobel planned to marry, he commissioned a dazzling crystal pendant as a gift. Fabergé was not able to complete the elaborate pendant in time for the wedding, so Emanuel got creative. Andri's husband-to-be was a young military officer stationed in Boden in northern Sweden, a place with a reputation for cold winters and many bears. As a provisional gift, Emanuel had Fabergé make a small bear made of black obsidian, with red rubies for its eyes. This expensive gag-gift remains in the Nobel family collection to this day. Lavish pranks aside, once the pendant was ready, Emanuel personally traveled with it all the way to Boden, where Andri met her beloved uncle on the platform of the train station to receive the wedding gift. It was these kinds of moments, large and small, that endeared the younger generation to their uncle, and Emanuel was deliberate in making his family members feel close and united during the uncertain times of an expanding war.

As Europe was burning, Stalin was freezing on the edge of the Arctic.

The Tsar's police, tired of the pattern of escape and recapture, had sent him to Turukhansk, a region that has made "Siberia" synonymous with Timbuktu. Turukhansk is a province in northern Siberia of nearly unfathomable remoteness. Winter temperatures would drop to –60 degrees Fahrenheit. Only a few thousand people populated a landmass larger than France and Germany combined. When Stalin arrived on August 10, 1913, it had taken him twenty-six days to get there from the other side of the Urals.

He spent his last roubles on shoes and warm clothes. He wrote letters to comrades pleading for money, begging to be remembered at all by the cause. Escape across this Arctic moat made of barren land seemed impossible. In early 1914, he and a Bolshevik colleague were moved even farther north to a tiny village called Kureika.

The thirty-five-year-old Stalin took as his mistress a thirteen-year-old orphan named Lidia.* Lidia's memoirs tell of the two drinking vodka and carousing in the frozen and desolate village. In December 1914, as artillery boomed across Europe thousands of miles away, she bore Stalin a child who died soon after birth. Even for an exiled criminal, Stalin's indulgences were frowned upon and Lidia's fellow orphans treated him like an outcast, further isolating him within this minuscule village.

He wrote to Lenin from the tundra, "How am I? What am I doing? I'm not alright. I'm doing almost nothing. And what can I do with a complete lack of serious books? . . . In all my exiles, I've never had such a miserable life as here."

Stalin was a nonfactor during the first years of the Great War, but still better off than millions of other descendants of serfs who were slaughtered in trenches or dying of starvation. Stalin was surviving. Living for his chance to fight a different kind of war.

---

* Fourteen was the age of consent in the Russian Empire. Then again, this was Siberia, which was only quasi-subject to Russian law. Stalin regularly had sexual trysts with teenage girls, both during and between periods of exile.

CHAPTER 14

The Tsar Cannot Be in Two Places at Once

ONLY ONE YEAR before the war began, Nicholas II had celebrated three hundred years of the Romanov dynasty. He'd commissioned a special Fabergé egg to mark the occasion. A celebratory mood seemed appropriate as the autocracy had been enjoying a period of political stability with the revolutionaries bottled up. Other than a sickly heir, all was on the upswing. Russia at that time was most aptly compared to America for its population size,* natural resources, and trajectory of industrial growth.

But then in a flash, only one year after the Great War began, the

* In 1914 Russia's population was 165 million, and equally astounding was how quickly the population was growing, having more than doubled the 1815 count of 72 million. In 1914 France and Britain had populations of only 40 million and 35 million, respectively, both populations larger by only a few million than the 1815 census. Germany's population in 1914 was 65 million, having tripled in a hundred years. Only America could compare to Russia, with a 1914 population of 100 million that was also experiencing rapid growth. (Going back to 1815 in America is quite tricky, though the number is less than 10 million, many of whom were slaves.)

empire seemed to be in a dramatic free fall. The population was starving; the military was disorganized and humiliated. The general sense of nationalism and zeal that Russians felt in support of their Tsar at the outset of the war was gone. Daily suffering and a run of bad news from the front lines led to a lack of confidence in the government. This time, the revolutionaries were ready to organize and, with good reason, could lay the blame for current troubles on the regime.

The Nobel factories were in overdrive. Emanuel's companies added extra shifts to deliver greater amounts of petroleum, munitions, and machines for the war. His limiting factor was available labor. As Russian soldiers were cut down by the hundreds of thousands on the fronts with Germany and Austria, the Tsar began to conscript men from the population of Siberian exiles. (Stalin avoided conscription due to his deformed arm.) As the Tsar threw more men into battle, labor for Russia's factories and farms became harder to find.

Of Russia's overall population of 165 million, about 18 million were eligible for military service, and the government conscripted 15 million of those. Labor on Russian farms fell by two-thirds, and many factories became deserted. Emanuel scrounged for labor, and because his businesses were critical to national security, he received some government help in doing so, but the government directed the primary flood of humanity into the war.

However, men without rifles and artillery don't win battles. The Russian army had some success in the south, where they won victories over the Austrians, but on the northern side of the front, the disciplined German army devastated the Russian forces in the battles of Tannenberg and Masurian Lakes. Churchill later declared the war on the Eastern Front to be the most terrible war in human history, "in its scale, in its slaughter, in the exertions of the combatants, in its military kaleidoscope."

From the rim of the Siberian Arctic in July 1915, Stalin read for the first time Machiavelli's *The Prince*, a gift from his comrade Lev Kamenev. He then wrote to his friend to say, "My greatest pleasure is to choose one's victim, prepare one's plans minutely, slake an implacable vengeance, and then go to bed. There's nothing sweeter in the world." As a bandit revolutionary who had worked the oil rigs of Baku, Stalin's two most-hoped-for victims would likely have been the Tsar, followed by his chief supplier of guns and petroleum, Emanuel Nobel.

One month after Stalin's letter, on August 21, 1915, Nicholas II would take an action that all but ensured Stalin an opportunity to topple the autocracy. The commander in chief of the Russian army was the Tsar's uncle, the six-foot, six-inch-tall Grand Duke Nicholas Nikolaevich, who had spent a lifetime in military service but had never commanded troops in the field. Twelve years older than the Tsar, the Grand Duke was an intimidating presence who berated subordinates, yet at the outbreak of war, among ministers and the regular military, he was the popular choice to lead the Imperial Army. The Grand Duke took the reins of a wholly unprepared military and, to make matters worse, proved to be inept. By the war's first anniversary, Nicholas had decided to replace his uncle. In itself, this appeared to be the right move. What became such a tragic mistake for the future of the Romanovs was Nicholas's decision to replace his uncle with himself.

In August 1915, Nicholas II left Petrograd for the front lines, specifically the Polish territory of the Russian Empire.* Would Nicholas be able to lead the government in Petrograd while also running the war from the front lines? His loyal advisors warned him that he could not be in two places at once.

Nicholas's decision to leave the capital to assume command of the army caused two problems. First, he no longer had anyone else to blame. By personally assuming the role of commander in chief, he eliminated any distance between himself and Russia's military failures. The Russian people associated all the military outcomes with Nicholas

---

* Poland was not an independent state during the war. Positioned between Russia, Germany, and Austria, it was the scene of some of the heaviest fighting of the Great War. Near the conclusion of the war in 1918, Poland became an independent republic.

directly. His hope had been that the presence of the people's demigod would inspire his troops and reinvigorate a feeling of Russian pride. This may have been the case for a brief moment, but Nicholas had less military expertise than his uncle, and of course the raw truth was that he was not at all godly. The bungled military planning continued, and the Russian people now blamed the Tsar.

The second problem was that by leaving Petrograd, the government was now in the hands of Alexandra and Rasputin. Though Nicholas had been an ineffectual leader, of that absurd trio, he had been the most steady. Alexandra relished the new power in her husband's absence and assured him that she was up to the challenge of leading the empire, writing to him that she had "trousers on unseen."

Yet her chief spiritual and political advisor was the peasant-turned-pilgrim Rasputin, who, when not directing ministers, was enthusiastically visiting brothels and offering rhetoricals to prostitutes and housewives such as "How can we repent if first we have not sinned?"

This grandiose and hapless pair running the government created a sentiment of no confidence from all corners of Petrograd that was observed even by foreign dignitaries stationed in the city. The French ambassador wrote to the government in Paris, "I am obliged to report that at the present moment the Russian empire is run by lunatics."

The Russian military loathed Rasputin. When he declared his intent to visit military headquarters in Mogilev, about five hundred miles from Petrograd, the commander wrote, "Come and I'll hang you."

The Russian press frequently ran cartoons that mocked Rasputin's influence over the monarchs and suggested a lecherous relationship between Rasputin and the Empress. Nicholas's reputation with the public seemed damaged beyond repair. A glorious triumph in the battlefield might have saved him, but that was not to be. The Tsar had abandoned his capital in wartime, relied on mysticism, was unable to heed good advice or absorb bad news. All this presented an opportunity for those who opposed him.

The Tsar still had a loyal contingent within the aristocracy, though. These people considered Rasputin to be enemy number one, and they resolved to take action against him. On December 29, 1916, the very wealthy bon vivant Prince Felix Yusupov sent an invitation asking Rasputin to join him that evening at Yusupov Palace. The prince had been plotting with several of his fellow aristocrats on how to murder Rasputin to free their emperor from his dark sway. According to Yusupov's memoirs, Rasputin seemed to have some unearthly power that made him hard to kill.

Yusupov's co-conspirators waited in a separate part of the palace* as the prince greeted Rasputin and showed him into the drawing room. Yusupov served small cakes that he had loaded with enough poison to kill a horse. But Rasputin seemed uninterested in eating anything, and the nervous Yusupov began to sweat, his courage for the entire endeavor beginning to fail. Finally, after some encouragement from Yusupov, Rasputin ate. Perhaps out of politeness he ate one, then two, then three of the cakes. Yusupov thought that ought to have settled the matter, but it didn't. The conversation continued, Yusupov starting to panic in the company of his guest, who he had thought would be dead by now. He offered Rasputin wine, also heavily poisoned, and Rasputin drank. The conversation continued.

Rasputin didn't appear to suffer so much as indigestion. Yusupov was shocked that his guest was still breathing and became desperate for other options. He excused himself from the drawing room and made for the chamber where his colleagues had gathered. They calmed Yusupov, then gave him a gun and a plan.

Yusupov returned to the parlor and told Rasputin how much he wanted to show him an important piece of art from his collection in the next room. Rasputin accepted, and as he viewed the art, Yusupov

---

* Though not all were in attendance at the Yusupov mansion, reportedly among the planners were Nicholas's cousin the Grand Duke Dmitri Pavlovich as well as members of British intelligence. The British wanted Rasputin out of the way because they feared he might influence the Tsar to withdraw from the war and negotiate a separate peace with Germany, which would allow Germany to focus all its efforts on the Western Front against France and Britain.

drew his gun and shot Rasputin in the chest. The monk fell to the floor. Dead. Or so Yusupov thought.

The prince returned to his friends to share the triumph. He had rid the empire of the scourge Rasputin. But the job wasn't done, because they still needed to dispose of the body. Yusupov returned to the gallery to assess the job. As he pondered, feeling proud of himself, Rasputin leapt to his feet. No longer a corpse, the furious monk attacked the prince. Terrified, Yusupov warded off blows and fled through the mansion, calling for help.

Rasputin gave chase all the way outdoors, where the entire group of plotters confronted him in the courtyard. There they beat him and shot him several more times, including one shot to the head. To be certain he was truly dead, they bound him and rolled him inside a carpet, then dumped the whole bundle into the icy Nevka River. The body was discovered beneath the ice on January 1.*

The enigmatic Rasputin was gone. Posthumously, his disciples argued that he had been a kind and peaceful man, loyal to his monarchs, his devotion to God sincere. Admirers acknowledged that he was flawed but said that the worst accounts of his behavior were invented by his enemies and jealous rivals (history has confirmed many of the stories about Rasputin were lies told by his enemies). But there is no doubt that Rasputin's presence was a destabilizing force in Russia. News of his death spread quickly from Petrograd to the edges of the empire.

On hearing of the murder, Nicholas reportedly felt both relief and disgust. It was a heinous act aimed at the highest rungs of power. And yet even Nicholas felt a burden lifted. Most in Petrograd believed the removal of Rasputin was essential and found moral justification in the brutal deed. There was scant police investigation during the disarray in the capital in a time of the war.

---

* Yusupov's memoir, *Lost Splendor and the Death of Rasputin*, first published in French in 1952, likely enhanced the drama of the events with Rasputin, but what is certain from contemporaneous medical records is that Rasputin had a bullet hole in his forehead, he had suffered cuts and bruising, and his corpse was found in the frozen river.

There are no letters or other documents to indicate whether Emanuel felt relief or dismay at Rasputin's murder. In the first hours of 1917, as Rasputin's body was pulled from beneath the ice, Emanuel was focused on his factories, his refineries, and his hospital for the troops. Incredibly, by the dawn of 1917, the Russian economy had recovered somewhat and was delivering massive quantities of war materials, thanks in large part to Emanuel and a handful of industrialists. Russia produced rifles, ammunition, and even aircraft. Many fighter planes designed by twenty-eight-year-old Ukrainian-born Igor Sikorsky saw action in the war. The stock market was way up and as Nobel Brothers closed the books on 1916 it would be a record year in both quantity of goods produced and profitability—by far exceeding the previous record in 1915. Even Russia's farms were producing ample food; however, the government failed to overcome wartime disruption to the rail system, which meant the food rotted in silos, unable to get to the urban populations that needed it.

In the end, Yusupov's killing of Rasputin did not bring needed political stability, or pave the way for more competent military leadership. If anything, it merely added to the chaos and equivocation in Petrograd. From afar, Stalin sensed that opportunity could be found in the tumult. More so even than Lenin, who had publicly wondered whether his generation would see the revolution, Stalin seemed to know the autocracy would fall in his lifetime. Stalin brooded in the Arctic, still with certainty that events would call him home. As his mistress, now fifteen, delivered another baby, Stalin awaited his orders and was ready to pounce westward to the capital.

The Tsar's domestic goodwill was nearly spent in full. Only weeks after the murder of Rasputin, unprecedented mayhem would engulf the Russian Empire and bring new heights of bloodshed and horror to an already war-weary people.

Russian aircraft designer Igor Sikorsky stands on the bow of his craft The Grand *with Nicholas II during a military inspection in Krasnoye Selo, July 1913.* The Grand *was the world's first multi-engine aircraft. Sikorsky established several "first-in-flight" milestones and, like the Nobels, was an example of world-class industrial achievement in tsarist Russia. Following the October Revolution, Sikorsky learned he was on a Bolshevik kill list and he fled Russia in December 1917, eventually emigrating to New York, where he pioneered the flying boats used by Pan Am, including the* American Clipper, *flown by Charles Lindbergh in 1931. Sikorsky also developed the world's first functional helicopters, including the Black Hawks used by the American military. The Sikorsky Aviation Corporation is now a division of Lockheed Martin.*

PART III

AN OIL COMPANY MASQUERADING AS A COUNTRY

1917–1922

Russia is an oil company masquerading as a country.

—US Senator John McCain, 2014

CHAPTER 15

February

THE YEAR 1917 would bring a new war to Russia, as well as an additional layer of complexity to the ongoing Great War. The battle-fatigued armies of the Central and Allied Powers were increasingly desperate for resources to continue the fight, and chief among their needs was oil. Emanuel Nobel, from his headquarters in the Russian capital, controlled more oil than any other single person on the planet.

In January, as Rasputin's corpse decomposed in a Petrograd morgue, many of the key figures who would come to dominate the year were nowhere near the city. Nicholas II was off at the front on a fool's errand to rehabilitate the military, leaving only a stunned Alexandra to lead the government without the aid of her spiritual muse and confidant.

Lenin was barking motivations from Switzerland. Stalin was in Siberia, straining at his leash. Trotsky had been expelled from France, escorted by French police across the border to Spain, where he was promptly rearrested, then put on a ship across the Atlantic. On January 13, 1917, Trotsky arrived in New York City, where speculations about the murder of Rasputin were still circulating in the newspapers.

Tireless for his cause, Trotsky got to work and quickly made underground connections with members of German intelligence who were embedded in the United States.

A primary aim of German intelligence was to remove Russia from the war by means other than artillery. Germany viewed Lenin and Trotsky as allies in this goal. A key tenet of the Bolshevik political platform was to end Russia's involvement by negotiating a separate peace between the two countries. This was perfectly aligned with Germany's hope to close down the Eastern Front and focus on the west. In New York, German operatives funneled $10,000 to Trotsky as an investment in his revolutionary work.

Emanuel was in Petrograd. His businesses had never been stronger, but the Russian Empire that was their home had never been so compromised. Government ministers had lost all confidence in Nicholas and openly mocked him in his absence. The Tsar's paranoia-driven fecklessness was so reliable that a top minister reported that anyone could set one's calendar by it. British agent Robert Bruce Lockhart reported a Russian minister's critique of the Tsar to London: "I have two months in which I shall be his favorite, two months in which he will suspect me, and two months during the course of which he will kick me out."

While the ship of government drifted rudderless, discontent fomented on the streets and out into the distant rural regions of the empire. Contributing to the upset of the peasants was the Tsar's plan to confiscate land from farmers and give it to army recruits in order to incentivize military participation. In return for military service, and in particular for medal-worthy bravery in action, the Tsar would reward soldiers who managed to return alive with arable acreage. If picking up a rifle could mean becoming a landowner, many found it a risk worth taking. But of course this land had to come from somewhere. At the beginning of the war, peasants owned roughly forty-seven percent of the empire's land, having purchased it in the decades since emancipation. The peasants had come to expect further land redistribution, but war brought the opposite. More than fifteen million acres were confiscated during the war—some taken from the nation's most productive farmers with little or no compensation.

If grievances over land and hungry bellies weren't enough, most of these people had multiple relatives who had been fed to the slaughter of the front, only to hear the news reports of Russia's poor military leadership and humiliating losses, all for a Tsar who seemed less godly by the moment, in part due to his lampooning in the press.

Years of Marxist agitation and preaching had made a ready foundation for revolution. Certainly, the urban workers and even many of the peasants had become conversant in socialist principles. These people could begin to imagine, to speak up for, and organize behind a movement for a different political and economic system.

For a population who had become weary to the bone of fighting a war, the Bolshevik promise that the first order of business would be to remove Russia from the war was well received by millions.

Emanuel could sense the unrest in the streets of Petrograd. In early 1917 his accountants tabulated the results of the prior year. The book value of the machine factory had doubled (seventy percent of the production of the machine factory was for the military—primarily Diesel engines). Nobelessner was way up too, but the success of the petroleum company was simply astounding. The dividend for Nobel Brothers yet again set a new record at forty percent. The roubles were pouring in, to the tune of seventy-five million in profit, of which Emanuel paid out fifty million in the dividend. But with the ire of the proletariat visible on every street corner, Emanuel understood that this was the kind of good news that one must keep to oneself. He made no public announcement of the dividend and ordered his directors to follow suit.

On February 23 (by Russia's Julian calendar, March 8 by the Gregorian calendar), resentment in the bread lines of Petrograd boiled over. Without the orchestration of Lenin or other revolutionary leadership, the people began to riot in protest of food rationing. Industrial strikers poured into the streets, adding to the bedlam, and faced down the police and uniformed imperial guards in a series of clashes that lasted for days. With the Tsar absent and his most loyal troops with him at the front, Petrograd was ill-prepared to handle riots on such a scale. Worse, many of the soldiers in the city's garrison were disaffected with the regime and sympathized with the protestors.

On the fifth day of riots, chaos reached a level unseen in the history of Romanov rule as the Petrograd garrison, meant to protect the government, officially switched sides. With this news, Nicholas II boarded a train leaving his military headquarters in Mogilev and started the more than four-hundred-mile journey to the capital to save his throne. The ineffectual leader was further compromised by a bad cold, for which he took cocaine as a remedy.

His return had all the wisdom of entering a house on fire without a fire hose, because on that same day, February 28, the Duma issued the statement: "In view of the grave situation of internal disorder, caused by measures taken by the old government, the Interim Committee of Members of the State Duma has found itself obliged to take into its own hands the restoration of state and public order." Two members of the Duma immediately left Petrograd with orders to intercept Nicholas's train. The intent was to persuade him to abdicate while leaving room for the preservation of a reformed monarchy in which a new constitution and parliamentary system would play a larger role than in the past.

Nicholas II made it to Pskov, about 185 miles from Petrograd, when the Duma members reached him to deliver their message. Nicholas stood before the two men, outraged at their impertinence. Though he likely would have banished them, he was stopped short by the arrival of two telegrams from his field generals that clarified Nicholas's position beyond any doubt. General Aleksei Brusilov messaged, "At this moment the only way to save the situation and create the possibility to continue to fight the external enemy . . . is to abdicate the throne." Simultaneously, General Aleksei Evert wrote to Nicholas that the Tsar could not rely on his army and that at present "there are no means whatsoever of stopping a revolution in the capital cities."

Nicholas stood newly humbled before the Duma representatives.

He had lost his grip on power and could see no way to regain it. From Pskov, he announced his abdication with his best effort at a positive spin:

> *At this moment, a moment so decisive for the existence of Russia, Our conscience bids Us to facilitate the closest union of Our subjects and the organization of all their forces for the speedy attainment of victory. For that reason We think it right—and the Imperial Duma shares our view—to abdicate the crown of the Russian state and resign the supreme power.*

The two immediate candidates for the throne were his younger brother Michael and his twelve-year-old son, Alexei, though his uncle, the recently fired commander in chief, was also a possibility. Nicholas initially thought to abdicate in favor of his son, but instead renounced the throne in favor of Michael, who refused to accept it the following day. The throne stayed empty while the new Duma, now emboldened after having ousted the Tsar, attempted to direct the affairs of the nation.

The Tsar's abdication did not satisfy the rising new order but rather only affirmed its strength. Back in Petrograd, the French diplomat Louis de Robien observed on March 1, "The revolution appears to have definitely triumphed. The troops are going to the Duma to take the oath [to the revolutionary cause]."

Officers in the military were now at the mercy of their long-aggrieved and vindictive men. Robien wrote, "Many [officers] were mutilated and soaked in icy water or petrol. Admiral Wirren was burnt to death in a barrel, and his eighteen-year-old daughter was raped before his eyes and then had her throat cut."

A more fortunate naval officer, better liked by his men, was granted a forty-eight-hour shore leave, though as evidence that a revolution brings the top to the bottom and the bottom to the top, the leave was granted and signed by the ship's cook.

Many of the mutineers took advantage of this upside-down

environment to loot and pillage the mansions, palaces, and businesses in the city under the pretext of looking for tsarist police and serving the revolutionary cause. The mob penetrated the wine cellar of the Winter Palace that held a stash of priceless bottles going back to the time of Catherine the Great. The French diplomat lamented, "And it has all been gulped down by these Vodka swiggers."

All the city prisons were thrown open, which liberated German officers alongside Russian common criminals. Robien saw that the army cars had fallen into the hands of the revolutionaries, who were now a mix of protestors and the soldiers of regiments who had thrown in with them. "There is a constant stream of motorcars along the quay, crammed with soldiers. On the front part of almost every car there are two men stretched out on the mudguards on either side, aiming their guns ahead of them with fixed bayonets."

The Duma declared that there would be no more tsars. Nicholas would not abdicate in favor of anyone. The Duma abolished the monarchy and quickly established a provisional government, which was formed essentially from an executive committee of the Duma. Senior Russian officers were marched to a makeshift tribunal that represented the new government and, in a humiliating display, made to pledge their oath to the revolution.

At this point the mobs that had forced revolution consisted of urban workers and a growing number of the farmers who were responding to the broad themes of socialism and Marxism. The socialist movement comprised numerous competing factions that included the Socialist Revolutionary Party, the Menshevik Party, and the Bolshevik Party, among others. A jumble of these factions with no clear leadership in place attempted to fill the void of power in Petrograd.

Nicholas was devastated by the lack of support from his generals and the loss of the throne. He wrote in his diary, "All around is betrayal, cowardice and deceit." By March 22, Nicholas II was back with his family in the Alexander Palace, where Alexandra was in hysterics. She had repeatedly visited the palace garrison to plead for their protection, but most of the men had deserted. The family was vulnerable to an invasion by the mob.

Two other events happened the day Nicholas reunited with his family. First, General Lavr Kornilov arrived at the Alexander Palace to inform the Tsar that he and the Tsarina were under house arrest, ostensibly for their own protection. The children remained with their parents, and the servants and staff were offered the choice to stay or go. Dozens elected to remain in confinement with the former monarchs. Second, the United States became the first foreign government to officially recognize the authority of the Provisional Government. America saw that "another country created through revolution" was a possible ally. Two days later Great Britain, France, and Italy also recognized the Provisional Government.

Nicholas II might have taken a proactive course with ministers and the public earlier in March, demonstrating leadership to quell the rebellion and rally support for the monarchy, albeit a massively reformed one, but he simply was not up to it. Instead, he submitted.

General Kornilov left the former Tsar under guard in his home. Inside the palace, Nicholas opened to the first page of Tolstoy's *War and Peace* and began to read. Outside, Russia began a period of wild upheaval.

In a matter of days, Emanuel Nobel had lost every one of his ministerial connections. In the empire's new political and economic reality, he was without a friend in power. He was also potentially without clear title to the assets of his own businesses. There had been no action to seize his assets as of yet, but the core tenet of the Marxist movement was for communal, rather than private, ownership. In the immediate wake of the Tsar's abdication, Emanuel's importance to the Provisional Government rested in his expertise in running businesses that were crucial to the future of the country. No matter who owned the oil, any successful leadership in Russia would need Emanuel's participation in extracting the crude and refining it for use.

The change to the social order was so significant that it seemed almost dreamlike to the people who walked the smoldering streets of Petrograd. The overthrow of the Romanov dynasty took less than two weeks, though it had been so long in the making that the February Revolution had the sensation of being both inevitable and abrupt.

As bullets continued to zing across the streets of Petrograd, one stray even killing the nephew of a Nobel executive as the boy watched the violence from the window of his home, Emanuel met with Finland's General Gustav Mannerheim at the Hotel Europa.

Finland was then a duchy of the Russian Empire and Mannerheim had served with distinction on the Eastern Front under the Tsar. The two men spoke in the comfort of an upstairs suite. Emanuel was then fifty-seven. Mannerheim was forty-nine, tall, athletic, fairly dashing, and an impeccable dresser. They discussed a range of topics, including whether the worst could possibly be behind them, what Russia's future in the war would be, the possible organization of the new government for Russia, whether provinces within the empire—such as Finland—would push for independence from the new government, and the security of Emanuel's oil business in Baku.

The two talked in relative calm, given the tumult happening on the streets below. Most rioters took vengeance on their proximate target—meaning their employers. But Emanuel's employees felt no animosity toward him, and, rather than attack him, they remained loyal, even protective.

A knock at the door interrupted their conversation. A porter entered with a dire warning. Men with bayoneted rifles were filing into the hotel, looking for former officers of the Tsar to arrest, or worse. Mannerheim, in his decorated uniform, would be a prized catch.

Emanuel leapt up and escorted his guest to a back stairwell leading to a side entrance where his carriage was waiting on the street. He took the general to the Petrograd head office of Nobel Brothers, only a few blocks from the hotel. Emanuel dispatched a driver to his home to bring a set of his clothes for the general. The two waited in Nobel offices, which were relatively safe because, as had been the case through the many riots in Baku, Emanuel's reputation for fairness to his workforce engendered merciful treatment.

The clothes arrived and were a poor fit for the taller, slimmer man but, at the moment, preferable to an officer's uniform. The general seemed quite undisturbed and deliberate when picking out which of Emanuel's ties to wear for his escape from the capital.*

About the time Emanuel was assisting General Mannerheim's dangerous exit from Petrograd, Stalin arrived in the city. Petrograd was unmoored, more like Baku than the capital of a European nation. Violence was ever-present, the tides of power shifted unexpectedly, and there was no political stability. It was precisely the kind of environment in which Stalin thrived.

Following the Tsar's abdication, Stalin was no longer anyone's prisoner. He was off his leash at last. Stalin came to the capital on March 27 by way of a three-thousand-mile trip on the Trans-Siberian Railway, with a typewriter under his arm, ready to agitate for the most extreme outcome possible.

After three years of silence while he had been isolated in the far reaches of Siberia, Stalin went on a writing tear. He took over as the editor of *Pravda* (replacing Lev Kamenev) and authored forty lead articles in the critical few months following Nicholas II's abdication. The language of the revolution that Stalin used began to shift from a foundation of Marxist terms to being a battle of good versus evil. He ginned up a win-at-any-cost class war rather than framing a contest of ideas and principles. He opposed the more moderate political voices that seemed to have an inside track in forming the Provisional Government. Portentously, the word *provisional* was used contemporaneously

* Finland declared independence from Russia in 1917, then suffered a civil war between the monarchists and Finnish Bolsheviks. Mannerheim led the monarchist side to victory. Finland adopted a republican constitution in 1919 and held its first election the same year. Mannerheim served as prime minister from 1944 to 1946.

to describe the new government. The forecasted lack of durability would prove true.

As Stalin published at a feverish pace, the most storied train ride in history happened. Lenin was in Switzerland when he heard the news of the Tsar's abdication. Remembering well the "dress rehearsal" of twelve years before, Lenin knew he needed to get to Petrograd as quickly as possible. Germany, aware of the Bolshevik pledge to pull Russia from the war, which would free up Germany's eastern flank, felt the same way.*

With German assistance, Lenin and his wife along with twenty-nine other political exiles secretly boarded a train in Zurich that passed through Germany, then met a ferry to cross the Baltic Sea to Finland, where the party rode horse-drawn sleds across the Russian border to another train and finally to Petrograd.

True to form, when Lenin reached Finland Station in Petrograd on April 3, he brushed aside any official greetings and made straight for the nearest armored car, which he climbed atop, then launched into one of his trademark impassioned speeches. He declared that the recently installed Provisional Government was deceiving the people, that the Bolsheviks must overthrow the unsteady new leadership and end the European war.

Lenin was making a bold break from the prevailing thinking of the revolutionary leadership. The All-Russia Congress of the Soviet was dominated by the more moderate Mensheviks and the Socialist Revolutionaries. These factions believed that true socialism would first come through a period of cooperation between the working class and the bourgeois (professionals, intellectuals) that would entail intermediate steps in capitalism and democracy. Even moderate Bolsheviks subscribed to this evolutionary plan. Alexander Kerensky, representing

---

* Colonel Vladimir Hurban, America's attaché to the Czech Legation, later testified to the Overman Committee of the US Senate in 1919 regarding Trotsky's work in New York City and remarked, "The German government knew Russia better than anybody, and they knew that with the help of these people [Bolsheviks] they could destroy the Russian army."

the Socialist Revolutionary Party, was elected prime minister of the Provisional Government. Kerensky was a lawyer whose family had been friendly with Lenin's family, the Ulyanovs. Kerensky's father had even taught Vladimir Lenin in his school years. But Kerensky was leading a government that was conciliatory to factions of the political right, which outraged the Bolsheviks.

Lenin arrived in Petrograd shouting his slogan that would become famous: "All power to the Soviet!" The implication of his demand was for the immediate and complete leap to socialism. Lenin quickly won the moderates of his party, then turned his focus on winning over the members of the other socialist parties that had been elected to the All-Russia Congress of the Soviet that controlled government appointments.

Simultaneously, Trotsky was trying to make his way from New York City back to Petrograd. Historian Antony Sutton describes President Woodrow Wilson as Trotsky's "Fairy Godmother" when he authorized an American passport for him—over the objections of the British, though certainly the Germans would have approved. The British officials in Nova Scotia detained Trotsky for a month. As Trotsky had a valid passport and there was no crime to charge him with, they released him on April 29. He reached Petrograd on May 17.

Now all the key players were together in the capital for the first time, and the Bolsheviks were trying to organize in time to seize the opportunity they had missed twelve years before. Yet the Russian Empire comprised so many different coalitions that the tumult of new leadership brought management challenges far beyond the politics of Petrograd. The construct of what had been the geography of the empire began to split at the seams. Provinces of the borderlands began to edge toward autonomy. Finland, Poland, and Ukraine talked of independence. The Baltic states in the west and the critical petroleum region of the Caucasus talked of splitting as well. In June 1917 the author Maxim Gorky wrote that the empire was "falling apart, like an old barge in a flood."

Emanuel observed this rush of events with trepidation. Like any rational person, he had recognized the corruption and weakness of Nicholas's wayward regime, and he held some optimism for what a stable constitutional government might bring. Should political moderates win out, and the moderates were nominally in charge, Russia might have a bright future. But the Bolsheviks were determined that their time had come.

Soviets, meaning elected committees, popped up all around the empire in haphazard fashion. A soviet could be tiny and local, or at a district or regional level, and many had no authority other than what they could physically enforce. Low-level pop-up soviets conducted meetings and gave speeches on nearly every street corner, electing and declaring a local soviet. Often the winners of these sham elections were thieves and prostitutes. In theory, all soviets served in a hierarchy controlled by a national soviet led by the All-Russia Congress that would control the government.

The Provisional Government itself, though, was a rabble of leading reformers. Appointed officials even included some constitutional monarchists, and the initial aim of Kerensky's government was to be democratic, not socialist. Trotsky, a moderate Menshevik, had come to believe that such a democracy would be dominated by the landowning aristocracy, and so his views evolved to adopt the more aggressive posture of socialist intervention that matched that of Lenin, Stalin, and the Bolsheviks. As the three men moved ideologically closer, as well as now being physically closer, Trotsky jumped ship from the Mensheviks to join the Bolsheviks.

In June and July 1917 the First Congress of the Soviets was convened and attended by delegates from regional and district soviets around the country. Seven hundred and seventy-seven delegates declared their party affiliation: the Socialist Revolutionaries won 285, the Mensheviks won 248, and the Bolsheviks won only 105, a victory for the moderates.

The Bolsheviks were in the minority in the congress, but within the party Stalin's star remained high. In the election of the Bolshevik Party Central Committee, Stalin took ninety-seven votes, third most, trailing only Lenin and Grigory Zinoviev, a long-standing and popular ally of Lenin's who had returned to Petrograd with him on the sealed train from Zurich.

Stalin had attained his strongest position yet within the party, but the democratic Provisional Government controlled Russia. Alexander Kerensky, leader of the Socialist Revolutionary Party and prime minister of the Provisional Government, had the helm. But then Kerensky took the strange (though possibly principled) action that exposed his belly to Lenin and the Bolsheviks.

At the First Congress, Kerensky announced a military offensive against Germany and the Central Powers. He would not end or even pause in fighting the war. Bizarrely, given the political climate, he proposed to send Russia's army back on the march. Conscription would continue, as would the confiscation of grain to feed the soldiers instead of feeding the starving people of Russia. Kerensky's action, of course, pleased the Allied Powers, whose support he needed, but this came at a steep price to his reputation among his own people and provided new fodder for Lenin's many speeches and Stalin's many articles.

Emanuel, meanwhile, remained in the capital through June, operating his businesses from his headquarters. He dispatched his top executive Karl Hagelin to Baku, which, in a role reversal, was quieter than the capital. After brief negotiations between management and the workers' committee, the employees at Nobel Brothers were back on the job, and oil prices were enjoying wartime highs.

In July, Emanuel traveled to the health resort in Yessentuki in the northern Caucasus. During summers before the war, he had enjoyed the spas of Western Europe, but the borders were closed during the war and advisors felt that a domestic retreat was best. He commented that accommodations in the town "match the expectations that one is allowed to have at present."

As the summer heat of 1917 rose, it seemed possible that the declarations of Lenin and Stalin could be dismissed as the ravings of fanatics, that war would continue to be hell, and that the Nobel businesses would continue as usual. But history is full of surprises.

1

An oil painting by Immanuel Nobel that captures the scene of the demonstration of his undersea mines to the Russian crown prince and senior military officials.

2

Immanuel Nobel painted this watercolor that shows men deploying his undersea mines from small boats. His sons Robert and Ludvig later performed this task in defense of Saint Petersburg during the Crimean War.

3

A map of the Caucasus in 1922.

4

Baku Harbor.

5

The interior of a turn-of-the-century oil derrick in the Baku oil fields that houses the drilling equipment and steam engine.

6

Emanuel Nobel, age twelve.

7

Emanuel Nobel and his employees welcoming the Imperial entourage to Nobel Brothers Petroleum Company during Alexander III's visit to Baku in 1888. The background shows the enormous scale of Emanuel's refining and storage operations.

8

The Baku oil fields, circa 1900. The large puddles visible in the photograph are not water but waste oil from gushers.

9

A street corner in the city of Baku, circa 1903. The streets were either mud or dust, theft and violent crime were rampant, and living conditions were dismal.

10

Employee housing at the Nobel Brothers Petroleum Company in the outskirts of Baku. The housing development included paved streets, electric lighting, and many amenities for leisure pastimes. Working conditions for the Nobelites were far better than those experienced by employees of other firms in Baku.

11

Oil wells in Baku experiencing the deadly inferno of a blowout in 1912.

12

Photograph of a Nobel Brothers distribution depot in Brussels, almost three thousand miles from Baku. This horse and cart that carried a cistern of kerosene represented the last leg in Emanuel Nobel's vision of bringing petroleum from his wells in the oil fields of the Caucasus to the wicks of the kerosene lamps in homes around the world.

13

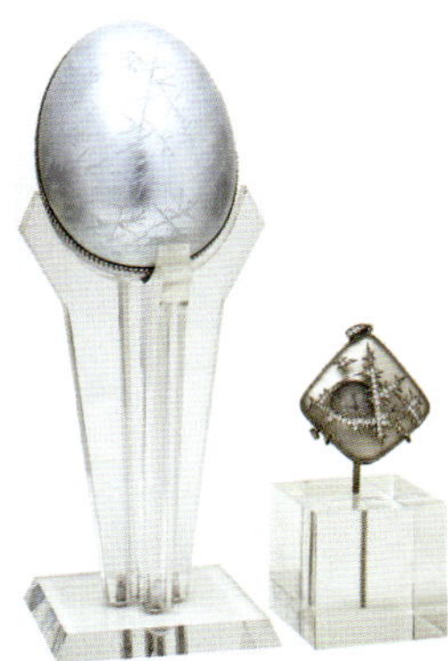

The Fabergé Ice Egg and accompanying Surprise pendant watch (the watch is a "surprise" placed inside the egg) produced by Peter Carl Fabergé in 1911 for his best customer, Emanuel Nobel.

 14

An oil painting of Emanuel Nobel at work in his Saint Petersburg office.

15

The interior of the Nobel factory in Saint Petersburg.

16

The mugshot of Joseph Stalin from his 1910 incarceration in Bailov Prison, Baku.

17

A Soviet propaganda poster from 1947 featuring Joseph Stalin, who was then General Secretary of the Communist Party. The caption of the poster reads: "Stalin's kindness illuminates the future of our children."

18

The image above shows Lenin as he motivates the crowd while Trotsky and Kamenev look on from the steps of the podium. Below is the same image after Stalin's propogandists erased his rivals from the iconic photo. Stalin used similar methods to vanquish the legacy of Robert, Ludvig, and Emanuel Nobel.

19

Communist propaganda poster showing Vladimir Lenin sweeping away kings, capitalists. and religious leaders.

Portrait of Emanuel Nobel by the Russian artist Valentin Serov, 1909.

CHAPTER 16

October

SUMMER TURNED TO fall, and still Emanuel stayed away from Petrograd. The revolution had placed a bull's-eye on capitalists, aristocrats, and the members of the bourgeois. Though the fever pitch of revolt had begun to settle down in the city as the Provisional Government tried to establish order in its first months, the capital was still too dangerous for Emanuel and industrialists like him.

He moved from Yessentuki to the nearby resort town of Kislovodsk. The Grand Duchess Maria Pavlovna, widow of the Tsar's uncle, was already in residence along with many others close to the court.

Emanuel's petroleum and machine businesses, critical to the future of Russia no matter who was in charge, continued to thrive, though the employees took precautions. Nobel's many Swedish and Finnish employees stayed on the job in Russia, but their wives and children evacuated. The hope was for all to return as soon as the new political system had restored order and safety in the streets.

Reflecting the Nobelites' dogged optimism, a popular read among Swedes in Russia was a new book by a Swedish author titled *How to*

Do Business with Russia. The book painted a charming image of what, in retrospect, nearly came to be. The author C. E. W. Petersson, who had sold equipment in Russia for nearly thirty years, claimed that the coming changes would be for the best and that "after many centuries of oppression and repression [under the tsars, Russia] will be opened to the capital, enterprise and energy of the West."

Not all were so optimistic about what the revolution would mean for the future. Britain's prescient diplomat and spy Robert Bruce Lockhart filed a report back to London in the first weeks after the revolution predicting that there certainly would be more revolutions in Russia to follow: "It is improbable that a country in the state in which Russia is at present can pass through so disintegrating an upheaval of her forces without further revolutions and counter-revolutions."

While Kerensky contended with his many political challenges, he approved a half measure of assistance to the deposed Tsar and his family, for whom he felt some sympathy. Kerensky stopped short of allowing Nicholas to leave Russia, which would have been an unpopular decision, but ordered that the family be moved from Petrograd across the Urals, where they would remain under house arrest in a place more easily protected from the mob.

Lockhart's prediction of counterrevolution played out entirely. Kerensky faced a potential coup from both sides of the political spectrum. On the far left were Lenin, Trotsky, and Stalin, who worked feverishly to build support but by the fall were the much smaller threat. Kerensky had thrown Trotsky in jail in August for leading a failed Bolshevik uprising in Petrograd. Lenin had retreated to Finland, and very few of the Russian people were moved by Stalin's extreme rhetoric. More concerning to Kerensky was a potential coup from the far right. Lavr Kornilov, the former general of the Imperial Army who had given Nicholas the news of his arrest, became the face of the counterrevolution. Though Kornilov did not intend to restore the monarchy, he favored wresting control of Petrograd by establishing a military dictatorship. Reviewing the confusing messages between Kerensky and Kornilov, it is unclear whether Kornilov actually intended to move against Kerensky's government, but there is no doubt he questioned Kerensky's strength as a leader. In any event, Kerensky, sensing a threat, real or imagined, declared Kornilov a traitor and ordered his arrest. Kerensky distributed forty thousand rifles from the armory to a militia made of factory workers to put down the counterrevolutionary threat from the right.

Kerensky jailed Kornilov and overcame the immediate threat, but the conflict weakened Kerensky and, predictably, was an enormous boost to the flagging Bolsheviks. Stalin described the Kerensky-Kornilov conflict as a gift to the revolution, writing in September 1917 that prior Marxist revolutions in Europe had lacked staying power and the ability to hold gains because of the "absence of a powerful counterrevolution that might have whipped up the revolution and strengthened it in the fire of battle." Stalin used the Kornilov affair to energize the people, warning that if the far right should retake the government there would be a return to rule by the aristocracy, that land redistribution would be reversed, that the perceived gains of the revolutionary process to lift the repressive boot of the Tsar would be lost. He published an article that framed the people's choice as "Either, or!" There could be no moderation or middle ground as represented by Kerensky. One must choose to back the aristocracy and the counterrevolution or side with the proletariat, the peasantry, and the "complete triumph of the revolution."

Fallout from Kornilov's challenge from the right proved to be the gift that kept on giving to the extremists on the left. The forty thousand rifles that Kerensky distributed to his new militia were now in play. Previously, nearly all striking workers and protestors were unarmed. There had been no such thing as a Red Guard. But these factory workers who were coming under Stalin's spell each now had a rifle. In the wake of the counterrevolutionary threat, Stalin was calling for a complete break from the Provisional Government. And he appeared now to be summoning an army to his side. From a July low point during which many key Bolsheviks were jailed or on the run, the Bolsheviks had emerged by early autumn as the primary threat to the Provisional Government.

The international community watched the shifting tides in Petrograd with great interest. Like the player of a shell game who follows the ball and not the shells that briefly contain it, the Allies and Germany held their gaze on Nobel Brothers and the petroleum of the Caucasus regardless of who held the scepter of power in the capital. British and German spies crawled around the region, subverting opposing causes and promoting their own.

Emanuel observed with equally rapt attention, wondering within which regime he would eventually need to lead his businesses. Any outcome but one, the Bolshevik, held some hope. For the time being, his thousands of employees continued to drill, refine, and distribute oil.

America's interest in the region manifested in the unlikely guise of the Red Cross. Purportedly a humanitarian mission of doctors to aid the ravages of war, the American Red Cross Mission to Russia was suspiciously light on doctors and heavy on industrialists with business ties to Standard Oil, J. P. Morgan, and other American companies. The July 1917 mission, working in Russia just months after the first revolution and while Stalin was publishing his missives, consisted of only seven doctors, outnumbered by fifteen lawyers and businessmen who inexplicably were eager to travel to war-torn Russia. More than half the members of the humanitarian mission came from the New York financial district. This contrasts strangely with the American Red Cross Mission to Romania, also of July 1917, which consisted of sixteen doctors accompanied by only two lawyers, one treasurer, and one engineer. Clearly the mission in Russia had a different composition of personnel because it had a different primary motive.

By August, all seven doctors of the mission to Russia quit in protest of the political activities of the mission and of Colonel William Thompson, who was in charge of the American delegation. Thompson, then forty-eight, was a financier who owned and operated several mines and railroads in the American West.

Thompson had indeed been active. While on the Red Cross mission, he met with Kerensky's government and agreed to provide a $2 million (approximately $50 million in 2024) contribution to a government committee to ensure that it "could have its own press." The chief propaganda aim of this press was to promote Russia's continued fight in the war against Germany. Additionally, J. P. Morgan cabled 425,000 roubles (approximately $40,000) to the Petrograd branch of National City Bank (a Morgan-controlled bank) for Thompson to use as he saw fit. Thompson would remain on the ground in Petrograd, constantly testing the direction of the winds and placing bets on the various groups vying for power using his remarkable access to American capital.

What the titans of Wall Street found so appealing about Russia in 1917 was the common economic outcome shared by monopoly capitalism (as one could describe the American industrial trusts for petroleum, steel, cotton, and tobacco) and the economic planning of a totalitarian socialist state. Which is to say, each of these political and economic environments offers a captive market. In fairness, for years the tsarist regime had preserved the Russian market as semi-captive to the benefit of the Nobels over foreign firms like those of Rothschild and Rockefeller. Now the Americans saw an opportunity to get into the good graces of a new regime that was weak and in need of international friends. This condition led to strange bedfellows—an unlikely alliance between the American capitalists and the international revolutionary socialists. Each represented very different means to the same economic end. Whether a population was controlled by a massive capitalist monopoly or by a communist government that bartered with a foreign industrial interest, the result was a captive economic market.

The socialists were of course aware of these unprincipled bargains being struck, but in their time of frailty, they needed any friends with money who came calling. Lockhart later described Trotsky's pragmatic bending of principle in a report to London: "He [Trotsky] hated British capitalism almost as much as he hated German militarism, but he could not fight the whole world at once. He was therefore willing to cooperate with us [the British] although he stated frankly this must be an agreement of calculation and not of love."

Stalin, the most radical of Lenin's comrades, continued to push a more aggressive agenda to seize power. While international diplomats-cum-spies and the many domestic factions vied for influence in the unstable empire, Lenin was again remembering the lesson of his missed opportunity in 1905. The key was to be decisive and unsparing. Lenin had earlier declared that "an oppressed class which does not strive to learn to use arms, to obtain arms, deserves to be treated as slaves." With greater popular support in the wake of Kornilov's failed counterrevolution, Lenin was determined not to miss his new opportunity.

During the first week of October, Lenin shaved his beard, put on a wig and fake glasses, and took the risk of leaving Finland and returning to Petrograd to attend a meeting of the Bolshevik Central Committee on October 10, his first since the Kerensky government's July crackdown against revolutionary incitement. Due to fear of arrest, only twelve of the twenty-nine committee members were present. Stalin was among them, and he supported Lenin, who delivered some of his most effective browbeating, so that by the end of the all-night meeting, ten of the twelve in attendance voted for immediate insurrection against the Provisional Government.

The two dissenting members, Zinoviev and Kamenev, published their rationale days later in a small newspaper. By publicly explaining their opposition to Lenin's plan, the plan for insurrection was now public as well. As the Menshevik, Bolshevik, and Socialist Revolutionary leaders began to filter into Petrograd for the Second All-Russia Congress of the Soviets, which was planned for October 25, they were split between the Bolsheviks' plan for immediate action and the opposing plan to wait and see.

Then Kerensky took another action that backfired and seemed to bolster the extreme position of the Bolsheviks. Because Kerensky had learned of Lenin's planned insurrection, on October 24 he ordered the arrest of several top Bolshevik leaders and shuttered two Bolshevik newspapers. This provoked Stalin's rank and file to action. The Bolsheviks had approximately ten thousand men armed with rifles, gifted by Kerensky in his action to put down Kornilov. Armed Bolsheviks organized and took to the streets. The officers of the Petrograd garrison who were in support of Kerensky—of which there were about fifteen thousand—strangely stood down and did not engage the insurrection. The defense of the Provisional Government was left mainly to an all-female battalion of 140 soldiers and 40 war invalids. The American diplomat DeWitt Clinton Poole reflected, "The Bolshevik stock phrase is 'seizure of power' but that is really too dramatic a phrase. The Kerensky government simply melted away." The delegates of the All-Russia Congress fell in line, and the Bolsheviks waltzed into power in the course of a single day, nearly unopposed.

By the end of the next day, October 25, Kerensky was out and Lenin was in. This change of control is called the October Revolution, coming only eight months after the prior revolution that ended Romanov rule. Lenin now controlled the government yet still lived the scrappy and humble life of a true and principled revolutionary—something later observed with admiration by foreign dignitaries who met with him. Rather than moving into a palace and drinking rare wines, Lenin made his bed in a makeshift office using a pile of old newspapers. Days after the October Revolution, he retired for the night next to Trotsky, who was on his own pile of newspapers. Lenin remarked to him as he drifted off, "It makes one's head spin to pass so quickly from persecutions and living-in-hiding to power."

With all eyes still on Nobel's petroleum, the international community didn't miss a beat in redirecting funds to keep cozy with those newly in the center of power. Thompson, who remained in Petrograd from July through November in his leadership role of the Red Cross, gave a whopping "personal contribution of $1,000,000" to the Bolshevik cause, as reported months later by *The Washington Post.* What happened behind the curtain was reported decades later in a biography of Thompson that revealed a photograph of the cable to him from J. P. Morgan that read, "Your second cable received. We have paid National City

Bank one million dollars as instructed—Morgan."* American industrialists recognized there was a new sheriff in town who needed friends perhaps more desperately than even Kerensky had. Though Bolshevik rule might still prove to be fleeting, a million dollars to the Morgans and Rockefellers was a small price to pay for favor with the new regime.

Lenin of course knew the tenuousness of his position but also knew where his advantages lay and how to press them. To his colleagues he predicted that the capitalists would fight among themselves to sell him the rope with which he would hang them.

Lenin's paramount advantage was predicated on the Bolsheviks maintaining control of the Caucasus and the petroleum therein. However, control of the petroleum was not simply a matter of military occupation of the region. Emanuel Nobel's company represented more than half the oil from Baku, but an occupying force couldn't just take over production. Without Emanuel's expertise and the cooperation of his workforce, the flow of oil could slow to a trickle.

Almost immediately upon Nicholas II's abdication, Baku had fallen under the sway of the Muslim Turks who had violently ousted their Armenian rivals. Then in the early weeks of 1918, the Armenians had their revenge as they joined the Bolshevik Reds to route the Turkish leadership of the city. The Muslims who did not flee were slaughtered; some estimates run as high as eighteen thousand deaths. Children were flung on sabers, women cut down in the streets, then left in bloody heaps.

Stalin had been in Lenin's ear incessantly over the years about the critical importance of the region, and, thanks in part to Stalin's work, the city of Baku was a Bolshevik stronghold. Stalin reiterated his position, declaring that with Finland and Poland breaking away from the empire in the west, holding Russia's "southern flank" of the Caucasus was more critical than ever. The dominant figure of the southern flank was Emanuel Nobel.

---

* When Lenin later issued the nationalization decree, the National City Bank branch in Petrograd was the only domestic or foreign bank that the Bolsheviks did not seize.

As Emanuel observed the events of October and Lenin's victory, trepidation turned to dread. He could work with an autocracy, he could work with a constitutional democracy, and he could work even with a moderate socialist government. But for an industrialist like Nobel, Bolshevism represented the end. With strict implementation of Marxist philosophy, the state would seize every asset, and private ownership would come to an end.

He remained in the resort town of Kislovodsk, sending and receiving myriad letters to manage the businesses. He lived quietly and peacefully. Several younger half siblings and their in-laws even found the opportunity to ride horses and play tennis. Soon after the October Revolution, his half brothers Gösta and Emil, now thirty-one and thirty-two, traveled from Petrograd to visit him. They had a happy family reunion over meals that were far less extravagant than had been the norm only a year before. Mainly there was work to be done. The brothers needed to consult with Emanuel in person, avoiding the delays in the exchange of written correspondence. In the spa town the Nobel family leaders spent long days around a table, reviewing the fast-moving events in the capital and speculating about the country's surprising new leadership.

The brothers celebrated Christmas together with a traditional Swedish meal, then stayed on with Emanuel into the new year. In early January, despite his concerns for their safety, Emanuel agreed that his brothers should return to the company headquarters in Petrograd, writing, "It is with a feeling of great unease that I allow them to go."

The Nobel businesses needed leadership on-site, preferably from a member of the family, but at present Emanuel could not be that person because Stalin's eye remained fixed on him. Emanuel lamented in a letter to his stepmother, "I cannot deny that our friends are justified when they press me with such urgency to keep away from Petrograd and from Baku as well as Grozny, where large crowds of workers are clamoring."

Emanuel was far too recognizable to walk those streets and too big a prize for Stalin. The Bolshevik leadership, especially Stalin, was aware of precisely where Emanuel had taken refuge. For the moment, they did not have the strength to reach him. Lenin was busy on numerous fronts: domestic rivals for power, foreign interference from the Allies, a lingering war with Germany, and splintering factions of the empire. But Lenin was ruthless and able to see several moves ahead. As his strength grew, he would come for Nobel.

CHAPTER 17

Campaign Promise Delivered

When Emil and Gösta Nobel returned to Petrograd, they felt as did most citizens of Russia and the world—that the Bolshevik putsch was a flash in the pan. As historian Anna Reid has written, the Bolshevik government was not quite stillborn, but was extremely fragile and did not enjoy widespread public support. American journalist John Reed, who was reporting on the revolution at the time, wrote that "it never occurred to anyone—except perhaps to Lenin, Trotsky and the Petersburg workers—that the Bolsheviki would remain in power longer than three days."

Many of the moderates and those on the right were persistently optimistic in the face of Lenin's gains; a brief period under Lenin's control could even be a good thing because a failed Bolshevik experiment might then rid Russia of the radical Marxist scourge forever. The Nobels felt that if they could simply keep their heads down, keep building Diesels, and keep the oil flowing, they might ride out the storm in a matter of weeks or months at most.

Lenin had other ideas, and all the momentum. True to his dictum, he was decisive this time around, not allowing rivals and enemies the space to breathe. To colleagues he reflected that there can be decades in which nothing happens, then weeks when decades happen. He aimed to maximize his narrow window of opportunity.

In one of the great ironies of the revolution, Lenin quickly censored the press. After years spent denouncing the Tsar's censorship and operating a network of illegal underground printing presses, once in power Lenin quickly shuttered more than sixty newspapers in one of his first government decrees. He explained that the repression "was of a temporary nature and will be removed by a special decree as soon as normal conditions are reestablished." Many correctly supposed that time would never come.

He founded the All-Russia Extraordinary Commission for Combating Counter-Revolution and Sabotage, known to history as the Cheka, its Russian acronym. This brutal domestic paramilitary force became Lenin's means of enforcing Bolshevik justice. Terror reigned, and the tactics of the Cheka were designed to incite fear to the point that even talk of subversion was unthinkable. Those suspected of disloyalty were imprisoned in horrific conditions. Louis de Robien observed with distress that when a suspect could not be apprehended, the Cheka imprisoned and tortured his wife and children until the suspect arrived to surrender himself.

This had been Stalin's favorite style of play, and alarmingly he now had government backing. He boasted the personal mantra, "Death solves all problems. No man, no problem."

Overnight, these actions sullied the lofty utopian socialist ideals that had been shouted on street corners for decades. They seemed a far cry from Lenin's humble bedding of newspapers or his habit of holding meetings around a plain table over a spare meal that had made a positive impression on foreign dignitaries in his early days of power. Denis Garstin, a captain of the British army, wrote, "If you look at what the Bolsheviks want to do you feel sympathetic, but if you look at what they've done, you're dead against them."

No matter how objectionable Lenin's repressive measures were, for the moment he held the keys to government, and therefore the keys to Russia's vast natural resources. To some extent, international governments needed to play ball. And yet, there was still a war on. There was still an Eastern Front. The German army was a colossal force, and the Russian army, especially in the splintering disarray of the revolution, was all but nonexistent. It seemed the dreaded Germans might march into Petrograd unimpeded.

Lenin had opened negotiations with the Germans, primarily through his lieutenant Trotsky, but there was no formal peace. The Germans wanted land, petroleum, copper, coal, and wheat. They decided that the more they could grab before reaching terms, the better the terms would be. The German army was on an eastward march to Petrograd.

France and Great Britain had a deadly fear of Lenin taking Russia out of the war, which would mean that 150 divisions of German, Austrian, and Turkish troops could move from the east to the west, where they would take up the fight. In addition, if Russia concluded a separate peace with Germany, Russia would release nearly two million prisoners of war back to the Central Powers to become soldiers again. And what's more, terms of a treaty between Russia and Germany could be sweetened with arms, fuel, and grain to support the enemies of France and Britain.

The Allied belief was that it was far more critical to prevent Russia from leaving the war than it was to persuade America to join it. The US Congress had voted to join the Allied side in April 1917, which was certainly welcome news, but America was an ocean away. America's military-industrial capacity had not yet ramped up. America had never fought a war in Europe, and American troops were unorganized and untrained, not seasoned and battle-tested like the hardened troops who already lined the trenches of Europe by the millions. Most believed that whatever contribution America could make would be too little and too late to be of consequence.

Great Britain debated these same fears at the highest levels. Foreign Secretary (and former prime minister) Arthur Balfour wrote in December 1917 of a general sentiment in Britain that "the Bolsheviks could only be regarded as avowed enemies, and to treat them as anything else showed a lamentable incapacity to see facts as they are." This seemed a clear and inescapable ideological reality. The Bolsheviks had openly declared themselves enemies, calling for the Marxist overthrow of every government around the world. Britain could hardly miss this warning, and indeed, at the time of Balfour's writing, Britain was quietly funding anti-Bolshevik causes throughout southern Russia, especially in the oil regions of the Caucasus.

Yet in the same memorandum Balfour acknowledged the dilemma presented by the Great War in dealing with this new regime in Russia whose stated mission was an end to the British way of life. He finished the memorandum with the conclusion that "no policy would be more fatal than to give the Russians a motive for welcoming into their midst German officials and German soldiers as friends and deliverers." Balfour believed the British would need to play nice with Lenin, because the worse of two evils was an alliance between the Germans and the Bolsheviks.

Prime Minister Lloyd George stopped well short of actual diplomatic recognition of the Bolshevik government, but Balfour's memorandum persuaded Lloyd George to make an outreach of support.

Weeks later Trotsky met with Robert Bruce Lockhart, who was in regular contact with Bolshevik officials and had become quite enamored of the charismatic Trotsky. Though Trotsky was pleased to see warmer messaging from London to the Bolshevik government, he was also aware of London's concurrent financial support of anti-Bolshevik causes. He remarked to Lockhart, "Your Lloyd George is like a man playing roulette, scattering chips on every number."

But the Bolsheviks played many angles, too. For years the Germans had supported Bolshevik reentry to Russia, which indicated a friendship in theory. Contradicting this theory were two undeniable facts: Lenin was actively inciting Marxist revolts inside Germany to spread Bolshevism and topple Kaiser Wilhelm II's authoritarian regime, and the German army continued its offensive against Bolshevik Russia, attempting to acquire land and resources from the broken empire.

The diplomatic signaling from Lenin and Trotsky was confusing. Lenin kept his options open as to whether he would be a friend to the Allies or to Germany.

Britain and America had a similar policy toward the Bolsheviks: nonintervention with a guise of friendliness that stopped short of diplomatic recognition. While they viewed the Bolsheviks as a threat, that threat was secondary, and their focus remained on winning the war first.

On November 28, 1917, Wilson officially ordered that there be no American interference with the Bolshevik Revolution. In January 1918, with America now nine months into the European conflict, Wilson gave his famous "Fourteen Points" speech, which was meant to lay out the principles for negotiations that would end the war. The entirety of point six addressed Russia. Wilson promised the chaotic remnants of the former Russian Empire, presently led by Lenin, a path "unhampered" by the international community to forge its own political future.

A month later, on February 16, Secretary of State Robert Lansing, an ardent anti-Bolshevik, mirrored the British policy when writing to the French ambassador Jusserand, "It is considered inadvisable to take any action which will antagonize at this time any of the people which now control the power in Russia."

Morgan and Rockefeller had heavy influence at the State Department, which seemed to permit (though not declare) a green light for Wall Street to stake out American interests in Russian markets. And Trotsky welcomed these rich American industrialists. His shaky new government needed foreign trade, investment, and capital. The lack of diplomatic recognition of the Bolsheviks was confounding him, starving him out.

Trotsky's official title was the People's Commissar for Foreign Affairs. Appointed by Lenin, who was Chairman of the Council of People's Commissars, Trotsky became the Bolshevik representative to the West and by accounts was impressive and reasonable to deal with. He also nominally held the keys to Russia's vast natural assets and seemed ready to make deals. This delighted Raymond Robins, who had replaced Thompson as the head of the American Red Cross Mission in Russia and was the face of Wall Street to the East. Robins joined Britain's Lockhart for lunch on February 12, 1918, and, reflecting the optimism many in the West still held for dealing with the Bolsheviks in their first months of power, declared Trotsky to be "the greatest Jew since Jesus Christ."

Robins wanted Wall Street to leap into Russia and grab the spoils of petroleum, minerals, timber, and grain. He knew that to move quickly—quicker than the Germans could exploit the situation—he needed Bolshevik support. Though capitalism and communism are diametrically opposed in theory, the reality of the German threat made strange economic bedfellows for the Bolsheviks.

In a statement from Robins to Lockhart, the American admitted:

> *You will hear it said that I am a representative of Wall Street . . . let us assume it is true. Let us assume that I am here to capture Russia for Wall Street and for American business men. Let us assume that you are a British wolf and that I am an American wolf, and that when this war is over we are going to eat each other up for the Russian market . . . but let us assume at the same time that we are fairly intelligent wolves, and that we know that if we do not hunt together in this hour the German wolf will eat us both up.*

These high-stakes hunting games advanced a disastrous outcome for Emanuel Nobel and the other Russian industrialists. Nobel was caught in a terrible trap. On one side were the commercial interests of the Allied Powers. If Morgan, Rockefeller, and others had their way, they'd abscond with Russia's treasures and leave Nobel with nothing. If the Bolsheviks could manage to gather independent strength without giving away the candy store to the Allies, the communist regime would simply confiscate and keep (per the instructions that are the very bedrock of communism) Russia's treasures and leave Nobel with nothing. The third and possibly worst of all options was that all of

Russia would soon be speaking German, at which point Nobel's fate would be anyone's guess. Emanuel's only card to play was the same card he'd always had—that he knew how to run a petroleum business better than anyone else in Russia.

As the world circled to pick the carcass of the Romanov Empire, Nobel represented the most prized assets. For someone like Rockefeller, who had been on the losing end of a struggle with Nobel for decades, this was a gift of the first order. Having been unable to break Nobel the old-fashioned way, now he might be able to let the Bolsheviks break Nobel for him, then have the State Department hand him the leftovers.

However, the Bolsheviks breaking Nobel and controlling Baku was by no means assured. Lenin was barely holding the capital. Just as Emanuel had felt unsafe in Petrograd, Lenin was also feeling uneasy living there, but for a different reason, and decided to leave as Nobel had done months before. Not wanting to be anywhere near for what seemed the inevitable arrival of the Germans, on March 12 Lenin moved himself and his government from the capital to the ancient city of Moscow, about 440 miles to the southeast.

The new government quickly made itself at home. The Hotel Metropol,* a jewel of Moscow initially designed to be an opera house, was renamed the Second House of the Soviets, and its 250 rooms housed many top Bolshevik officials. Lenin established the center of power in the Imperial Senate building of the Kremlin, which had been commissioned in the time of Catherine the Great. After a two-hundred-year hiatus, Moscow again became the capital of Russia, as it remains today.

Lenin enacted further rebranding, a tactic that would be a hallmark of the Soviet regime. In February he dropped the Julian calendar of the tsars and adopted the optically more modern Gregorian calendar of the West. This put an end to the confounding thirteen-day difference in recording events in Russia that has been a thorn to historians.

---

* The Hotel Metropol is the setting for the Amor Towles novel *A Gentleman in Moscow.*

He also took the action to rebrand his own party by dropping the word *Bolshevik*. On March 8 (Gregorian), Lenin took the formal action of swapping the name *Bolshevik Party* for the *All-Russian Communist Party*. The word *Bolshevik* had come to be associated internationally with radical and brutal methods. And communism had always been the goal. The long-held axiom of Marxist doctrine was that capitalism would be replaced by a transitional period of socialism (bringing equal distribution of wealth and property), which would in turn be replaced by communism (eliminating private ownership of productive property).

Diplomats of Western Europe stationed in Petrograd watched as the greatest treasures collected by centuries of tsars were transported from the capital of the tsars to the capital of Lenin. In a single day, Lenin's men loaded the most valuable items of the Winter Palace (today better known as the Hermitage, which functions as a museum) into twenty-seven train carriages and sent them off to Moscow. The mind-boggling diversity of the artifacts reflected the hundreds of disparate cultures that, by force or by treaty, had been rolled into a fragile concept of unity since the thirteenth century when Genghis Khan and his Golden Horde swept from China and Siberia across the plains to the borders of Europe, linking territory that would mostly become Russian by the time of the Romanovs.

Wealthy aristocrats sought to make a fire sale of prized possessions in order to acquire cash that would be easier to take with them on the run. Louis de Robien, who appreciated fine art, lamented that such precious items might fall into the hands of those who didn't fully appreciate beauty. Aware of a priceless bust of Marie Antoinette that decorated the parlor of a Petrograd mansion, he wrote, "It is a unique example, the others having been destroyed during the French Revolution, and it would be highly desirable if the Versailles Museum could buy it, rather than it should one day grace the parlor of a Transatlantic pork merchant."

Treasure was not all the Bolsheviks took from the halls of the former regime. Trotsky entered the foreign office and demanded to see all secret treaties between Nicholas's government and his counterparts in France and Great Britain. Trotsky obtained treaties that outlined the terms (upon victory in the ongoing European war) to divvy up the spoils, mainly the stretch of territory connecting the Black Sea with the Mediterranean, critical to global commerce. To expose the imperialist plans of the former Tsar—and Russia's Provisional Government, which had maintained the secrecy—Trotsky publicly revealed the treaties, which were published in a number of newspapers, including *The New York Times*.

The Bolsheviks' capacity to exert international military force was negligible, though fortunately for Lenin the calamity of the European war-in-progress seemed to solve more problems than it presented. Lenin's way forward was to keep the international community friendly and guessing. He had come to power with the Russian people in large part by riding his promise to pull Russia from the war, but to exit the war would mean terminating any friendship with the Allies, such as it was. His hope was that the fighting on the Eastern Front might simply pause, then stop altogether, perhaps with a wink and a nod rather than a formal treaty. Trotsky began publicly to advocate a position of "neither war nor peace," in which there would be no official peace that would violate Russia's commitment to the Allies, and there would be no ongoing war that would violate Lenin's commitment to Russia's peasants and proletariat.

Lenin was prepared to capitulate to the Germans, painful as the terms of the Germans would be, but he gave Trotsky some leeway to see if his noncommitment to any side might work. Trotsky's fence-straddling proved unacceptable to the Germans, who already distrusted the Bolsheviks, especially since they were actively provoking socialist uprisings in Berlin. On February 18, Major General Max Hoffman restarted the eastward march of the German army toward Petrograd. The Germans also supported Finland's General Mannerheim, recently assisted out of Russia by Emanuel Nobel, to overthrow the Bolshevik-supported Finnish Socialist Workers' Republic.

With Germany back on the march, Lenin capitulated within days. On February 23, he received Germany's redrafted terms by courier. It was an ultimatum far worse than the terms offered before Trotsky's attempt at an informal peace. Among the terms now demanded by Kaiser Wilhelm II was recognition by Soviet Russia of the independence—and German occupation of—Finland and Estonia, which came with strategic ports on the Baltic Sea; Ukraine, with all its wheat production; and, most prized by the Kaiser, the oil regions around the Caspian Sea. Certain Caucasian lands, including the port of Batum on the Black Sea taken by Alexander II forty years earlier, would return to Germany's ally, the Ottoman Empire. The treaty also called for the Bolsheviks to disarm and pay a massive indemnity.

Lenin was ready to sign, but Trotsky and other senior Bolsheviks, including Stalin, objected. The Germans had given only forty-eight hours for an answer, and about half of that was used up by the travel of the courier to deliver the message. In the frenzied persuasions, Stalin came around to support Lenin and the treaty as proposed by the Germans. The fact was that Lenin could muster no army to oppose Major General Hoffman's advance. He was over a barrel, and if the Germans chose to exploit the situation with harsh terms, there was nothing he could do to stop them.

On March 3, only a day after the German army seized Kiev, Lenin's government signed the Treaty of Brest-Litovsk and concluded a separate peace. The bitter Russians taunted that the Allies would still likely prevail in the European war and reverse Germany's fortunes with equally punitive terms. The Russian representative Karl Radek portentously remarked to General Hoffman, "In the end the Allies will put a Brest-Litovsk treaty upon you."

From the Allied perspective, the Treaty of Brest-Litovsk confirmed Bolshevik treachery. This massive betrayal closed down Germany's Eastern Front. The German army was now free to throw its full strength against the French and British with the hope of knocking them out of the war before American troops could arrive in force.

Politically, the treaty marked a shift in the way Allied governments treated the Bolsheviks. Many early supporters of Lenin, Trotsky, and Stalin—people like Britain's Lockhart, who had argued there was advantage in forging commercial and diplomatic relationships with the Bolsheviks—began to change their tune, now believing that the Bolshevik government was dangerous and untrustworthy and must be opposed.

International distrust in Lenin grew as governments became aware that Lenin was true to his word in his desire to provoke socialist revolutions around the world. His machinations behind the scenes to incite revolt were not limited to Finland, Germany, and an abortive Bolshevik revolution in France in 1918. Stalin's old playbook to keep the printing presses active in the Caucasus had moved to countries in the West, including Britain and America. American universities began to teach courses in Marxism and socialism. As Marxist literature became more prevalent in America, the public became more concerned about the movement's growth. American media began to scrutinize industrialists, including Henry Ford and J. P. Morgan (as recorded by financial journalist John Barron), and accused them of having Bolshevik sympathies.

But sometimes business is just business. Socialism, as long as it remained in Russia, was incidental to the American tycoons. American industry was typically on the side of the greatest financial gain. Journalists and American congressional hearings had already begun to explore clandestine Wall Street and State Department involvement in the 1903 revolution in Panama for purposes of exploiting the canal; the 1912 revolution in China in return for the commercial advantages that Sun Yat-sen might deliver should he prevail; and financial support for Pancho Villa in the Mexican Revolution of 1914–15.

Wall Street was not ideological. In fact, during the Great War, the Morgan-controlled banks Guaranty Trust and American International Corporation made loans to both sides in the conflict. Military intelligence provided a summary of American loans—some illegal—to German interests during the war in a report to the 1919 Overman Committee of the US Senate.

But while Wall Street was not particularly moved by ideology, people were. From inside the Bolshevik borders, Maxim Gorky felt that Lenin and Stalin had abandoned revolutionary ideals in favor of a police state. He wrote in April 1918, just after the Treaty of Brest-Litovsk, "They are cold-bloodedly sacrificing Russia in the name of their dream of the world-wide and European revolution." He lamented that "we Russians make up a people that has never yet worked in freedom" and that, in deposing the Tsar for Lenin, Russia had traded one dictator for another.

The charge that Gorky, Kerensky, and many Russians leveled against Lenin and Stalin was that these revolutionaries valued Marxism above Russia, that their true aim was not national but international, and in order to see Bolshevism spread around the world they were willing to sacrifice Russia and its people. In what was called Leninism, the Bolshevik leadership, especially Stalin and Lenin, prioritized support for Bolshevik uprisings in countries around the world.

Political and military leaders of nations in Europe and the Americas were coming to recognize Bolshevism as their greatest threat. Even while war still raged in Europe, Churchill went so far as to say that the Allies should prepare to bolster Germany back up in a postwar Europe as a bulwark against Bolshevism.

As suspicion and outright opposition mounted, Lenin continued to practice duplicity. On March 1, only two days before the signing ceremony for the peace treaty with Germany, Lenin took a chair across the table from Robert Bruce Lockhart. It was the first meeting between the two men, and Lenin was in a desperate situation. He had made the decision to betray his alliance with the British, yet he needed continued British aid. Lenin tried to assure Lockhart that Russia was still very much for the Allied cause, that Germany was the true enemy, and that the treaty with Germany was only a necessary expedient to halt the German march on Petrograd.

Lockhart, still on good terms with Trotsky, listened intently. Lenin promised that even after the treaty, Russia would implement a policy of "passive resistance" against the Germans that could possibly cause Germany to keep more troops in the East even than a declared war against the beleaguered Bolshevik army would have. When Lockhart seemed reassured, Lenin went a step further to ask his new friend if Britain would persuade her ally Japan not to attack Russia from the Pacific side, and that if this could be done, Lenin would even provide safe passage to a Japanese force to travel across Russia and create a new Eastern Front against the Germans. Lockhart of course loved the (unlikely) plan and reported it back to Britain.

Per the Treaty of Brest-Litovsk, the Baku assets of the Nobel Brothers Petroleum Company were in theory, though not in practice, now in German-controlled territory. Given Stalin's obsession with Nobel's oil, this concession seems impossible, and it was. Lenin and Stalin never took this term of the treaty seriously. Baku was theirs, and on this term in particular Lenin's commitment to continue resisting Germany was sincere. Although Soviet Russia did not live up to its Allied commitments, Lenin and Stalin also never stopped treating Germany as the enemy.

The treaty was only weeks old when Lenin made another capitulation of sorts—this time to Emanuel Nobel. With the war nearing its fourth anniversary, all the major powers were desperate for fuel. This included the Bolsheviks, who inherited Imperial Russia's reserves that were depleted by the war effort despite Nobel's continued production. Lenin of course knew where in the ground the petroleum was, but he needed someone to drill for it, refine it, and deliver it to the places that required it. His ramshackle government had no ministry in place to take on the task, and so as much as Stalin might have wished to imprison or execute Emanuel, he knew the Soviets needed Nobel. Perhaps prison or execution could come later. Instead, they would send Nobel a summons.

Both Nobel and Stalin had anxiously watched from afar as varied and desperate forces fought for control of Baku. In March 1918, a new player emerged to govern the city's treasures on behalf of the Bolsheviks who had wrested Baku from the Turks.

Stepan Shaumian was an Armenian Bolshevik born in Tiflis. At thirty-nine, he was the same age as Stalin, and the two had collaborated many times over the previous decade for the Bolshevik cause in southern Russia. After the Bolshevik Revolution, Shaumian became chairman of the Baku Council of People's Commissars and oversaw the period of the Baku Commune that took control of Baku in March.

Per the terms of the Treaty of Brest-Litovsk, the Ottomans received land concessions in the Caucasus that included Batum, but there was no direct mention of Baku in the treaty. Adding to the confusion over territorial claims, Azerbaijan, Armenia, and Georgia all rejected the treaty and instead declared independence. The Bolsheviks also effectively rejected the treaty as it applied to Baku and attempted to hold Baku and its oil for Lenin's government.

Shaumian's main objective was to secure the petroleum and send it north to Tsaritsyn, then on to the rest of Russia. The most daunting obstacle to meeting this objective was, of course, the Ottoman Empire, which had the fiercest military presence in the region and was determined to retake Baku by force. The Ottoman Turks were moving so aggressively toward Baku that even Germany, their ally in the war, was growing wary of what they viewed as Ottoman greed for the petroleum region. The Turks had an army of twenty thousand soldiers marching through Transcaucasia, about twice the number Shaumian could call to arms. While Shaumian trained and outfitted a Red army in Baku for what seemed an inevitable clash with the Turks, he tried to stabilize the oil industry. Though he agreed with Stalin on the long-term course of full nationalization, for the time being he made no change to the existing structure that kept the pre-revolutionary industrialists like Nobel in charge.

On April 12, 1918, Lenin and Stalin directed Isidor Gukovsky, the new finance minister and commissar for oil matters, to send a demand letter by courier to Emanuel Nobel in Kislovodsk. By this time, there were many armies in Russia, including the Russian Whites for the old regime, the Russian Reds for the Bolsheviks, the Germans, British, and Turks. Civil unrest and looting were so widespread that there was no postal service connecting Petrograd with southern Russia, and telegraphic connections were mostly cut off; all communications between Nobel and people in Petrograd or Moscow happened by courier.

Moscow addressed the April letter to "Citizen Emanuel Ludvigovich Nobel" and summoned him to Moscow. The newly named communist government wrote in the letter that they required Emanuel's presence to address "pressing issues concerning the Nobel Bothers Petroleum Company with regard to the delivery of liquid fuel to Volga, Moscow and Petrograd."

Even if Moscow had been a safe place for Nobel—which it was not—this would have been a perilous journey through vicious battle lines in which many of those doing the fighting were snatching industrial chiefs like Nobel for ransom, prison, or worse. Anticipating Nobel's concern for his safety, the letter assured that Lenin had ordered all Soviet officials in the realm to guarantee safe passage from Kislovodsk to Moscow for Emanuel and his family. The Soviets needed his help.

Yet the Soviet request for partnership, like the Soviets' negotiations with the British and Americans, was a partnership of reluctant calculation, not ideological alignment. It was a capitulation by Lenin and Stalin, one that could be revoked at any time, possibly the moment Emanuel set foot in communist-controlled Moscow.

No doubt, Emanuel recognized this trap. He refused Stalin's summons. His half brothers Gösta and Emil were in Petrograd, but Emanuel remained in Kislovodsk through the spring, waiting. Emanuel still believed that these upstart radicals—Lenin, Stalin, and Trotsky, who had no training or experience in running a nation—could not last long. If the Germans didn't take them out first, certainly the Allies would not tolerate this communist government that had already avowed itself an enemy of the West.

CHAPTER 18

Burn Down the Mast

ONE MONTH AFTER Emanuel declined the summons to Moscow, the first train in five months readied to leave Kislovodsk in the Caucasus, and Emanuel's executive team assumed he'd be on it. He could be safely in Sweden within days. Instead, Emanuel gave up his seat to Vladimir Kokovtsov, who had been finance minister under the Tsar and who had decided he'd had enough. Emanuel's decision to stay in the Caucasus in May 1918 seems foolhardy more than one hundred years later, but at the time his calculation to remain had sound logic. He was tucked within a vast region controlled by the White Army, which opposed the Bolsheviks. And although Baku was under communist control, it was but an island of red in a sea of white.

The anticipated wane of Bolshevik strength seemed to be underway. On May 16, upon reading a German intelligence report that outlined Lenin's many predicaments, Kaiser Wilhelm II wrote in the margin, "He is finished." Lenin's challenges were myriad.

On May 28, from Tiflis, the majority-Islamic population of Azerbaijan that had been under the rule of the tsars for a hundred years declared independence from Russia and created the Azerbaijan

Democratic Republic. Georgia and Armenia quickly declared independence as well. Stalin saw his southern flank coming apart, but with so many crises he was powerless to do anything about it.

Stalin and Lenin's adversaries were internal as well and included those who also occupied the far left of the political spectrum. The Socialist Revolutionaries, whose strength came mainly from the peasant farmers rather than the urban-centric Bolsheviks, had briefly supported Lenin but then split with him over Brest-Litovsk. The leader of the Socialist Revolutionaries, Maria Spiridonova, wanted to continue to fight the Germans. A day after publicly denouncing Lenin and his peace policy, she dispatched two assassins to penetrate the office of the German ambassador to Russia, where they blew him up with a grenade, then escaped through a window. She hoped the assassination would infuriate the Germans and reignite the war. But Germany determined that a new invasion of Russia was pointless—Bolshevism was doomed anyway, and Germany needed her troops elsewhere.

Lenin held on to the strings of power, but barely. One of the few dynamics in his favor was that the many factions that opposed him also opposed each other. These factions were united in their loathing of his regime but had almost no other common ground, and he still had more power than any other single group within the disarray.

Reflecting the confusion over who was in power, when the Japanese landed a force in Vladivostok along Russia's eastern edge, it was with the stated purpose, as Britain's Balfour said, to "help the Russians." But nobody in Russia knew which Russians the Japanese meant to help. As a result, leaders of the Reds and the Whites were equally suspicious. Of course, both were correct to be on their guard because Japan's primary business inside Russia, as was the case with all of Russia's powerful neighbors, was to help themselves to land, minerals, timber, and Nobel's petroleum.

Also opposing Lenin from the east was the Czech Legion, an experienced fighting force on the side of the Allies in the Great War. The unit was made up of volunteer soldiers from the Czech region that had been a part of the Austro-Hungarian Empire and whose goal was to become an independent Czech state. The Czechs suspected the Bolsheviks of sympathies with Germany and so opposed them in the Russian Civil War. The Legion's numbers had grown to fifty thousand after the release of Czech prisoners of war per the terms of the Russian peace with Germany. Joining with Siberian peasants and Cossacks, by the spring, the Czech Legion became one of Lenin's fiercest threats and had taken over large stretches of the Trans-Siberian Railway.

To the south in the Caucasus, by the end of May, a large Turkish force had gathered in Elizavetpol, a neighboring town to Baku, and was making preparations to seize the city. The Germans held Ukraine and the nearby territory around the Black Sea, while the Ottomans held neighboring Batum, and the British general Lionel Dunsterville* was stationed in Hamadan, a few hundred miles south of Baku in present-day Iran. Dunsterville had several thousand troops, forty-one Model-T Fords, and orders to "prevent German and Turkish penetration" in Baku. By the summer of 1918, the oil city was an active theater in the European war.

Shaumian knew he was outmatched by the Turks and pleaded with Stalin, who was in the process of securing Bolshevik control of Tsaritsyn, midway between Baku and Moscow and critical for distribution, to send military aid. Stalin, to his own and Shaumian's dismay, had scant troops to spare, and when Shaumian realized that he could not summon nearly enough Bolshevik support to withstand the coming Turkish assault, he and his advisors considered inviting Dunsterville's British troops into the city to fend off a massacre at the hands of the Turks and a forfeiture of the oil fields. Many of the terrified members of the Baku Commune favored an invitation to Dunsterville, but Lenin, due to diplomatic tensions with Britain, refused the idea.

Dunsterville's mission was not to seize Russia's oil for the British as much as it was to prevent Germany from controlling it. The British soldiers who came to be known as the "Dunsterforce" had to navigate

---

* Dunsterville attended school with the author Rudyard Kipling and was the inspiration for the character Stalky in Kipling's stories *Stalky & Co.*

xenophobic, warlike, and well-armed bands of Azerbaijanis, Armenians, and Turks who each believed in a birthright claim to the region.

In the chaos of small armies, the flood of updates to Lenin was overwhelming, and in a speech to the national Soviet (hereafter referred to as the Soviet) he complained that "one fool can ask more questions than ten wise men can answer." He recognized that his own survival depended on draconian decisiveness, and a good measure of paranoia. Rather than treat an enemy as though he might soon be a friend, as the old adage goes, he treated friends as though they would soon be an enemy. And he tied off loose ends. In a momentous and irrevocable act born of insecurity, he tied off the biggest loose end of all.

By the time the ink was dry on Brest-Litovsk, Nicholas II and his family had been held captive about a year, living modestly yet comfortably under house arrest in Tobolsk, Siberia. Kerensky had allowed this and even expressed worry for the Tsar's safety. But Lenin knew that a living tsar was a threat, a banner around which the Whites could rally. Word had also reached Lenin that the Bolshevik guards had grown quite cozy with the royal family and that there had been much mutual flirting between members of the guard and the teenage princesses.

Lenin issued a directive to move the royals west, closer to Moscow, to the compound of a wealthy merchant in Ekaterinburg, where Lenin assigned a more cold-blooded guard detail to enforce the house arrest. He planned to bring all the Romanovs who were in line for the throne to Ekaterinburg, where he would orchestrate their trial for crimes against the state, a trial that would have a predetermined guilty verdict. He intended for the trial to be a show that was worthy of an international audience, and preparations for apparent legitimacy of the spectacle would take some time.

Amid the military and political tumult, Lenin attempted to impose Marxist economic policy on Russia. Under Kerensky, the Provisional Government had introduced the concept of a labor exchange. Then, with the Bolsheviks in power, on February 18, 1918, Lenin mandated that in cities with a population greater than fifty thousand all hiring of employees must happen through a labor exchange comprising Soviet-appointed officials. Each urban center would have its own exchange.

The exchange had four primary responsibilities: to register the supply and demand for labor, to set the appropriate wages, to actively mediate recruitment and job placement of workers, and to collect and record information on the state-owned labor market.

In support of the disparate labor markets around the country, the government confiscated thousands of private homes in the cities and moved workers in from the industrial outskirts, repartitioning these homes according to the size and need of the new families who were to supply the labor.

For a government nearly paralyzed by crises, the central planning of the labor markets was an impossible task. The labor exchanges were organized by people who were incapable of doing the job, not only because many of them were inept, but also because nobody knew how to organize a labor market—such an endeavor had never happened before at any time or place in history. Plans were repeatedly drawn up, discarded, then redrawn all while industrial efficiency waned and corruption waxed. The madness was compounded by the fact that a huge swath of Russia, in particular Siberia and the steppe region (modern Kazakhstan) of eastern Russia, was not under Bolshevik control but was occupied by forces of the White Army.

Nowhere in Russia were the stakes higher or the bedlam greater than in Baku. As chairman of the Baku Commune, a large part of Shaumian's job was to develop sources of revenue to pay the salaries of soldiers in the Red Army. Shaumian needed money immediately, before economic reforms could realistically be put in place, so he turned to levying taxes. Shaumian settled on a fifty-million-rouble tax* per capitalist, and when the tax was not paid voluntarily, Shaumian

---

* This was a period of hyperinflation in Russia, and equivalent values are difficult to determine. For example, the largest printed Russian banknote in 1918 was ten thousand roubles. By 1921, Russia printed banknotes for ten million roubles.

directed that the tax be collected by force, which led to moments that were so haphazard as to be farcical. Anastas Mikoyan, the editor of a socialist newspaper in Baku who worked with Shaumian to collect taxes, recounted his adventure demanding the tax from a bank that refused to pay it: "I had heard there were such things as safes, but had never seen one." Mikoyan entered the local bank with Shaumian's fourteen-year-old son and several Red Army soldiers carrying rifles. Mikoyan reported with a sense of unreality about the seriousness and peril of events, "We shouted: 'Hands up! Everybody stand!' It was funny and very exciting. Then I asked 'Where are the safes?'" The deputy manager of the bank came to open the safe, but only one of two required keys was on the premises. Having done nothing but cause a scene, Mikoyan simply returned to the offices of his newspaper.

While the tax collection efforts continued with some success, Shaumian also worked to bring the oil industry under control of the Soviet. The Baku Council of People's Commissars met three times per week from 10 p.m. to 3 a.m., and the first order of business at each meeting was to review the quantity of oil shipped north to central Russia. Lenin remained skeptical of any changes that might disrupt the supply of oil from Baku. As the weeks slipped by from May through July, even though Shaumian and the Baku Commune controlled the city and Lenin had officially approved nationalization,* the oil industry continued to operate independently because Lenin had not fully edited and approved the preliminary agreement for the labor contract.

The Baku leadership that emerged from this disorder was not only inexperienced but preposterous. The newly appointed minister of war was a former asylum inmate whose first acts included the election of a donkey to represent oppressed animals. An illiterate sailor became superintendent of schools, and a prominent pimp held oversight of public welfare.

---

* Upon Lenin's order of nationalization in June, he sent a separate telegram to Shaumian to clarify that he had approved the nationalization order but that Shaumian should delay the implementation with regard to the oil industry.

On June 4, Stalin rallied five hundred troops from Moscow and traveled south to the Volga valley, which had been a critical transportation artery for Russian industry, especially for Nobel's petroleum. By June 7 he had set up headquarters in Tsaritsyn.* Stalin's mission was to supply Moscow with the abundant resources of southern Russia. On Stalin's first day he cabled Lenin that he would soon send eight express trains loaded with grain to feed Moscow, which he managed to do.

Stalin became the boss of the Tsaritsyn Cheka, whose brutal interrogation and intimidation methods included scalping, crucifixion, removal of limbs with handsaws, and impaling prisoners on stakes. He also assumed leadership of the entire regional Red Army of the south, and because of the critical nature of his mission to feed and supply the nation, he was given wide latitude, even semi-autonomy from Trotsky, who was war commissar and increasingly Stalin's bitter rival for the number two spot behind Lenin in the Communist Party hierarchy.

Despite all the turmoil and expanding responsibilities, Stalin's gaze never seemed to deviate from Nobel's oil fields. Stalin believed it was time to implement war communism, a more aggressive approach to state control of the economy that included a broader scope of nationalization, stricter centralized economic management, and full state control of foreign trade. Stalin presented a plan to party leadership to nationalize the entire Russian oil industry. This proposal was a remarkable turn in his journey, going from living in the Baku slums as a lowly hand on the treacherous oil derricks of Nobel and Rothschild to being the military and political leader who was attempting to seize this industrial colossus with the stroke of a pen.

But Lenin and the central government resisted Stalin's urging to seize the oil industry. They knew that the steady flow of petroleum was necessary for national security and that there was no one in the

---

* Tsaritsyn was founded as a fortress city on the west bank of the Volga in 1589 and became an important commercial center under the tsars. The Soviet regime renamed the city Stalingrad in 1925 to honor Stalin, then in 1961 the regime of Nikita Khrushchev renamed it Volgograd—its present name—as part of Russia's de-Stalinization movement.

communist regime who was an expert in oil extraction and production. Therefore, to seize the industry and maintain supply levels would require the cooperation of the current industrialists. Emanuel, the most critical figure for such a transition, had already refused a summons to Moscow. There was no precedent or example for how to organize such cooperation, as there was no state-owned oil industry anywhere in the world* and all acts of nationalization and central planning to date had led to steep declines in productivity.

While Stalin and Lenin were exchanging messages between Tsaritsyn and Moscow that would determine the fate of the Russian oil industry, Emanuel was still biding his time in Kislovodsk behind a protective curtain of the White Army in the Caucasus. While Emanuel's community of refugees was safe and even had time for leisure activities such as painting, playing cards, and racket sports, they had run out of legal tender. The absence of cash was causing their microeconomy to grind to a halt. Emanuel was best equipped to solve this problem, and the town selected him as chairman of an ad hoc finance committee.

Emanuel arranged for new currency to be printed at a bank in the neighboring town of Pyatigorsk, then he established a system of exchange to distribute paper currency in return for the deposit of stocks, bonds, and other valuables. The grateful townspeople once again had cash in their wallets and named this currency "Nobel Notes." Having resolved this simple but fundamental need, the town's economy became fluid once again. On June 17, Emanuel wrote to his stepmother, Edla, "We have already printed and put into circulation over 28,000,000 roubles, so in this place there is hardly any other money in the population."

Only three days later, crushing news reached Nobel. Lenin had relented and given Stalin his way. On June 20, Russia nationalized the oil industry. Generations of Nobel vision, investment, and execution

* Britain's purchase of a fifty-one-percent ownership stake in the Anglo-Persian Oil Company was mainly to ensure purchasing contracts that guaranteed future pricing rather than government operational control.

became a state monopoly overnight. A labor exchange guided by a Soviet-appointed committee would take over. Emanuel might have noted the perverse inversion of Lenin's earlier observation about decades when nothing happens followed by weeks when decades happen. In Emanuel's case, there had been decades spent forging an industry, to be lost in only moments.

One week later the communist government nationalized select large industrial concerns. Among these was the machine industry. Lenin nationalized more than 9,500 businesses by simple decree—the largest confiscation of private property in the history of the world. By the end of June 1918, Emanuel found himself robbed of his Russian conglomerate.

Stalin delighted in the decrees that advanced war communism, yet no one seemed to know what to do next. The central government founded a National Oil Board (*Glavkoneft*), with the mission to take over the formerly private industry. This new regulatory body had a twelve-member board of directors. Six of these were members of the Communist Party, appointed to the board by Lenin. In recognition of where the true expertise lay, the remaining six seats went to directors of Nobel Brothers. Among these six members was a begrudging Gösta Nobel, who was living exposed in Petrograd.

After the six directors of what had been Nobel Brothers finished their first day of meetings as members of the newly founded National Oil Board, they lamented to one another, "They're asking us to arrange our own fourth-class funeral, one in which the corpse himself drives the hearse."

For the moment, the board did little more than insert its own commissars into the management of private oil companies to act as eyes on the ground. It was impossible to make greater changes due to the absence of qualified people in the Communist Party. In these early days, the board directed that oil operations continue largely as before. The employees of Nobel and the other oil companies stayed on the job, paid wages as they had been before. Besides, Lenin had other concerns. He still needed to address his greatest rival for the leadership of Russia.

Only weeks after the nationalization decrees that Stalin so eagerly sought, Lenin recognized that he needed to take a drastic measure to put down the White armies. Cumulatively, the White Army comprised more than a million soldiers, larger than the Red Army, but the Whites consisted of several uncoordinated factions that included the Volunteer Army, the People's Army, the Siberian Army, and the Unification Army. These sub-armies shared no political or ideological goals other than anti-Bolshevism. They had no other unifying force, and Lenin benefited from their disorganization.

Yet there was one living banner that could inspire a plurality of these forces to come together. While Nicholas II read novels to his children under the watchful eye of Bolshevik guards, factions of the White Army had been making gains in pockets around Russia. In particular, the Czech Legion was causing problems in the East. This fifty-thousand-strong army had already taken Vladivostok and removed its Bolshevik leadership. By the end of June the Legion controlled major stretches of the Trans-Siberian Railway and was driving westward through Siberia—getting dangerously close to Ekaterinburg, where the Tsar was being held.

Lenin's plan had been to put the Romanovs on trial and convict them of crimes against the people. He would cast the Bolsheviks as the defenders of the common man, then, as the final act of this theater, execute the royals. With the advance of the Czech Legion, Lenin was running out of time, but he had taken a precaution. He had made clear to the guards that if the unfolding of events should make such a trial impossible, the imprisoned Romanovs should be summarily executed rather than liberated. He had essentially issued an open kill order as a fail-safe.

While the gains of the Czech Legion might have been taken as encouraging news to the Romanovs, unknown to Nicholas and his family, it was a death sentence. The Soviets decided they needed to cut short plans to present a sham trial to an international audience. At two in the morning on July 17, the grim Bolshevik guards, most of them already drunk, entered Nicholas and Alexandra's bedroom and rousted them from under the covers. From the second-floor bedrooms they also gathered the Grand Duchesses Olga, Tatiana, Maria, Anastasia, the Tsarevich Alexei, the family physician, and three servants. Under a pretext, they led these eleven confused though increasingly wary men, women, and children to the basement. Outside, the guards left the engines of the trucks running, hoping to cover the sound of gunfire. These murders were to be secret. Lenin knew in advance that the reaction of the international community to this heinous act would be harsh. He meant to keep these murders unknown for as long as possible.

The hail of gunfire ripped into the bodies of the Romanovs and their attendants. Several of the bullets strangely deflected off the bodies, the result of large precious gems that the children had sewn into the seams of their nightclothes. The family had taken to referring to their treasure of jewels as their medicine, so that upon hearing the approach of guards the parents would cautiously whisper for the children not to forget their medicine.

Wearing these semi-bulletproof nightclothes, several of the victims, including the young daughters, were wounded but not killed. The drunk guards, having hurdled their initial hesitation to murder and now feeling a greater thirst for blood, stepped forward with bayonets and carved away any remaining life. The bodies were carried to the waiting trucks that took them deep into the woods, where they were burned with fire and acid, then buried. A week later the Czechs arrived and took Ekaterinburg.

Perhaps more than any other Bolshevik act, the murder of the Romanovs burned down the mast of the ship. It was a turning point for the way Allied governments and the public came to view Lenin and Bolshevism. More so than ousting Kerensky's government, more than the brutal tactics of Stalin and the Red Army (which were no more brutal than the pogroms that the White armies visited on Russia's Jews and other minority populations), and more than nationalizing private industries, it was the massacre of the royals—especially the young, sick Tsarevich—that soured both the governments and the public sentiments of the West.

News of the atrocity spread quickly. The local Soviet commissar had been bragging around town about the murders. In a haunting explanation of the killers' motives, one Ekaterinburg resident remarked, "After all, you don't get many chances in the course of an ordinary life to shoot an imperial family."

In Great Britain, advisors warned King George V, a cousin to the murdered Tsar, not to attend a memorial service at the Russian church in Marylebone. Many feared Britain's own cells of Bolshevism and worker unrest and felt that a show of sympathy for the Tsar might provoke domestic troubles. This was the reason why King George and his prime minister, Lloyd George, had in the preceding months refused to grant Nicholas II asylum in Britain. While the King hadn't saved the Romanovs with an offer of asylum, after the murders he did find the resolve to overrule his advisors and take the comparatively minor step of attending their memorial service.

In the wake of the murders, others in the West began to oppose the Bolsheviks openly. A general sentiment arose that to attempt cooperation with such a brutal regime would be futile.

In August, less than a month after the executions and little more than three months before the end of the European war, a British force landed in Archangel along the White Sea in the frosty reaches of northern Russia. An American force would soon follow, planning to fight the Bolsheviks and move south toward Moscow. Meanwhile, in the Caucasus, after less than four months in power and with no reinforcements available from Stalin, Shaumian accepted the impossibility of holding Baku against the Turks.

Shaumian and twenty-six of his fellow commissars fled for their lives by sailing across the Caspian Sea.* Their departure opened the

---

* Shaumian and his colleagues were arrested on August 16 by anti-Bolshevik forces and placed in a Baku prison. Mikoyan, who had failed to open the bank safe to collect the Bolshevik tax for Shaumian months before, and a small group of Bolsheviks broke Shaumian out of prison and he again attempted to escape by ship. This time he was arrested by soldiers supporting the Socialist Revolutionary Party, who executed Shaumian and all twenty-six of his commissars by firing squad on the night of September 20 along a remote stretch of the Trans-Caspian Railway.

door for General Dunsterville, who, by August 4, occupied Baku. The British, for the moment, upended Bolshevik plans for a state-run economy in the oil region as well as either German or Turkish control of the oil fields. In the port of Baku, Dunsterville and his staff boarded the *Kruger*, where they pulled down the red communist flag and raised the flag of the Tsar's navy. The steamship was nearly twenty years old and had been an oil cargo ship owned by the Russian shipping company Caucasus & Mercury.* The Bolsheviks had briefly used the ship until Dunsterville captured and commandeered it, making it the flagship of the British Caspian Flotilla and mounting four field guns in the cargo hatches.

Dunsterville held Baku, but the situation was volatile. Ottoman Turks and Azeri forces, collectively the Caucasian Islamic Army, fought to retake the city. Additionally, a southern faction of the White Army, supplied by the Germans, was camped in the region with eyes on the prized petroleum.

With the British troops in place, the remaining management of Nobel Brothers still in Baku immediately dispatched emissaries to Kislovodsk to speak with Emanuel in the hopes of persuading him to return to the city. They would escort him safely back to the Caucasus, where the industrial titan would be welcomed by the British and he could resist the Bolshevik order of nationalization, just as most of eastern Russia, under control of the White Army, was also resisting.

But Emanuel saw things differently. The country was unstable, particularly in the south. Though the British had arrived, they were not fully committed to a long-term diplomatic plan in Russia. The Germans and Turks were circling near Baku and the fighting was vicious. The Bolsheviks had lost Baku but were making gains elsewhere in the Caucasus, bringing them closer to Kislovodsk. Cities were

---

* Caucasus & Mercury was one of the largest shipping companies on the Volga, boasting a fleet of forty-four river barges and eighteen steamships (a small fraction of the size of Emanuel's own fleet that he had integrated with the petroleum company). The Soviets later nationalized the shipping company and in October 1923 renamed it the Soviet Caspian Shipping Company.

changing hands abruptly, and Emanuel was growing more of the mind to get out of Russia rather than deeper in. He decided to stay in Kislovodsk and wait things out a bit longer.

Emanuel's intelligence regarding Stalin's gains in southern Russia was correct. The Bolsheviks continued to fight for territory, and Lenin, in violation of the terms of Brest-Litovsk, had not withdrawn forces from Transcaucasia. Emanuel knew that in the long run Stalin would not accept British control of Baku. The fight was not yet done. Only for the moment were Lenin and Stalin powerless to oppose Dunsterville while they had so many other problems to attend to first.

Confronted with a cascade of adversaries, Lenin sought a friend. Fresh from concluding the Treaty of Brest-Litovsk with Germany, Lenin returned to the Germans to appeal for help against what he now viewed as his greatest threat—the British and American forces on Russian soil in the north, south, and east.

On August 27, 1918, as Dunsterville held Baku, Lenin signed a supplement to Brest-Litovsk that sweetened the deal. In return for German military action against the Allied forces in Russia and a promise not to occupy Petrograd, Lenin gave up six billion marks, Estonia and Lithuania (then called Livonia), and twenty-five percent of the output of the Baku oil fields.

Lenin despised having to call on Germany for aid against the Allies, but he realized that German aid was available and necessary. He penned a handwritten note to his Bolshevik envoy to Sweden about his predicament, explaining that with Germany at present "there was a coincidence of interests."

Joining his interests with Germany came with a domestic cost to Lenin. There had already been numerous plots to assassinate top Bolsheviks. Even the British Secret Service Bureau got in the game, employing a pretext to arrange a meeting between Stalin and a Russian-born spy whose plan was to shoot Stalin point-blank (though this meeting never came off). Then on August 30, three days after the supplemental agreement with Germany, Lenin delivered an hour-long speech at the Mikhelson Machine Factory in Moscow. After he finished his speech, he walked toward his waiting car. Fanya Kaplan, a twenty-eight-year-old member of the Socialist Revolutionary Party, intercepted him. She fired three shots, hitting him twice, once in the neck and once in the chest. Lenin would survive, and his guards quickly captured Kaplan. Before her execution she declared that she'd been motivated to act by Lenin's authoritarianism and his betrayal of revolutionary ideals. Lenin's methods and alliances proved unpopular to many, and he undoubtedly compromised his own ideals when he deemed it necessary to maintain power.

As the European war dragged on through August, Germany's prospects grew dimmer, and some in Britain began to look toward the prospects of a postwar Europe, recognizing that a productive southern Russia would be key to the prosperity of all Europe. Of particular interest to Britain was control of the Transcaucasian Railway connecting Batum on the Black Sea to Baku on the Caspian. Robert Bruce Lockhart explained the imperative to preserve Russia's productive potential in a letter to Foreign Secretary Arthur Balfour:

> *By restoring order in Russia not only are we preventing the spread of Bolshevism as a political danger but we are also saving for the rest of Europe the rich and fertile grain districts of the Ukraine which in the event of half-measures will be rendered sterile by anarchy and revolution . . . [O]rder in Southern Russia is of extreme importance.*

Lockhart estimated that a successful British intervention in Russia to "restore order" would require fifty thousand troops in the south landing along the Black Sea and another fifty thousand coming via Siberia. Currently, the northern British force in Archangel plus the Dunsterforce in the south totaled less than three thousand troops. This was not a compelling show of force.

America's private industry was likewise looking for Allied-led stability and a helping hand to access new markets. These corporations hoped for their government and military to pave the way in. As

Rockefeller famously wrote in his memoirs, "One of our greatest helpers has been the State Department in Washington. Our ambassadors and ministers and consuls have aided to push our way into new markets to the utmost corners of the world."

While a massive commitment of troops was a big ask of the war-weary governments and people of Britain and America, espionage was more easily achieved, and Baku was crawling with spies. General Dunsterville's sparse brigade was at least equipped with terrific military intelligence. In his memoirs he wrote, "Through our agents, we were at all times thoroughly in touch with the general situation." He noted that in a confidential letter intercepted by British spies, the enemy had written despairingly, "The English hear even our whispers."

But the spy game was not enough. As it turned out, the Dunsterforce remained in Baku for a period of only weeks. Too small a force to maintain order in Baku, Dunsterville moved out of the city on September 14 amid protests from the population both for and against his presence. He left the city's Bolshevik leaders in jail. The day following the British departure, armed Azerbaijani Turks, lying in wait in the outskirts, raided the city, looted homes and businesses, and massacred every Armenian they could find. It was yet another round of reciprocating ethnic revenge, and nearly ten thousand people were slaughtered in their homes and in the streets.

Nobel's petroleum assets continued to be spared the worst of the damage because even in a bloodlust frenzy the Turks knew not to destroy the infrastructure critical to oil production. But the fighting in the Caucasus that Trotsky once called a "gigantic ethnographic museum" was severe. Emanuel's decision not to return to Baku proved to be a wise one.

The Allies were winning the war. Even with Germany free of the Russian front, many of its troops had to remain in the east to hold occupied territory and extract food and materials. Additionally, Austria-Hungary had all but collapsed (and even considered signing a separate peace with the Allies behind the backs of the Germans), and the

Americans entered the conflict with greater speed and force than anticipated.

But while the war began to wind down, to Emanuel's dismay, by the autumn of 1918 the Russian Civil War began to heat up. The size of the forces of both the Whites and Reds grew, and the scale of the tragic conflict expanded.

As bloody as the Great War had been for Russia—by some accounts claiming the lives of two million soldiers—the Russian Civil War was far worse. The war for the future of Russia would ultimately claim ten million lives—most of them civilians.

CHAPTER 19

Run for Your Life

EMANUEL CONTINUED TO monitor events from Kislovodsk through the fall of 1918. He managed patchy communications with his executive team to the south in Baku (which had been in Turkish hands since Dunsterville had evacuated in mid-September) and with his half brothers to the north in Petrograd. Parallel wars ruled the business environment in Russia. The great European war was going very badly for the Central Powers. This would have been terrific news for a tsarist Russia, which would have been poised to take its share of new land, reparations, and other spoils of war. But post-tsarist Russia had abandoned the fight, and their claim to compensation in return for years of prior effort as an ally was unpersuasive. In the meantime, though Russia's status in the war had changed from participant to bystander, the country was still vulnerable to the desperate armies in need of war materials. Worse, the civil war was destroying vast infrastructure as the combatants, evenly matched in strength and viciousness, were determined to rule.

The Bolshevik Red Army suffered heavy losses, especially in the north and east, but offset these with gains elsewhere. Lenin had the loyalty of the proletariat and therefore had his greatest influence in the major cities. Stalin made gains as the leader of the Red Army in the south. Bolshevik troops were spreading across the Caucasus. By late 1918, Bolshevik patrols were spotted near Kislovodsk.

On October 30, 1918, the Ottoman Empire, Germany's ally, formally surrendered. Among the terms, the Turks abandoned claims to lands in southern Russia, including Baku. After only two months under Turkish control, the British again returned to occupy Baku.

On November 3, Austria-Hungary surrendered, and Germany stood alone. The Armistice finally came at 11 a.m. on November 11, 1918. The Great War was over.

The worst calamity in human history, the origins of which confound historians to the present day, came to an end twenty months after Tsar Nicholas II abdicated, twelve months after the Bolsheviks assumed power, eight months after the Bolsheviks pulled Russia from the war by signing the Treaty of Brest-Litovsk, and less than four months after drunken guards massacred Nicholas II and his family. The speed of change in Russia was staggering.

For the Allied troops still stationed in Russia who were participating in a quasi-intervention of the civil war, news of Armistice Day meant very little. A soldier of the Czech Legion sat with his rifle inside a bunker in western Siberia, awaiting an imminent Bolshevik attack. A messenger arrived with a slip of paper. The commanding officer read the message and announced with little enthusiasm that an armistice had been signed in France. The soldier recorded that he "listened politely . . . and went on shuffling to keep warm." A treaty in Paris meant nothing. He expected bullets from the Bolsheviks soon.

Private Scheu of the US Army's 339th Infantry stationed in northern Russia didn't even learn of the Armistice until eight weeks after the fact. Nor did it matter once he did, as the news arrived along with orders to retake positions in the north. Scheu remarked that "the Armistice doesn't mean a damn thing over here."

The Armistice brought joy to the leadership of the British war cabinet that was tempered by the knowledge that Bolshevism was not going away. Lenin's stated intent was an international revolution of the proletariat, and what was becoming agonizingly clear to all in the West was that the momentum for global communism seemed to be building. Communist newspapers and organizational infrastructure were growing inside each of the Allied Powers—Britain, France, and America.

On the evening of November 10, the day before the Armistice, French premier Georges Clemenceau had sent a telegram to British prime minister Lloyd George informing him that the Germans were facing revolution at home. Kaiser Wilhelm II had abdicated on November 9, and many in Germany feared the outbreak of Bolshevism in his place.* Upon reading Clemenceau's telegram, Lloyd George commented that events in Germany "were taking a similar course to that which had taken place in Russia in 1917." Bolshevism was hopping borders.

On November 11, as the leaders of France and Great Britain exchanged telegrams and announced Armistice Day, Emanuel Nobel was in the midst of a life-and-death attempt to escape from Bolshevik-controlled Russia. In the weeks before the Armistice, he and his colleagues had hatched a daring, desperate plan. Most of the aristocrats and extended Romanov family who had sheltered in Kislovodsk had left long ago. In October, just as Germany's allies were falling away, Emanuel had finally decided to make his getaway.

As he had done with his businesses, Emanuel had planned every detail. Kislovodsk seemed about to fall to the Bolsheviks, and the escape

---

* Wilhelm's fate was very different from that of his cousin Nicholas. After Wilhelm abdicated, he boarded a train the next day along with numerous railcars full of gold, priceless art, and other treasures. He traveled to the Netherlands, which had been a friendly neutral during the Great War. Months later the Treaty of Versailles called for the prosecution of Wilhelm for war crimes, but the Netherlands refused to extradite him. Britain and France had by then lost any zeal for a trial of the Kaiser, and rumors swirled that by unofficial channels Britain had communicated to the Dutch that they would welcome the refusal. President Woodrow Wilson also opposed extradition, arguing that a prosecution of Wilhelm would destabilize the peace and the international order.

route had become dangerous. On such a journey death could come as easily in the form of an emissary of Stalin as it could from a common bandit. Escorting Nobel were Mikhail Yevlanov, a former army officer and son of a Nobel Brothers executive, and Vladimir Nazansky, a longtime friend of Emanuel's who was the former police chief in Baku in the time of the tsars. Since Gösta Nobel was in Petrograd while his family was in Kislovodsk, Emanuel intended to bring with him Gösta's wife, Zhenya, and their three children—the youngest only two.

The family needed passports and exit permits. The name Nobel was famous and impossible to use. Yevlanov and Nazansky doctored false passports under assumed identities, with disguises to match. The problem of acquiring exit permits was solved through a stroke of luck. The local official who oversaw the permits was a former policeman who had worked under Nazansky. This connection, combined with a stack of roubles, secured exit permits that matched the false passports.

Emanuel was widely known to be unmarried and childless. As a part of the ruse, Zhenya pretended to be Emanuel's daughter, the three children his grandchildren. Yevlanov, the former soldier, pretended to be Zhenya's husband. But despite having passable paperwork, they couldn't begin their escape from Kislovodsk, where they would be easily recognized. Instead, days in advance, they packed only necessary items in plain sacks that they sent ahead to a farm outside the city. Then, on the agreed-upon afternoon, they split into groups and set off in different directions for a casual stroll. Once safely out of sight, they converged on the farm, where two wagons awaited.

In dim evening light, the Nobels and their escorts, disguised as farmers, climbed under the canvas roofs of horse-drawn carts. They rode twelve miles to nearby Yessentuki. And there, as the entourage hastened down the street, a passerby seemed to recognize Emanuel. In the insecure and paranoid environment of a community under brutal authoritarian control in which reporting on one's neighbor is rewarded, word of Emanuel's presence in the small town quickly reached the authorities.

Police apprehended the Nobel party for investigation. The enormously wealthy industrialist was a prize. Local businessmen rushed to his defense and appealed for his freedom. Directors from the People's Bank in Pyatigorsk, who had coordinated directly with Emanuel in the effort to establish the Nobel Notes, submitted a letter that referenced Emanuel's work, which had delivered economic stability to the region, declaring that for the previous months "with his knowledge, his experience and unusual energy [he] rescued us and the whole district from this difficult predicament."

The authorities were unmoved, and the investigation continued. Emanuel was the prisoner of Stalin's henchmen in southern Russia, but because of the compromised communications in November 1918, Emanuel's only hope was that Stalin himself would not learn that he held in his clutches the embodiment of all he opposed. The local Soviet officials determined that Emanuel had no savings in the bank. They demanded of him a war tax of 170,000 roubles, which he managed to scrounge together. After three days in custody in Yessentuki, the police let him go.

After escaping what would likely have been a death sentence, Emanuel and his companions wasted no time in traveling 125 miles northwest to Stavropol, held by Pyotr Glazenap of the White Army. From there the Nobel party boarded a third-class train to Rostov, inching ever farther west and north. In the first week of November, Rostov was a Russian city under German control, during what were clearly the final days of the German Empire. News of a possible end to the war drove excited conversations in every town.

In Rostov, Emanuel met the Swedish consul, who assisted in obtaining passports for travel to Kiev. The German command in Rostov issued papers for "the well-known and top industrialist Emanuel Nobel with his family and secretary [Nazansky] who is on his way from Rostov to Kiev on a journey of interest to the German Empire."

In Kiev, also controlled by the Germans, the Nobel party secured a similar letter ensuring safe passage to Warsaw. It was on this leg of the journey, a day's travel from Warsaw and as the calendar hit November 11, that the German Empire formally surrendered.

As the Nobel party arrived in Warsaw, the entire European rail system experienced intense congestion with postwar reorganization. The remainder of Nobel's escape route—which took them through Berlin, then on to Stockholm—was safe and uneventful, but quite slow. Only in early December did Emanuel arrive safely back in Sweden, the birthplace of his grandfather. The epic saga of the Nobel family in Russia that had begun eighty-one years before seemed to be at an end. Only Gösta and Emil remained behind.

From the Grand Hotel in Stockholm, Emanuel and Zhenya now prayed for the survival of the young half brothers who were caught in a Bolshevik web in Petrograd. Their predicament was unlike the circumstances of Emanuel's brief detention in the wilds of the Caucasus.

The Swedish government had arranged for an evacuation of the colony of Swedish nationals in Petrograd that took place in October and November 1918, the very time Emanuel had begun his escape from the Caucasus. Gösta and Emil hesitated to join the Swedish-sponsored evacuation. They felt a responsibility to Emanuel and to the future of the petroleum company, the machine factory, Alfa-Nobel, and Noblessner. Staying in Petrograd would cost them dearly.

On October 30, as Emanuel was negotiating with police in the Caucasus, fifteen hundred miles to the north, the Petrograd Cheka arrested Gösta and Emil. Armed agents dragged the brothers to a cell in the Peter and Paul Fortress,* which had been used as a prison for political prisoners in the time of the tsars. Once in their cells, the Cheka went to work. Varvara Yakovleva, infamous for her diabolical cruelty, was head of the Petrograd Cheka and led the interrogations.

Unlike Emanuel's detention in Yessentuki, Stalin had knowledge of the Petrograd arrests and that he had captured the young Nobels. He had issued the arrest order to the Cheka under the pretext that Gösta had been in league with the British (who were occupying Baku per the terms of Ottoman surrender in the war) to engineer the arrest

* Peter the Great established the fortress in 1703 on an island in the Neva River. It is currently a museum.

of a top Bolshevik in the Caucasus. Stalin, after a youth spent among the street gangs of Tiflis and in the oil fields surrounding Baku, now had the famous Nobels locked in his prison.

Despite Gösta's denials and the fact the there was no evidence against him, the brothers remained hostages of the Cheka. Stalin aimed to use the Nobels as bargaining chips if he could and kill them if he couldn't. But Stalin and the Petrograd Cheka had miscalculated.

In the wartime frenzy of misinformation, Stalin and the Cheka had believed that Gösta and Emil were Russian citizens. They were not. Only Emanuel was a Russian. Gösta and Emil were Swedes, and the Swedish government was prepared to come to the rescue of two of their most famous citizens.

Oscar Lundberg, the official representative of the Swedish government, informed the Cheka that the Nobels must be immediately released or Sweden would arrest the Soviet representative in Stockholm, Vatslav Vorovsky.

The Bolsheviks had a shaky grasp even on internal conflicts, and they certainly didn't have the muscle to pick fights with sovereign nations. Under threat from the Swedish government, the Cheka set the Nobels free, though the terms of release guaranteed that Gösta and Emil would remain in Petrograd. But on December 6, just as Emanuel's harrowing escape ended safely in Sweden, the Swedes broke off diplomatic relations with Soviet Russia. Importantly for the Nobels, this break meant that Gösta and Emil no longer enjoyed diplomatic protection. They quickly began plans to escape.

On December 17, in the dead of winter, the brothers traveled through the outskirts of Petrograd, by dogsled and on foot, toward the Finnish border. Any misstep could lead to capture and a horrifying interrogation and torture. To escape meant the difference between salvation in Sweden or a return to a furious and unrestrained Cheka in Russia—worlds apart yet separated by only two hundred miles.

The brothers trekked across an expanse of forested and snow-covered trails in the bitter cold. Furtively, they covered mile after mile. Finally, as Gösta took the determining step into Finland, he noted the eerie intangibility and strange significance of political borders that have driven human behavior: "The border itself consisted of an ordinary ditch extending over an open field. When I passed over this ditch I understood for the first time the real meaning of a border. For me, the one side probably meant death, the other side freedom." There was no passport control, no man-made marker, no difference in the grass, trees, or air. It was simply one step.

Once in Finland, the brothers made for Helsinki, where they boarded the steamship *Oihonna*, bound for Sweden. They joined Emanuel in Stockholm on December 22, in time for Christmas. Family letters reveal that it was a joyous reunion, and the Nobels celebrated with plenty of food and drink. But they were haunted for the rest of their lives by the events of 1918.

Gösta reported to a Swedish newspaper on December 28 about the conditions on the ground in Moscow and Petrograd: "Not even the most intense imagination could . . . depict the situation as it actually appears. Both cities are in a death fever, which has sunk its claws into them, and is expressing itself as the most dreadful nightmare."

As the calendar turned to 1919, all the Nobels were gathered in Sweden, out of Stalin's reach. Yet the Nobel industrial empire remained fixed, deep behind enemy lines. Emanuel began to devise plans to subvert the Bolshevik takeover of his life's work.

CHAPTER 20

Civil Is the Worst Kind of War

EMANUEL WAS SAFELY in Sweden, outside the borders of Russia, where the Bolsheviks could not capture and coerce him. To get what they needed from the oil magnate, Lenin and Stalin would need to come to the negotiating table.

Robert Bruce Lockhart traveled through Stockholm on a diplomatic and intelligence-gathering effort for Britain. Naturally he made plans to see Emanuel Nobel while there, and Lockhart recorded his impression of the meeting in his memoirs. "[Mr. Nobel] had formed a more accurate estimate of the situation [in Russia] and was convinced that Bolshevism had not yet reached its apogee . . . and [he] visualized Bolshevism as a world danger. With other Swedes he had joined a rifle club in order that he might take his place behind the bourgeois barricades in the event of a proletarian rising in Sweden."

Both Lenin and Nobel recognized that oil was the key to Russia's economic recovery. At that time, the Caucasus oil fields had suffered only minor structural damage despite the monstrous bloodshed in the region. With investment in new drilling and refining technologies, and proper management, Russia could once again be a world leader in oil production.*

But before Lenin could focus entirely on Russia's economic prosperity, he needed to win a civil war. As with the economy, oil was also vital to the war effort. As Britain's Lord Curzon said after the Great War, "The Allies had floated to victory on a wave of oil." Lenin intended for Soviet Russia to ride the same wave. While it is true that Lenin never planned to abandon the oil region of the Caucasus to the Germans per the Treaty of Brest-Litovsk, he still did not occupy it. From the time of the Armistice and the withdrawal of the Turks, the British held Baku.

Lenin needed to come to terms with Stalin's old adversary Nobel. He reached out to Emanuel with a proposal. Lenin and Stalin offered a deal in which the Soviets would return assets of the Nobel company if Nobel's company would provide oil that was critical to the Soviets' ability to win the civil war. The terms of Lenin and Stalin's offer are captured in a letter sent by Emanuel via the US minister to Sweden, Ira Nelson Morris, to the American delegation in Paris, with a copy given to Foreign Secretary Balfour, who was leading the British delegation at the Paris peace conference at Versailles.

The long process of peace negotiations (ultimately lasting five months) to conclude the Great War had begun on January 18 in France. Emanuel initiated communication with Morris on March 28, 1919, and Balfour received his copy of the letter on or about April 3.

Morris relates as context in a cover letter to Emanuel's message that "as the [Peace] Mission is aware, The Nobel Company in Russia is comparable to the Standard Oil Company in the United States." Morris relayed that "the Bolshevists held between 200 and 250 boats belonging to the Nobel Company, most of which were lying in the

---

* Nobel and Lenin would be proved correct. By 1927, with the Caucasus largely back online, petroleum represented twenty percent of all Russian exports by value and was the single-largest source of foreign exchange. As of 2024, Russia is the world's third-largest oil producer, accounting for over twelve percent of global crude oil production.

Volga." Stalin had been holding a Mr. Levestam, an executive of the Nobel Company, prisoner in Petrograd for the last six months. As a negotiating ploy of the Bolsheviks, Levestam "had just arrived in Stockholm after having been released by the Bolshevists in order that he travel to Stockholm to inform Mr. Nobel that the Soviet authorities were willing to release the Nobel Company's boats, if in return they could arrange for the shipment of oil from Baku and other oil depots on the Caspian to Russia to be distributed there."

This was quite a change in messaging from Lenin and Stalin to the Nobels. The change was not driven by ideology or a desire for long-term cooperation with Nobel. The reason was purely short-term desperation. Stalin lacked the military might to enforce policy in southern Russia. Emanuel noted the change in Soviet attitudes in his letter to the Allies, writing that despite Soviet authorities having declared that they would take over and administer all Nobel Brothers assets, the Soviets now found it "necessary to make an appeal to the Company in order to secure oils."

Emanuel was loath to make a deal with the devil, and he certainly didn't want to enter into any bargains with Stalin and Lenin without first coordinating his response with the Allies. He wrote to the Americans and British that he was "not in the least eager to send any oil into Russia without the full approval of the Allied governments."

Nobel's tone to the Allies then turned to one of caution—echoing the same notes Winston Churchill had been sounding before the Armistice. Emanuel wrote that if the Soviet government did not acquire sufficient oil by summer "their whole transportation system would collapse completely and that in all parts of Russia which are more densely populated, starvation on a tremendous scale would occur." He added that logically "the downfall of the Soviet Government will unquestionably result."

Emanuel knew that Stalin and Lenin would not allow a failed business negotiation for his petroleum to lead to a Soviet downfall, and therefore they would act to acquire the oil by any means necessary before a projected summertime collapse. Emanuel wrote of his "absolute certainty that the Bolshevists will resort to force to procure oil." This meant a Bolshevik attack on British-controlled Baku. At this point in the letter, Emanuel makes his direct appeal to Balfour and his prime minister, Lloyd George. Emanuel's closing analysis was that he "very much feared, should a Bolshevist attack on Baku take place, that the British forces at present stationed there would not be in a position to afford protection to the town and that the Bolshevists would destroy it." As summer was only a few months away, Emanuel was predicting to Balfour that unless Nobel Brothers delivered the requested oil, a Bolshevik attack on British troops in Baku was unavoidable and imminent.

Morris then offered his conclusion to the letter. "Hence Nobel was very eager to know what answer they would make to the Bolshevist proposal submitted to them."

Britain and America, in the midst of concluding the peace to the greatest war in history, needed to decide if they were willing to begin yet another war. The Bolsheviks were decidedly an evil, but perhaps not worth a war.

Lockhart, a Russian policy expert who was respected at the highest levels, gave the British war cabinet a matter-of-fact summary. He estimated that the Bolsheviks likely had popular support from only about ten percent of the Russian people, but that one "cannot deny their energy and party discipline." Further, the opposition groups within Russia, when looked at individually, had even less support. These disparate groups loosely affiliated as the White Army had nothing to unify them other than their opposition to the Bolsheviks and could be broadly grouped into monarchists, constitutional monarchists, republicans, and socialists. Alongside these domestic opposition groups, the Americans had troops in Russia in the north and east, while the British had troops in the north and held Baku in the south.

Lockhart proposed to his government that the Allies had three choices:

1. *To abandon intervention and come to a working arrangement with the Bolsheviks*

2. *To abandon intervention but to support the anti-Bolshevik organizations with arms and money*
3. *To intervene immediately on a proper scale*

The Allies had previously stated that the reason to place troops on Russian soil was to keep Russia's petroleum and other war materials out of German hands. With the Armistice in place and Germany defanged, a continued Allied military presence in Russia was difficult to justify without a formal declaration of opposition to the Bolshevik government. With regard to the spread of communism (the name more frequently used than *Bolshevism* as Lenin's rebranding effort took hold), the Allies needed to declare a position.

In the early months after the war, the Allied policy had involved aspects of all three of Lockhart's options. The overall policy was muddled and shifting, caused by fractured and competing domestic interests in Britain and America, not least of which were powerful corporate interests inside these nations. Many of the corporate interest groups encouraged their own governments to offer diplomatic recognition of the Soviet regime,* which would legalize commercial dealings in Russia. While official diplomatic recognition did not come, extralegal business deals did proceed nonetheless, including loans from Morgan-controlled banks as well as technology and consulting from Rockefeller-controlled oil interests.

There was also plenty of Allied subversion inside Russia. As proposed in the second option, Allied governments supported opposition groups that were collectively the White Army. Option three also remained on the table as Allied troops were still in Russia in the summer of 1919, though not at the levels Lockhart would have considered the "proper scale."

---

* The United States did not formally recognize the Soviet government until 1933. Technically, all American loans to Russia prior to that point were illegal. In 1919, as American troops opposed the Bolsheviks in Archangel in northern Russia, Morgan's Guaranty Trust assisted in the formation of the Soviet Bureau in New York—which was technically not illegal, though it was certainly playing both sides. Churchill declared in 1919 that if Lloyd George were to recognize the Bolshevik regime he "might as well legalize sodomy."

The White armies not only lacked a unifying motivation; they had mostly *opposing* motivations. The primary cause for war for many of the disparate White armies was nationalist at heart, yet they were a collection of different "nations." Now that the Empire had crumbled, they were seeking their long-hoped-for independence. Azerbaijan, Armenia, Georgia, Poland, Finland, Estonia, Latvia, and Lithuania all wanted to be sovereign states. They certainly didn't want to be rolled up into a Soviet empire ruled by Lenin, nor did they want to return to the Russian Empire of old. And yet that was the motivation of the monarchists and constitutional monarchists who made up a large element of the Whites with whom they were tenuously allied. In their push for central and total control of an empire, the tsars and Bolsheviks were two sides of the same coin.

The prospects of the generals of the White armies, in the estimation of the Allies, seemed to rise and fall. In addition to being uncoordinated, these armies became famous for corruption and cruelty. They seemed equally prepared to kill innocent Jewish populations as they did Bolsheviks. As news of these gratuitous and barbarous pogroms of Jewish communities by the Whites reached America and Britain, formal support of the Whites became increasingly difficult politically.*

As with the distractions of the Great War, the young and relatively weak Bolsheviks benefited from the distractions of those opposed to them in the civil war. The Bolsheviks remained energetic and disciplined. And they simply had better propaganda. Lenin's message when first rising to power had been succinct and effective: "Peace, Land, Bread."

Allied policy toward Russia remained one of equivocation. Lenin renewed his vows not to melt away as had the Kerensky government. Lenin also held the radio transmitting station in Moscow and developed wireless receiving stations at key points in the country. The abil-

* The American public was more outraged by the antisemitism than was the British. By contrast to the White Army, the Bolshevik Red Army was known to treat the Jewish people much better—Trotsky was Jewish, and historians believe Lenin to have had some Jewish ancestry. For a closer examination of this war, see Anna Reid's 2023 book *A Nasty Little War: The Western Intervention into the Russian Civil War.*

ity for messages to hop the enemy gave the Reds an intelligence and military advantage. The American diplomat DeWitt Clinton Poole noted after the civil war that if the Reds had "been dependent upon mail by railroad and by wire telegraph [that can be intercepted] their history might be different."

On April 7, 1919, only four days after Balfour read Emanuel's letter about the Soviet need for oil, and less than nine months after the brutal assassination of Nicholas II and his family, the British government assisted the harrowing escape of the remaining royals from Russia. It was to be the last flight of the Romanovs. In the port city of Yalta in the Ukrainian territory of Crimea on the shores of the Black Sea, an entourage of eighty people met the British battleship HMS *Marlborough*. Forty-four were members of Nicholas's extended family; the rest were attendants who scrambled around the docks with hundreds of pieces of luggage filled with jewels, art, and clothing. Aided by British seamen, the panicked royals and servants boarded the ship and sailed past Constantinople, then out to the Mediterranean, far from Lenin's clutches.

Among the royals on the ship were Nicholas's mother, the Dowager Empress Maria Feodorovna, as well as Rasputin's killer, Prince Felix Yusupov. Also aboard was Nicholas's six-foot, six-inch uncle, the Grand Duke Nicholas Nikolaevich, who had led the Imperial Army during the Great War.* Now nearly all vestiges of the imperial regime were dead or on the run.

On June 22, 1919, Emanuel Nobel turned sixty. As a backdrop to his birthday celebrations, the Red Army had begun to gain momentum, the international community felt a growing "Hands Off Russia" movement beginning with regard to military intervention, and Lenin had found a brilliant engineer-cum-diplomat, Leonid Krasin, as his

---

* British assistance was forthcoming as the royal family likely still felt shame for failing to save Nicholas II from his awful fate. From outside Russia, the Grand Duke became the figurehead of Russian monarchists and was even appointed Emperor of Russia (disputed) in July 1922. Therefore, by some accounts, Nicholas Nikolaevich was the last tsar.

negotiator with the West to make the most of Russia's resources—particularly its oil. Tall and thin, with angular features and a sharp, trim beard, Krasin was a longtime Marxist. He was a friend to both Tolstoy and Gorky, the latter describing Krasin as "shrewd-looking, his face for all the world like an old icon." He was perhaps more skilled even than Lenin at playing opponents against each other. But as Emanuel predicted, Krasin was working within a tight timeline. The summer deadline for Bolshevik acquisition of oil was drawing near.

Emanuel was festive nonetheless. Though he retained only a small fraction of his overall wealth, he had access to funds held in international accounts and assets that were out of reach of the Soviets. As patriarch of the family, Emanuel took his nephews and the two sons of his top executive Karl Hagelin with him on a yacht cruise to Norway. He was a father figure to all of them. Traveling north, they visited North Cape and Hammerfest—the northernmost city in the world, where in June the sun shines bright at midnight. These white nights were a hopeful metaphor that they could find a light in the darkness of the Caucasus. They poured champagne and the younger generation made toasts to Emanuel's health.

From the birthday party Emanuel traveled to Paris, to the Hotel Meurice. Though Emanuel's father had once deployed underwater mines around the Baltic to destroy ships of the British and French during the Crimean War, Emanuel now made France his temporary home. Paris had become the de facto center for most Russian oilmen and industrialists in exile who were attempting to navigate a way back to their empires. Emanuel arrived just in time for the conclusion of the prolonged Allied peace negotiations at Versailles on June 28.

Lenin's government had been excluded from the talks to the very end. Emanuel had refused to deliver his oil to the regime, and the prediction he made in his March letter to Balfour proved uncannily accurate. In August, the Red Army forced the British from Baku. Stalin once again had control of the city. The British military presence had been insufficient to oppose them, and Lenin now had the oil he needed to fight his civil war.

This last change of control in Baku concluded a crazed and bloody period of revolving rule. In summary, the mercurial instability began in 1917 when the oil city had belonged to the tsars until Nicholas II abdicated in March and the Russian Empire collapsed. The Turks then took control through the balance of 1917 until March 1918, when a combined force of Bolsheviks and Azeris violently expelled the Turks and formed the Baku Commune under Shaumian, which lasted three months until the end of July, when Shaumian and his twenty-six commissars fled before the advancing army of the Turks. Shaumian's flight made room for Dunsterville and his British troops to take Baku, though they managed to hold the city for only six weeks before they too evacuated and fled from the Turks. By mid-September, the Turks again occupied Baku, but this lasted less than two months, until the Ottoman Empire formally surrendered to the Allies in the Great War and turned Baku back over to the British in November. The British imposed martial law while the Azerbaijan Democratic Republic became stable enough to rule independently. Baku then became the capital of independent Azerbaijan, briefly, until the Red Army invaded in August 1919. Lenin formally annexed Azerbaijan into the Soviet Union in April 1920, which would remain the case until 1991. A head-spinning amount of tumult, particularly for the primary owner of Baku's petroleum, Emanuel Nobel.

To recap, in a period of only *twenty-nine months*, as Emanuel observed from Petrograd, then Kislovodsk, then Stockholm, the order of control in Baku was: Nicholas II, Provisional Government (nominally), Turks, Bolsheviks, British, Turks, British, Independent, Bolsheviks (Soviet Union).

The Nobel employees who had worked the fields and refineries during the peaceful British occupation mostly stayed on during the Bolshevik occupation. The city had already changed hands so many times, and these workers wrongly believed that this final period of Bolshevik control might be brief. They still hoped it was only a matter of time before the assets would revert to Emanuel's control and life would finally return to normal after twenty-nine months of hell.

Likewise, Emanuel and Gösta worked feverishly to make this so. The family set up a new official headquarters in Stockholm, where Emanuel also established a residence in a large flat adjacent to the Grand Hotel. But most of the serious work and negotiations took place in Paris.

The Nobel family had left behind and lost for good extensive personal possessions. Prior to fleeing, Marta Nobel, Gösta's older sister, had left her jewels and valuables in the Volga Bank, believing the bank would be safer than in her luggage or in a vault in the family home back in Russia. But the Volga was one of the first banks sacked by the Reds, plundered for war treasure.

Personal possessions were a minor matter, however. The prize was the business empire, presently mismanaged by the communist regime. Emanuel continued to fight for restitution. But the idea that Emanuel would again take the reins looked increasingly unlikely. There was a chance, of course, and the Nobels began to shift strategy to use their indeterminate claim to the assets in Russia as a negotiating tool. The international market still believed the Bolsheviks could lose control of the region and that the Nobels could establish a rightful claim. There was value in the Nobel claim, even if it would be difficult to enforce. Because Emanuel no longer had the government of any nation as a sponsor, he had little sway on the international stage.

For decades Emanuel had refused to sell his company. His final financial masterstroke was to recognize at the right time that a sale of Nobel Brothers to a foreign company, one that had the full support of its government—a government powerful enough to exert influence in Russia—would be the best use of his assets. Perhaps a value and a price could be agreed on for Nobel's company while there was still the possibility that Lenin's government would fall.

Two companies emerged as interested buyers, one from Britian, the other from America. Henri Deterding led the British firm Royal Dutch Shell. Deterding had already purchased the Rothschilds' Russian assets. He considered himself an expert in conducting business in Russia and believed he would ultimately block Soviet nationalization of his oil interests. Deterding also believed Bolshevik power was fleeting, writing to his colleague Calouste Gulbenkian that "the Bolsheviks will be cleared, not only out of the Caucasus, but out of the whole of Russia in about six months." Deterding saw opportunity.

All manner of Russian treasures were selling at bargain prices. Immensely valuable artwork was sold on the cheap by Russian émigrés in desperate need of cash. The West was picking over Russia's goods like collectors at an estate sale. Deterding aimed to become overlord of Russian oil. He first contacted the British Foreign Office in the autumn of 1919, asking for a guarantee of political support to enforce his purchase. The government stopped short of a guarantee but informally encouraged Deterding to acquire Nobel's Russian assets, in essence suggesting that the government would recognize Nobel's claim to the petroleum rather than the Soviets'. Deterding opened negotiations with Emanuel.

The other suitor was Standard Oil of New Jersey (the largest of the Baby Standards after the 1911 Supreme Court ruling that divided the oil trust). In early 1919 Standard had already negotiated with the independent government of Azerbaijan* to purchase eleven plots in Baku to prospect for oil. When rumors reached 26 Broadway that a consortium of Royal Dutch Shell and the Anglo-Persian Oil Company was negotiating the purchase of Nobel Brothers, the Rockefeller team moved swiftly.

Standard's management in New York immediately sent their head of overseas production, Everett Sadler, to Batum and Baku to kick the tires on Nobel's company. He visited the oil fields, the refineries, and the depots. He interviewed local members of industry, politics, and the military. He then compiled a detailed report for 26 Broadway that confirmed Emanuel still had some cards to play. He confirmed that Nobel Brothers was by far the most important petroleum company in Russia,

---

* In May 1918, as Russia fought its civil war, Azerbaijan declared independence as the Azerbaijan Democratic Republic (ADR). The new republic granted suffrage to women and gave women political rights equal to men. Independence lasted only twenty-three months.

accounting for about half of all production, twice the size of its nearest rival, Royal Dutch Shell. He added that despite the violence and destruction of recent years, Nobel's plants were in remarkably good shape, and that while there was political instability, the opportunity far outweighed the risk.

To drive home his message, he wrote to New York that Baku represented "a dream for an engineer and a paradise for a swindler."

CHAPTER 21

Woe to the Vanquished

Nobel brothers and Standard Oil of New Jersey engaged in formal discussions. Emanuel preferred this path over working with Deterding and Royal Dutch Shell. Standard was the global industry leader and Emanuel especially liked how cozy the American company was with the US State Department, a relationship similar to the one he'd once enjoyed with the Tsar's government.

The two petroleum giants started coming together in small steps. Walter Teagle, president of Standard Oil Company of New Jersey, served as negotiator for the American firm. Emanuel, with his heir apparent Gösta at his side, shuttled between London, Paris, and Stockholm to represent Nobel Brothers. In November 1919, Standard and Nobel Brothers signed a cooperative deal for the Nobel assets and distribution network in Poland, where Emanuel's ownership was outside Soviet control and was not contested. Standard purchased fifty percent of the Nobel assets in Poland, establishing Polnobel—the Standard-Nobel Company in Poland.

Following this successful model, 26 Broadway and the Nobels made a deal for another peripheral asset of Nobel—this time for the territory of Finland. By April 1920, the parties agreed on terms to establish the second Standard-Nobel venture, and Standard was eager to do more. By far, the main assets of Nobel Brothers were the oil fields, refineries, and distribution network inside Russia. The continued belief internationally was that the Bolsheviks would not last. Standard Oil saw Deterding and Royal Dutch Shell—who already had a claim to significant assets in Russia—as a rising threat and believed that a venture with Nobel Brothers, while the company was compromised by political unrest, was the best way to enter Russia and prepare for the coming fight with Deterding for the global oil market.

And yet the Soviets were still nominally in charge of all Russia. Lenin had already nationalized the petroleum assets of every company in the Caucasus. Anything there that Emanuel proposed to sell and that Standard proposed to buy was nothing more than thin air. If the Soviet had its way, it was Lenin who would broker the deals for what generations of Nobels had built. And he did.

In May, one month after the completion of Standard-Nobel in Finland (which was profitable for both Standard and the Nobel family for many years), Lenin's trade representative Leonid Krasin was in London for what he hoped would be official meetings. With the title Commissar for Foreign Trade, the suave and persuasive technocrat (and former executive of the Baku Electric Company—a successful capitalist himself!) hoped to establish trade relations with the West for the Soviet regime that was starved of cash and technology.

May 31, 1920, proved to be a pivotal day for the balance of history. Prime Minister Lloyd George invited Krasin to 10 Downing to discuss relations between Russia and Great Britain. This marked the first occasion that the head of a Western government received a Soviet emissary. The meeting started off thick with tension.

Though Lloyd George had wanted the meeting, many were opposed even to discussions with the Bolsheviks. Chief among those opposed was Lord Curzon, the new foreign secretary. As the handsome Krasin (who was apparently a ladies' man) entered the meeting room at 10 Downing, Curzon elaborately turned his back on the Russian.

Refusing to shake hands, Curzon moved to the fireplace and stared into the flames. Only when Lloyd George barked "Curzon! Be a gentleman!" did an awkward meeting begin.

Each party wanted something from the other. The Russians needed industrial expertise and technology to develop domestic production, and they needed foreign exchange (other countries buying their goods, which required recognition and official trade relations). Britain wanted access to Russian markets and natural resources. There was plenty of room for a deal, but little trust on either side. Lenin wrote to Krasin in preparation for talks with Lloyd George, "That swine Lloyd George has no scruples or shame in the way he deceives; don't believe a word he says, and gull him three times as much."

While Krasin was bartering with Nobel oil assets, so were the Nobels. At the same time Krasin was in London meeting with Lloyd George, Emanuel Nobel was in London meeting with Walter Teagle. Both Krasin and Nobel maintained their rights to negotiate with the very same petroleum assets in Russia. In one of the most bizarre corporate acquisition processes in history, not only were the parties uncertain who might be the buyer; they were also uncertain who might be the seller.

Standard Oil operated under the presumption that Nobel's claim was valid and that if Standard acquired the Nobel assets and the claim became at all difficult to enforce, the State Department would step in and, by intimidation or other means, help enforce Standard's ownership. Therefore, Teagle continued negotiations with Emanuel and Gösta to acquire the prize that Rockefeller had coveted for decades.

As a backdrop to these negotiations, grabbing newspaper headlines around the world were the Allied and White Army updates from Soviet Russia. Anton Denikin's White Army in southern Russia had been losing ground all year. By April he turned over command of his withering force and fled to the United Kingdom. In the north, British and American troops had withdrawn, and the Soviets had routed the remaining local opposition forces and occupied Archangel. In the east, the remaining American troops departed Russian soil from the port of

Vladivostok.* Finally, and most importantly for Teagle's talks with Emanuel, Stalin still had control of Baku.

Only a smattering of British troops remained in Batum on the Black Sea; then in June these last British troops left Russia for good. Any influence the West might have in Russia would now need to be exerted through economic means. The soldiers were all gone.

This might have given pause to the executives at 26 Broadway, but their mindset was still one of a dog after a bone. The opportunity was massive, the price cheap. And even if the Bolsheviks should hang on, Standard still had the mighty State Department on its side. In the wake of the Great War, America had emerged as a dominant world power and was starting to act like it.

Rockefeller's team was better plugged into the State Department than any private citizen in the world. The State Department explained that it could not offer any help directly to the Standard acquisitions in Russia but encouraged Teagle's work and, as the British had with Deterding, blessed the deal. Teagle moved forward.

Eight of nine board directors, including John Rockefeller Jr., voted to approve the deal with Nobel, believing that the opportunity to enter Russian oil production and thereby shore up Standard's European market might never come again. And the risk of an alliance between Nobel and Royal Dutch Shell was simply too great.

On July 30, 1920, the parties signed documents. For fifty percent of the Nobel Brothers holdings in Russia, Standard paid US$11,500,000.† The Nobels and the Americans were now equal partners in the Rus-

---

* The British campaign in Archangel had lasted more than a year, and many of the troops had become friendly with the local population that opposed the Bolsheviks. When orders to withdraw came from London, there was a tearful goodbye as the soldiers knew this to be a death sentence for the people left behind. The American withdrawal from Vladivostok was similar in that the departing commanders feared for the population of Russians that had supported their presence. Soviet reprisals were brutal and unsparing.

† When converting this value to the present day using the method of comparable salaries or percentage of GDP, Standard paid the equivalent of about $2 billion—an absurdly low number for the true value of the assets if there had been no political risk.

sian oil business, or perhaps partners in nothing at all. In August, Teagle briefed Secretary of State Bainbridge Colby, who expressed his satisfaction with the deal.

Krasin, Lenin, and Stalin brushed aside the July transaction. According to the Soviet regime, by all rights the Nobel business in Russia was theirs to operate or sell, not Emanuel's. Krasin acted as such. He continued to meet with the British government and with Deterding, still playing Western rivals against each other as he used Russia's oil as a carrot.

In November 1920, three years after the Bolshevik Revolution, Lloyd George's government took a major step toward cooperation with the Soviets by authorizing an official trade agreement. Lloyd George gave Lenin what he needed just when he needed it most—de facto recognition of the Soviet regime. The opening of foreign trade between Russia and Great Britain would come with the much-needed cash and technology essential to rebuild Russia.

Britain's willingness to cooperate with Russia economically may seem foolhardy and driven by the short-term desire to grab resources, but there were those who believed in a long-term rationale to keep the Soviets in power. In a diabolical and counterintuitive play, the more paranoid of Western industrialists liked having a dysfunctional political system in Russia. To install an efficient, Western-style government in the huge and resource-rich country that boasted a massive population would only create a powerful economic and military rival. Russia might be feared again, as Germany had come to fear Imperial Russia in 1914. For American and British corporations, it might be better to keep Russia functioning as a third-world nation with resources to exploit. Maintaining what the West believed to be a backward political system with state-controlled economic planning could ensure Russia remained underfoot.

Of course, Lenin would take power any way he could get it. He was desperately trying to keep his government afloat, and if he found support, he didn't bother to question the motive behind it. His working assumption was that anyone not of pure Marxist ideology was not to be trusted. Even some Marxists needed to be handled with caution. Increasingly, he found Stalin to be one of those.

In 1921, Lenin's health began to fail, likely due to residual effects of the two bullets he took in the failed assassination attempt three years before. While Krasin handled foreign diplomacy and Lenin's energy began to wane, Stalin expanded his power. Having enjoyed Lenin's favor in the early years of the civil war, Stalin had been something of a rogue operator, even defying an order from his frustrated boss and War Commissar Trotsky, who attempted to recall him to the capital.

By this time, the Red Army was on top. Success was in part due to Trotsky's ability to persuade many of the top commanders who had fought for Nicholas II in the European war to come fight for Lenin instead. The White Army was in shambles and the conflict with Poland, the last of the Western and Central European powers to oppose the Soviets militarily, finally ended in 1921 with the Treaty of Riga, which partitioned disputed territory between the two nations. With Soviet control firming up and Lenin's health becoming an issue, a quiet power struggle for succession began to take shape in the background. Trotsky, then forty-two, about the same age as Stalin, was the most likely successor.

While Lenin had previously defended Stalin from Trotsky's criticisms, he began to favor Trotsky and sour on Stalin. Lenin became increasingly concerned about Stalin's brutalism and his strategy for Russian expansion. The different visions of the two men came to a head in February 1921 with regard to Georgia—Stalin's country of birth. Soviet Russia had recognized Georgia's independence only one year before in the Treaty of Moscow, and Georgia had elected a social democratic government led by Mensheviks.

Once on stronger political footing, Lenin's hope for a larger plan was eventually to establish a federal system controlled by Russia in which the independent governments of neighboring nations like Georgia would operate in a two-tier government system with the Russian government as the primary tier. Stalin had other ideas.

Stalin knew that because Georgia was strategically located on the Black Sea, it was a point of vulnerability. Governed by Mensheviks who were sympathetic to exiled Russians, Georgia could become a stepping-stone for a Western invasion of Russia. With the civil war wrapping up and a Red Army stronghold in Baku, Stalin could push his forces west from the oil city through the Caucasus and take Georgia.

On February 12, the Red Army invaded Georgia. Continuously urged on by Stalin, Lenin had finally relented and given consent for the advance. The war lasted a month and six days. Russia annexed Georgia, dismantled the elected government of social democrats, and installed a communist government reporting to Moscow.*

The invasion capped an ironic and comprehensive transformation of a soul. The child who had nicknamed himself Koba after the hero of Georgian independence, and who had reviled the laws of the Russian oppressors to snuff out the Georgian language, would never have believed that his future self could *become* the Russian oppressor who invaded and annexed his native Georgia.

Though his military action succeeded, Stalin's bureaucratic skill was perhaps greater than his skill as a field commander. His influence grew, as did his reputation for barbarous methods. Reflecting his ruthlessness and disinterest in actual justice, he remarked to colleagues that it was better to have "ten innocent people suffer than to let one enemy of the people escape."

Fully in control of the Caucasus with no threat of Turkish, German, or British opposition, Stalin's forces were unrelenting. In a region accustomed to savagery, a haunting new form of organized, methodical terror began. In Baku, Stalin authorized "a week of plundering" in which citizens were invited to sack the homes of "capitalist bloodsuckers and their parasites." Any person opposed to the state-sponsored plundering was subject to arrest and execution.

---

* Georgia reemerged as an independent state upon the collapse of the Soviet Union in 1991. Putin later invaded Georgia in 2008, which was the first Russian military action against an independent state since the fall of the Soviet Union. The war lasted sixteen days and Georgia remained independent, as it does to this day.

While Stalin continued to operate unrestrained, Lenin and Krasin continued their efforts to acquire the money and technology needed to sustain a nation. Krasin continued to wheel and deal around Europe using the riches of the Caucasus as his ace in the hole. Krasin's tactics were duplicitous, and his intended mark was the British government. In Document 65 of the Politburo Resolution dated January 26, 1921, the first agreed point is to "conclude an agreement [a commercial agreement for British ventures in the Caucasus] on the principles advocated by Krasin." The following points of this confidential document reveal that Lenin had no intention of honoring the agreement. Point 4: "Dispatch envoys to Baku to explain that the attack on British imperialism must be pursued even more vigorously, though not in our name." Point 7: "Henceforth, communicate everything that is hostile to England only in a special code." Then Point 8 made very clear, "Inform all the eastern peoples, only verbally, through envoys, without a single piece of paper, that we shall dupe England."

By early 1922, Krasin was deep in discussions with Deterding for the sale of Soviet petroleum assets in Baku. These discussions took place mainly in London, and the British government had thrown their unofficial support behind Deterding and Royal Dutch Shell. The problem was that the assets Krasin had on offer were the very same ones Nobel had already sold to Standard Oil of New Jersey in a deal that had the support of the State Department.

This presented quite a problem for these formerly allied powers. Lenin's nationalization of industry, which Nobel viewed as theft, had been holding, but how could Deterding buy up the very same oil assets from the Soviets that Standard had already bought from Nobel two years before? Who owned what? Rumors about Nobel's oil business were circling the globe.

The State Department, urged on by 26 Broadway, aimed to find out what Krasin and the British were up to. On May 4, 1922, Secretary of State Charles Hughes sent a telegram to Ambassador Richard Child, who had an opportunity to meet with members of the British cabinet. Hughes instructed Child, "In informal conversations with British representatives, endeavor orally, discreetly and in the most friendly way . . . to ascertain the precise terms of the reported oil agreement between Soviet representatives and Royal Dutch Shell, and its effect on the rights now held by an American company in production, transportation, marketing and exploration."

Standard was angry with Deterding and the British for what the Americans viewed as an end-around deal with an illegitimate Soviet claim. The US government was also upset, and Hughes further instructed Child to give Lenin a brushback. "You may also see that word reaches Soviet representatives that this Government will not countenance any arrangements to the prejudice of American interests in Russia." Hughes then concluded, "Keep Department informed in detail."

As usual, the State Department had Standard's back, or at least projected as much. But what did "not countenance" really mean if Lenin decided that the State Department's threat was only a bluff?

As the governments of Great Britain, America, and Russia eyed each other warily, Krasin worked his wiles in hopes of a longer-term payoff. There was no watershed sale of assets and no formation of an international joint venture in Baku. Rather, he aimed to gather small investments of cash, consulting, and technology so that over a brief period of years he could resuscitate Russian oil production to prerevolution levels and do it all under communist control and ownership. He had plenty of economic rewards to dangle in return.

Emanuel demonstrated his shrewdness and once again proved to be a step ahead. He saw Krasin's plan and attempted to thwart it. There were a limited number of international petroleum companies that could assist in the redevelopment of Baku. Emanuel gathered them. In July 1922, only two months after the telegram from Hughes to Child, members of Nobel Brothers, Standard Oil, and Royal Dutch Shell met in London to discuss a coordinated strategy against the Soviets. The result was the London Memorandum, in which the parties agreed that the Soviets owed full compensation for confiscated property. Further, the parties agreed not to negotiate separately with Soviet Russia, and that should a Soviet representative attempt to contact any of the parties, that party would alert the others. Nobel hoped to put a stop to Krasin playing them all against one another. Emanuel had spent decades competing against the most powerful and sophisticated corporations in the world. He was still a master of the game.

In the coming months, the alliance of the London Memorandum grew stronger. By the end of 1922, thirteen additional petroleum companies whose Russian assets had been confiscated by the Soviets joined with Nobel Brothers, Standard Oil, and Royal Dutch Shell to form the Front Uni (United Front).

The standoff against the Soviets grew increasingly tense and had implications for ordinary citizens around the world. On the one side, Russia was desperate for cash and foreign assistance to rebuild its oil industry. On the other, with the international consortium of refiners refusing to tap the massive supply of Russian oil, Europe was becoming oil-starved, and prices were rising.

The threat to the United Front was that any of the parties would act out of self-interest to make a sweetheart deal with the Soviets. Anyone who might import bargain-priced Russian oil to supply Europe would make a fortune. Emanuel, Gösta, and Standard argued fiercely to hold the line, knowing that only through continued pressure on the Soviets would restitution of the confiscated assets be possible.

In the end, Deterding cracked. Royal Dutch Shell bought a massive quantity of cheaply priced oil and sold it for a huge profit. Although Deterding was roundly criticized for the betrayal, others would follow suit. Krasin's temptations were too great. The Front Uni died—and along with it any hope of the Nobels reclaiming what generations of the family had built in Baku. In the boardroom of 26 Broadway came the recognition that in purchasing Nobel's assets they had effectively bought a corpse.

On May 26, 1922, as Krasin was deploying his countermeasures against Nobel's coalition, Lenin had a stroke. He suffered aphasia (loss of speech) and loss of function on the right side of his body. He made a slow and partial recovery, to the point that he regained most of his speech, could hold a newspaper in his right hand, and could publicly present himself as being in charge of the government. On December 22, he suffered a second stroke that completely paralyzed his right side, permanently took his speech, and reduced his political career to that of a figurehead. By this time, the Soviets firmly held power in Russia and were enacting Lenin's New Economic Policy (NEP). Lenin, in an effort to rebuild the country that had been devastated by years of both European and civil war, had backed off the communist policy of extreme centralization and would allow capitalism, subject to state control, as a temporary expedient. (Stalin would later reverse NEP.)

In these years Stalin often visited Lenin at his home, where Lenin employed a chef named Spiridon Putin, who would often tell the story that he had prepared dinner for the monk Rasputin years before Lenin took power. The strangely charming Rasputin had joked with the chef about the similarity of their surnames. The chef cooked regularly for Lenin, and Stalin would occasionally join his boss to discuss the future and enjoy meals together. None could then know that years later Spiridon Putin would have a grandson named Vladimir Putin, who would ultimately succeed the man for whom his grandfather cooked.

On March 23, 1923, Lenin had a third stroke. When Lenin finally died on January 21, 1924, Trotsky was in the Caucasus. Stalin sent a telegram to Trotsky giving him the incorrect date for Lenin's funeral. When Trotsky arrived at the capital, having missed the funeral, Stalin had already made critical alliances in secret and outmaneuvered Trotsky for succession.*

Stalin would vanquish all his enemies. Of the seven original members of the party executive committee, called the first Politburo, at the time of the 1917 revolution (the members were Lenin, Trotsky, Stalin, Zinoviev, Kamenev, Bubnov, and Sokolnikov), Stalin won the support

* Trotsky remained in government as a popular and vocal critic of Stalin, but Stalin eventually managed to have Trotsky expelled from the Politburo in 1926, from the Communist Party in 1927, then finally exiled and deported in 1929. The charming and determined Trotsky continued to flit about the globe as an antagonist to Stalin and became an international superstar until an agent of the NKVD dispatched by Stalin caught up with Trotsky in Mexico City on August 20, 1940, and drove a mountaineering ice pick through his skull.

of two and murdered three. There has even been speculation by Russian historian Lev Lurie in 2012 that Stalin murdered Lenin by poisoning, known to be Stalin's favorite method of killing a rival. If true, he murdered the majority of the first Politburo.

Stalin's Communist Party controlled the Soviet, such that the party and the Russian government were effectively one—much the same as the Nazi Party would later control the German government. Stalin's tactic was to defeat, discredit, and erase. The single exception to this formula was Lenin, only because it served Stalin's purposes to support a cult of Lenin, as Stalin was the successor of that cult. Cultism was the communist version of tsarist godly anointment. Five days after Lenin's death, the Soviets renamed Petrograd Leningrad.

All other credit and praise accrued to Stalin. The following year, on April 10, 1925, the Soviets renamed Tsaritsyn Stalingrad to honor their supreme leader.* Stalin would name six more towns in the Soviet Union after himself, as well as towns in Albania, Bulgaria, East Germany, Hungary, Poland, and Romania. Stalin eventually even added his name to the national anthem (it was removed after his death).

Stalin continued his effort to discredit and erase individuals of the tsarist era, then appropriate their achievements for himself and the Soviet.† The tactic of renaming was applied here as well. The Ludvig Nobel Machine Factory became Pervij Sawod Russkiy Diesel (First Russian Diesel Engine Factory), which was the largest machine factory in the Soviet Union. Nobel Brothers Petroleum Company became

---

* In 1961, Stalingrad was renamed Volgograd. Leningrad became Saint Petersburg (again) in 1991.

† Unsurprisingly, Stalin was not as productive with Russia's resources as Nobel had been. Below is a comparison of the production of war materials during 1916 under Emanuel Nobel's leadership versus the year 1919 under the Soviet as Bolsheviks ran these same urban factories to supply the Red Army during the civil war:

Rifles:	(1916) 1,300,000	(1919) 460,000
Field Artillery:	(1916) 8,200	(1919) 152
Shells:	(1916) 33,000,000	(1919) 185,000 (less than one percent of 1916)

the Soviet Petroleum Company. The Petrograd location of the Swedish company Ericsson Telephone and Telegraph continued under the ominous name Red Dawn. Lessner Brothers became the Karl Marx Machine-Building Association.

Anyone who had been present for the Russian Civil War would be shocked some years later to read how little Trotsky had contributed to the Red Army, according to Stalin's official historians. Stalin went so far as to have Trotsky's image removed from photographs that pictured him next to Lenin during the glory days of the revolution. Stalin's actions inspired George Orwell to write chilling passages in his novel *1984* (published in 1949):

> *Every record has been destroyed or falsified, every book has been rewritten, every picture has been repainted, every statue and street and building has been renamed, every date has been altered. And that process is continuing day by day and minute by minute. History has stopped.*

In Baku and Leningrad, plaques and signage that identified the Nobel family or companies bearing their name were stripped away. All evidence of their existence was gone without a trace. To the extent that locals in Baku or the descendants of Nobelites might share memories of the boom years of Emanuel's time, the Soviets aimed to head off such remembrance. A Soviet history book published in 1980 did Stalin's posthumous bidding by writing, "Nobel Brothers was the leading capitalist predator in the Russian oil business. The degree of monopoly that they achieved brought its bosses large profits through an unprecedentedly refined exploitation of the workers."

This text is richly ironic when one considers that the Nobel family pioneered enlightened labor practices in Russia, that their workers proudly identified themselves as "Nobelites," and that many of Emanuel's workers risked their lives to protect him and aid his escape from Stalin's prison. Yet Stalin succeeded in vanquishing the Russian Nobels for a hundred years.

The world has known the name Standard Oil, but not Branobel. There are countless biographies of John D. Rockefeller, and the surname Rothschild has passed to legend such that we hardly bother with the given names of Rothschild family members. Not so with the Nobel family. The achievements of Immanuel, Robert, and Ludvig Nobel are unsung. Emanuel Nobel, with greater proximity to Stalin's revision of history, suffers a deficit of appreciation even more extreme than his forebears. Though both Rockefeller and Rothschild had waved the white flag before Emanuel, he brushed aside their entreaties to partner. For Uncle Alfred, he defied the King of Sweden as a matter of principle and duty to his family. He led the greatest industrial empire in Russia, perhaps in all Europe, yet the world does not know his name.

EPILOGUE

At Last

IN HINDSIGHT, ONE might have anticipated that Alexander II's reforms to freedom of assembly and the press would serve only to catalyze the institutions that opposed him, that the sons of the serfs he freed in 1861 would be the ones to murder him, that these assassins would employ dynamite as their weapon—an invention of the Nobels, who would also become their target.

To an outsider, these outcomes seem cruelly ironic. The chance for constitutional monarchy had often been so near but each time was savagely rejected. But perhaps for an insider, for one who understands the Russian people, who does not view Russians through a Western lens, the answer is that all along these violent outcomes were not ironic but inevitable. Nearly two hundred years ago, Tsar Nicholas I declared that the only way to rule Russia was as a lion, that the Russian people needed something different from what Western governments provide. Vladimir Putin, having studied centuries of Russian history in which attempts at reform have been unavoidably double-edged, seems to agree.

Emanuel Nobel understood Russians. He spent his adult life in

Russia, and for more than thirty years was a Russian citizen. Despite his familiarity with the political environment, one could forgive Emanuel for not having anticipated his own ouster at the hands of the communist regime, for believing that Lenin and Stalin would not prevail. So many others inside Russia believed as he did.

To break the Romanovs' literal godlike grasp on the empire required extraordinary events. It was not nearly enough to have the sudden death of Alexander III due to kidney disease that launched onto the throne one of the most feckless monarchs ever to rule in Europe. It also required a hemophiliac tsarevich, a bizarre mystic, a world war, two revolutions, and a civil war so catastrophic that it caused more than ten times the number of deaths as the American Civil War.

All of these individually colossal developments took place within just a few years and created such a black hole of chaos that foreign powers feared intervention. The Russian people experienced social change at the extremes: from governance by the far right to governance by the far left, from a deeply religious society to a violently secular one, from a capitalist economy to a nationalized and centrally planned system. The only constant was authoritarianism, and a foot on the neck of the people. Or so it would appear through a Western lens.

Emanuel certainly had a Western-leaning view of the world. He renounced his Russian citizenship in 1923 and once again became a citizen of Sweden. He also moved from Paris, which had been his primary residence for about two years while he and Gösta resolved the future of the family businesses in Russia, and made Stockholm his permanent home. With the political constraints of the Great War over, traveling to Germany was again possible, and Emanuel frequented the Golf Hotel at Oberhof, a favorite mountain health resort. He also took trips to Egypt, Sicily, Capri, and as far as India and Ceylon (Sri Lanka).

He maintained a close friendship with the Dowager Empress Maria Feodorovna, widow of Alexander III and mother of Nicholas II. The two had first met in 1888, all those years ago, when the royal family visited Nobel Brothers in Baku and concluded the visit by honoring Emanuel with the offer of citizenship. The two could marvel bitterly at the transformation of the Russian Empire that had occurred in such a brief period. The former tsarina, born a Danish princess, had returned to her home country and lived peacefully in Copenhagen. Emanuel made her a regular gift of caviar, which the Empress's secretary wrote "always gave great pleasure to Her Majesty."

Emanuel also remained close with his old friend and investor Marcus Wallenberg, the Swedish banker and industrialist who had been a business partner to both Rudolf Diesel and Emanuel, and focused more on entrepreneurial investing. Together with Karl Wilhelm Hagelin, perhaps the most talented executive at Nobel Brothers in its final decades, Emanuel established Cryptograph Ltd., a Swedish-based venture that designed and manufactured encrypting machines. He installed Hagelin's son Boris, who had built Diesels during the Great War in Nobel's Petrograd factory, as the chief engineer and executive. Emanuel's initial hope had been that he would recover his assets in Baku and that he and Standard Oil could use the encrypting machines for confidential communications with his executives in the Caucasus. This never came to pass, but Boris led the company to terrific success. The machines found an international market, including the US Army during World War II, and Boris Hagelin became a legendary figure in cryptography.*

Emanuel also reconnected with his friend Hugo Junkers, the German inventor who had pioneered advances with both the Diesel engine and aircraft design. In 1920, Emanuel invested in a regional airline developed by Junkers to connect Sweden with the Baltic states and other regions that were formerly a part of the Russian Empire. Nobel and Junkers were early to recognize that the airplane, which does not require the construction of roads or railroad tracks, would play a critical role in opening up the disparate regions of the former empire.

---

* Boris's great-grandson is the ice hockey star Carl Hagelin, who played as a professional for eleven seasons in the NHL and also won the silver medal for the Swedish team at the 2014 Olympics.

In addition to Emanuel's travels and his investments in new and existing ventures, he worked diligently to support the legacy of Uncle Alfred's prizes. From attending ceremonies to unofficially participating in the selection of recipients, Emanuel saw to it that the Nobel Prize became arguably the most prestigious award in the world. As was always his way, he contentedly worked without desire for credit or attention and pushed only the name Alfred Nobel into the limelight.

After such a sudden uprooting from the life he'd known in the time of the tsars, Emanuel's first days in Stockholm must have felt dreamlike. Then, after years in his new reality, as communism marched across Europe, perhaps he began to wonder if it was his once-celebrated years in Russia that were only a dream. In 1929, Emanuel turned seventy and the family threw the most lavish party yet for the patriarch. The scale of the party was perhaps due to a noticeable decline in Emanuel's mental acuity and a sense that his end was not far off. The celebration took place at the Golf Hotel. Among those attending or sending birthday wishes were King Gustaf V and Prince Carl of Sweden, Finland's General Mannerheim, Henri Deterding, Marcus and Knut Wallenberg, the former Russian finance minister Vladimir Kokovtsov, Albert Einstein, and Max Planck. Emanuel printed thank-you cards in four languages.

Emanuel died on May 31, 1932. In his last years he had quietly taken up with a lady friend who had accompanied him, as part of a larger entourage, on several of his vacations. The significance of the relationship became more pronounced upon the reading of Emanuel's will, which named her as a beneficiary. Antoinette Jerzykowicz received twelve percent of the tangible assets dispersed. Emanuel had spoken to Wilhelm Hagelin, asking his friend to ensure that the estate paid out the money to Jerzykowicz as Emanuel knew his family viewed the woman as a charlatan and opportunist. Lief Nobel, Emanuel's nephew, who had been part of the traveling entourage on the trip to India, wrote that Jerzykowicz was "a real devil of a woman, sour and lazy."

In gratitude for lifesaving services, Emanuel left a sizable pension to Vladimir Nazansky and Mikhail Yevlanov, who had helped Emanuel escape the Red Army. With still a glint of hope, Emanuel also noted that should any of the real estate, personal property, or assets of the businesses in Russia revert to the original and true owners, then full ownership should pass to his three half brothers, Rolf, Emil, and Gösta.

The size of Emanuel's true fortune—what he managed to scrape back to Stockholm and what was captured by Stalin—is impossible to reconstruct. In addition to his ownership of the four primary Nobel businesses in Russia, he had massive investments in numerous companies, including the nitroglycerin company founded by his uncle, extensive real estate holdings taken by the Soviets in various Russian cities, government bonds, furniture, jewelry, and artwork.*

Emanuel's stepmother, Edla, made a restitution claim for her confiscated assets in Soviet Russia. As such, a contemporaneous effort was made to ascertain the total value of her holdings, which comprised real estate, stocks, bonds, and personal property. The figure was more than 45 million roubles, which, converted to dollars and adjusted for inflation (which is a very conservative method that undervalues the original amount), equates to about $150 million today. Other methods to determine the present value of her fortune would place the figure well into the billions. Emanuel never filed a claim for restitution, though his fortune was far greater than Edla's.

The family held a Mass to honor Emanuel's life at the Russian Orthodox Church in Stockholm. The following day, on June 6, the family held his burial service at the nearby St. Jakob's Church. This concluded a sad separation from his father, Ludvig, whose remains

---

* Emanuel's art collection included paintings by Anders Zorn and the famous Russian artist Valentin Serov, who had also painted a portrait of Emanuel. Serov's other portraiture includes that of Maxim Gorky and Tsar Nicholas II. Serov's 1909 portrait of Nobel was exhibited in Moscow and Saint Petersburg in 1914. The provenance lists the painting "by descent" to Sotheby's London in 1988, and the Nobel portrait most recently sold through Christie's in 2002 for US$240,500. The portrait is currently in the collection of Petr Aven, a Russian businessman and art collector.

were buried on the opposite shores of the Baltic Sea in Saint Petersburg. Of all that Emanuel was forced to leave behind, this was among the most heartbreaking.

Communism had been only the musings of Karl Marx until Lenin put it into practice for the first time anywhere in the world in 1918. Then Stalin made sure it stuck. By the end of Stalin's thirty-year reign, he had made the Soviet empire one of the world's two superpowers.

The anarchist Mikhail Bakunin first met his communist rival Karl Marx in 1844 in Paris. The two met several times, usually in a dark pub while smoking clay pipes and drinking from tin mugs of beer. The exchanges often became fiery between them. Bakunin abhorred the central control espoused by communism, believing that too much power would accrue to a government authority and that trading a monarchy for communism would simply be trading one kind of autocrat for another.

Stalin seized the communist system that Marx designed. Bakunin never met Stalin. He died in July 1876, two years before Stalin was born. But Bakunin didn't need to meet Stalin in order to anticipate him. In 1844, between pulls on his pipe and sips of beer, Bakunin said to Marx, "A communist state would be no better than a capitalist one. Leadership would still be concentrated in the hands of a few. And if the country is led by workers, they would soon become as corrupt and despotic as the tyrants they overthrew." The error in Bakunin's prediction was that there might be any period at all without corruption and despotism.

In its first years, communism in Russia had plenty of help from abroad. A powerful tool to resuscitate the Soviet economy had been surreptitious support from the West. On May 7, 1919, police raided the offices of the Soviet Bureau at 110 West 40th Street in New York City at the behest of the US government. The socialist Ludwig Martens headed the Soviet Bureau in New York (Lenin had appointed Martens his ambassador to the United States in January 1919, though this was an unofficial position as the United States did not recognize Lenin's government), where US agents found a trove of information that connected American industrial interests to Soviet Russia. The American government shared the findings with the British, who were cooperating in the investigations of Bolshevik insurrection. Scotland Yard's Basil Thomson wrote of the unearthed files in New York that "there are grounds for believing that the [Soviet] Bureau has received financial support from [J. P. Morgan's] Guarantee Trust Company."

Thomson's report concluded that "[Martens's] organization is a powerful weapon for supporting the Bolshevik cause in the United States and . . . he is in close touch with the promoters of political unrest throughout the whole American continent."

Martens initially went underground after the raid, for a time hiding out at the home of Julius Hammer and his son Armand. Julius Hammer was a Jewish emigrant from the Russian Empire who came to the Bronx in 1875, where he built a successful medical practice, supported Lenin and Bolshevism from abroad, and was a founding member of the Communist Party USA.*

By February 1920, a subcommittee of the Senate Foreign Relations Committee investigating Soviet activity in America called Martens to testify. Martens confessed to revolutionary activity with the hope of overthrowing America's capitalist system. He also bragged to the media that his aim had not been to incite the American proletariat but, cynically, to persuade American big business interests to support Soviet Russia. He claimed that already US Steel Corporation and Standard Oil were assisting his effort to get the US government to offer diplomatic recognition to the Soviets. *The New York Times* published his remarks.

---

* Julius Hammer was already under federal surveillance for suspected Bolshevik sympathies. He was arrested in 1919 for charges related to a botched abortion in his clinic and sentenced to three years in Sing Sing. From Russia, Lenin criticized the charges against Hammer as a pretext. While in prison, Julius sent Armand to liaise with Soviet Russia. Armand Hammer controlled the family company, Allied Drug, which was in actuality a clandestine import-export company that smuggled equipment and cash into Russia and brought out raw materials (like fur pelts) to sell in the West. Hammer also laundered money to fund underground Soviet agents in the US, Britain, and Germany. He later became an oil magnate and chief executive of Occidental Petroleum. His great-grandson is the actor Armie Hammer.

In 1923, just as Emanuel renounced his Russian citizenship, the Soviets formed Ruskombank, the first international bank in the Soviet Union. The new bank would appoint Morgan-controlled Guaranty Trust as its agent in America, and Max May, a vice president of Guaranty Trust, became a director of Ruskombank. Stalin was succeeding in bending the West to his will. The economic benefit in working with the Soviets was too great to resist. Steadily, Stalin managed to acquire the foreign investment and technology to rebuild industries, including the petroleum industry in Baku, which by 1927 was approaching prewar production levels.*

Like Lenin before him, Stalin had to deal with internal rivals for power. But Stalin had a firmer grip on power than Lenin, who had to contend with powerful antagonistic political factions inside Russia as well as foreign armies on Russian soil. More securely in charge, Stalin dealt with political opposition far more ruthlessly.

William Faulkner wrote, "The past is never dead. It's not even past." There is no better example of this truism than the relationship between Russia and Ukraine. When a Ukrainian national movement gained traction in the late 1920s, Stalin aimed to nip it early. In 1929 he ordered the arrest of five thousand leading Ukrainian cultural and religious leaders and academics whom he charged falsely with plotting an armed revolt. With no trial, the prisoners were shot or deported to concentration camps.

When the Ukrainian peasantry resisted Stalin's policy of collectivization, which mandated the transfer of individual peasant farms to a

---

* In the early 1920s, industrial development in Soviet Russia came from the unlikeliest of places: Germany. Russian aviation pioneer Igor Sikorsky, a friend of Tsar Nicholas II, fled for his life in 1918, which left Russia bereft of critical aviation expertise. Fortunately for Lenin, the Treaty of Versailles made bedfellows of Germany and Russia. The treaty outlawed Germany from building aircraft, both military and civilian. This untenable condition led to a deal, made in secret, between Weimar Germany and Bolshevik Russia, in which the German inventor Hugo Junkers built a factory on the outskirts of Moscow where the Junkers firm produced aircraft away from the prying eyes of Allied inspectors and, critically for Lenin and Stalin, trained Russian engineers. Hugo Junkers and the Germans were the foundation of the Soviet air force.

collective controlled by the state, he engineered the Holodomor, the man-made famine of 1932–33 that effectively forced the deaths by starvation of an estimated seven to ten million Ukrainian people (according to a 2003 joint statement to the United Nations that marked the seventieth anniversary of the Great Famine).

Political rivals throughout Russia, real and imagined, met grisly ends. Stalin's paranoid and brutal Great Purge in the years 1936–38 resulted in the murders of 750,000 to 1,250,000 "political enemies."

In 1939, he struck a deal with Hitler. On August 24, Stalin and Hitler signed a nonaggression pact called the Molotov-Ribbentrop Pact. These two nations, both still bitter about their poor treatment under the Treaty of Versailles, agreed to a defensive alliance in which neither would attack the other in the event of war, and then they agreed to a plan to divide between them the nations of Eastern and Central Europe: Poland, Lithuania, Latvia, Estonia, Finland, and Romania. The two dictators intended to absorb Europe. A week after signatures, on September 1, Hitler invaded western Poland. On September 17, Stalin invaded eastern Poland. By October 6, the fighting was over and the two invaders annexed their shares of Poland.

Stalin had never fought in the Great War, so perhaps he never developed a reflexive hatred of the Germans. Possibly he even felt some gratitude to Germany for shuttling Lenin to Petrograd in 1917 to help spark the revolution. However, Hitler had served on the front lines in the Great War and never thought of Stalin and the Russians as anything but a natural and eventual enemy. On June 22, 1941, Hitler betrayed his pact with Stalin and launched a massive surprise attack against Soviet Russia.

Knocked on his heels by Hitler, Stalin joined an unlikely alliance with the democratic, capitalist nations of the West and took up the fight against his former co-conspirator for world domination. As has been the custom with Russia, it was an alliance not driven by ideology but by desperation and coincidence.

In this war, once again, Russia's greatest defense proved to be distance and a seemingly endless supply of men to fight. Soviet Russia fought valiantly and suffered terrible losses. As had the armies of Napoleon and Sweden's Charles XII, Hitler's army withered away in the cold and barren Russian plains. Stalin came out on the winning side, and in a world turned upside down by war he emerged a hero. His dominion over Russia was absolute, his acceptance by the international community complete, his selective erasure of the past—both his own misdeeds and the good deeds of his rivals—seemingly all but assured.

For his efforts to end World War II, a war he and Hitler started, Joseph Stalin was nominated for the Nobel Peace Prize in 1945 and 1948.

A NOTE ON DATES

In 1582, Pope Gregory XIII introduced by papal bull a new calendar to replace the Julian calendar that Julius Caesar had established in 46 BC. The purpose of the new calendar was to correct a slight solar inaccuracy that caused the seasonal dates to regress by about one day per century.

By the time the Protestant British Empire officially adopted the Gregorian calendar in 1752, much of the world was using the pope's calendar. A notable exception was the Russian Empire, which continued with the Julian calendar, also then referred to as Old Style (O.S.). Due to more than a thousand years of solar inaccuracy, by the twentieth century the Julian calendar marked events thirteen days earlier than the more precise Gregorian. Therefore, Russia's February Revolution began on February 23, 1917, by the Julian calendar but March 8 by the Gregorian calendar observed by much of the world outside the Empire.

On February 14, 1918 (by the Gregorian calendar), Vladimir Lenin abandoned the Julian calendar and adopted a modified version of the Gregorian calendar (called the Soviet calendar or Western European calendar) in Russia to conform more closely with the West.

In this book I have recorded the dates of events in Russia as Russians experienced them—by the Julian calendar before Lenin's decree and by the Gregorian after.

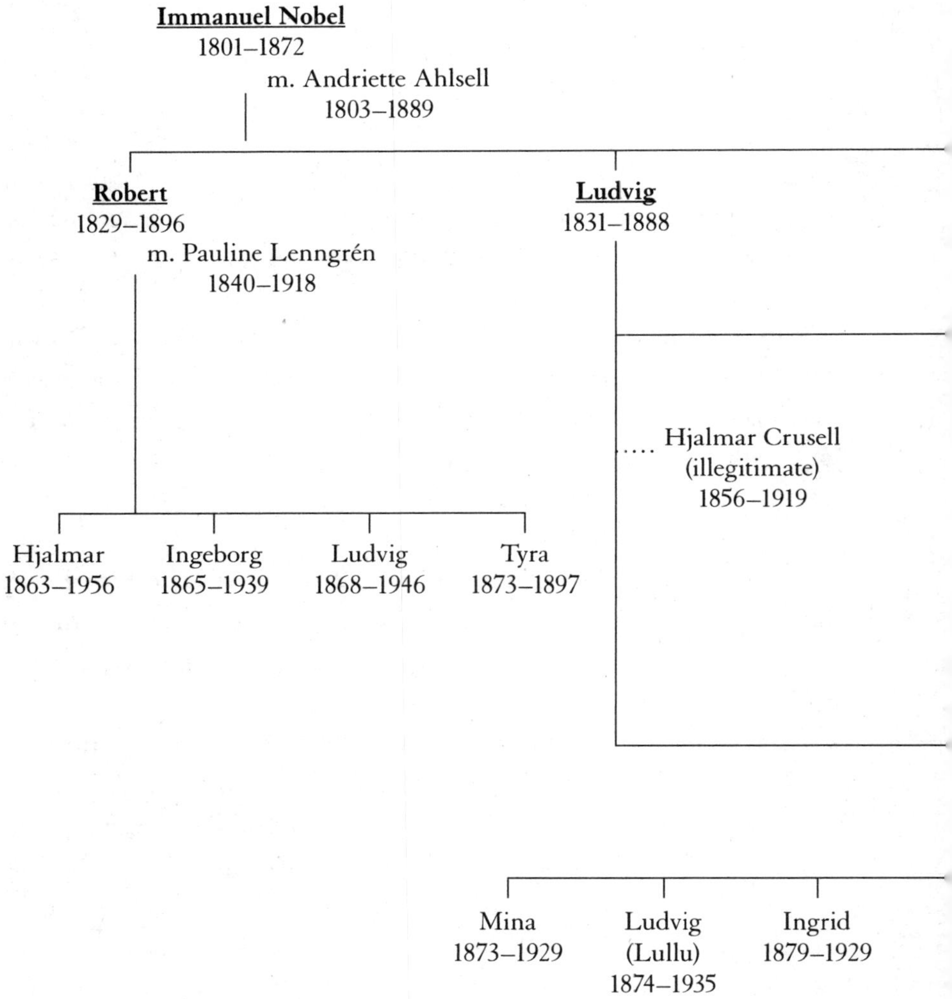

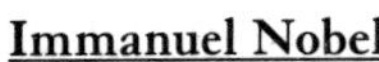

Immanuel Nobel
1801–1872
m. Andriette Ahlsell
1803–1889
Robert
1829–1896
m. Pauline Lenngrén
1840–1918
Ludvig
1831–1888
Hjalmar Crusell
(illegitimate)
1856–1919
Hjalmar
1863–1956
Ingeborg
1865–1939
Ludvig
1868–1946
Tyra
1873–1897
Mina
1873–1929
Ludvig
(Lullu)
1874–1935
Ingrid
1879–1929

NOBEL FAMILY TREE*

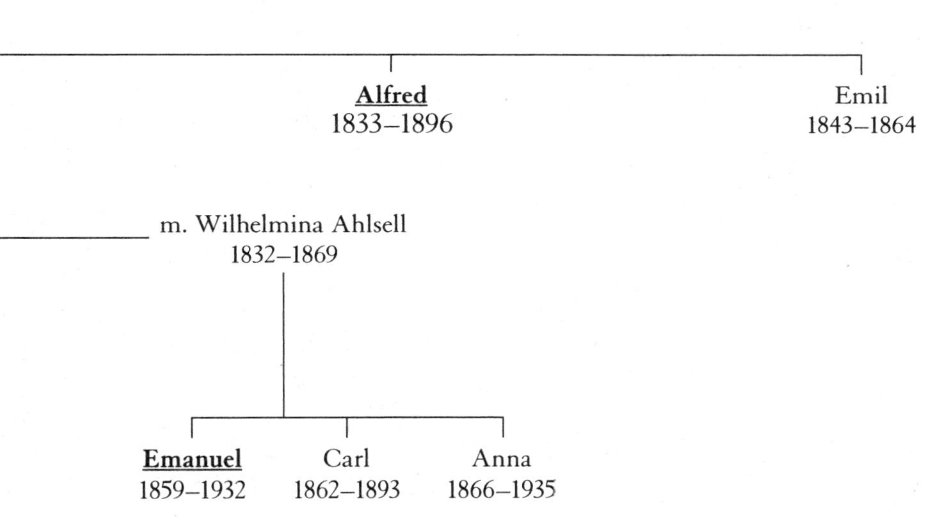

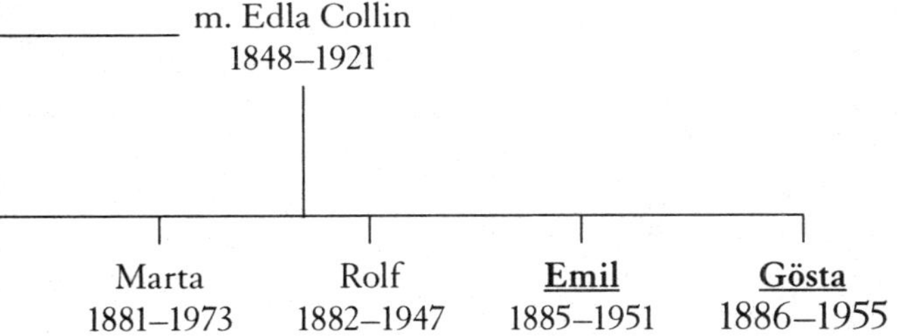

* Does not include family members who died as young children.

A NOTE ON THE NOBELS TODAY

Immanuel Nobel (1801–72) and Andriette (1803–89) had four children: Robert, Ludvig, Alfred, and Emil. Alfred and Emil (who died in a laboratory explosion at the age of twenty) never had children.

Robert Nobel and his wife, Pauline, had four children (names listed on page 304).

Ludvig Nobel and his first wife, Wilhelmina, had three children: Emanuel, Carl, and Anna.

Ludvig and his second wife, Edla, had seven children, including Emil and Gösta.

The Nobels today can trace their lineage back to the children of Immanuel's sons, Robert and Ludvig.

SEVERAL NOBEL ORGANIZATIONS AND PRIZES REMAIN ACTIVE:

Nobel Family Society: Thomas Tydén, a descendant of Carl Nobel's eldest daughter, serves as chairman. The function of this organization is to promote and protect the Nobel family history and the Nobel Prize. As such, the organization supports the Nobel Foundation (described below) but opposes the Nobel Sustainability Trust (also described below) and all other organizations and prizes that trade on the Nobel name because the society believes that the creation of new entities that attach the Nobel name dilutes the significance of the Nobel Prize and causes confusion such that, as Tydén says, "people cannot determine the real and the not real." Currently there are more than three hundred descendants of Robert and Ludvig Nobel who are members of the society.

Nobel Foundation: Established in 1900 per the terms of Alfred Nobel's will, the Nobel Foundation oversees both the financial standing and the prize-awarding institutions of the Nobel Prize. The foundation awards annual prizes in the categories of physics, chemistry, medicine, literature, peace, and economic science. From 1901 to 2024 the foundation has awarded the prize 627 times to 1,012 people/organizations.

Nobel Sustainability Trust: Formerly known as the Nobel Charitable Trust, the organization was founded in 2007 by members of the Nobel family with the mandate to encourage the research, development, and implementation of environmentally sustainable solutions. The trust is separate from, and at odds with, the Nobel Family Society and the Nobel Foundation. Board members of the Nobel Sustainability Trust include(d):

Peter Nobel (b. 1931) currently serves as chairman. He is a Swedish human rights lawyer and descendant of Emanuel's half sister Mina.

Michael Nobel (1940–2024) was a descendant of Marta Nobel, Emanuel's physician half sister. He earned numerous honorary degrees and served as board member or board chair for more than a dozen international companies in the fields of medicine and energy.

Erik Nobel (b. 1979) is based in Stockholm. He is currently a managing director for the international investment firm Levine Leichtman Capital Partners.

Stephanie Nobel (b. 1987) is a teacher in Sweden.

Johan Nobel (b. 1986) is based in Stockholm and is a client executive for the state-owned bank Swedish Export Credit Corporation.

The trust awards prizes at an annual summit, the most recent having been held in San Francisco, Munich, Paris, and Bergen. https://www.nobelsustainabilitytrust.org

Ludvig Nobel Prize: The nature of this prize has evolved over time and currently recognizes contributions to Russia. The 2024 winner was Ramzan Kadyrov, leader of the Chechen Republic, which is in the northern Caucasus between the Black Sea and Caspian Sea, for his efforts to support Russia's war in Ukraine. Prior winners include Vladimir Putin in 2008.

AUTHOR'S NOTE

History is most interesting when it sheds light on the present. As the world entered the 1980s and America enjoyed Michael Jackson, *The Bonfire of the Vanities*, the San Francisco 49ers, and the fall of the Berlin Wall, many historians had come to believe that the Russian Revolution was the most important event of the twentieth century. This acknowledgment came even with the sense of a receding threat during Gorbachev's perestroika. But Russia's history demonstrates a persistently alternating pattern between reform and repression, and Gorbachev's perestroika was not the final word.

Now, as the world moves deeper into the twenty-first century and the lens of history widens, we might reconsider the Russian Revolution as the most important event of the last five centuries, at least. But for the improbable emergence of Lenin, Stalin, and the Bolshevik Party in the autumn of 1917, how else would we have experienced Communist China, the Berlin Wall, wars in Korea and Vietnam, the Cuban Missile Crisis, NATO, and the Iron Curtain?

As horrific as we know Hitler to have been, he was only the third-worst mass murderer in world history—a distant third behind Stalin and Mao, both products of this singular event.

The Soviet regime that followed the tsars rewrote Russian history to fit the ideological agenda of the new government. Among the casualties of Stalin's erasures are members of the Nobel family. Many around the world recognize the Nobel name from the prestigious Nobel Prize, yet few know that Alfred's older brothers and nephew were the most powerful industrialists in the Russian Empire. For a time, Russia's industrialists and the Romanovs seemed to be leading the empire along a path of gradual reform to a constitutional monarchy. Then, through a confluence of bizarre events and incredible twists, such reform was arrested, and the people who supported the reform were deleted. This book is an attempt to reconnect the present with its heritage, to restore the Russian Nobels from their status as unpersons during the Soviet regime and bring them to their rightful place in world history.

TIMELINE

March 24, 1801: Immanuel Nobel born near Stockholm, Sweden

August 14, 1829: Robert Nobel born in Stockholm, Sweden

July 27, 1831: Ludvig Nobel born in Stockholm, Sweden

October 21, 1833: Alfred Nobel born in Stockholm, Sweden

December 20, 1838: Immanuel Nobel arrives in Saint Petersburg, Russia

March 30, 1856: Crimean War ends with the Treaty of Paris

June 22, 1859: Emanuel Nobel born in Saint Petersburg, Russia

March 3, 1861: Alexander II emancipates the serfs of Russia

October 1, 1862: Founding of Ludvig Nobel Machine Factory in Saint Petersburg

January 1, 1863: Abraham Lincoln emancipates the slaves of America

July 15, 1864: Alfred Nobel awarded the patent in Sweden for the blasting cap

April 16, 1866: Dmitry Karakozov attempts the assassination of Tsar Alexander II in Saint Petersburg

1873: Robert Nobel purchases land in the oil fields of Baku

1875: Nobel Brothers Petroleum Company incorporated

June 9, 1878: Nobel Brothers launch the *Zoroaster*, the world's first oil tanker

December 18, 1878: Joseph Stalin born in Gori, Georgia; birthname: Ioseb Besarionis dze Jughashvili

March 1, 1881: Alexander II assassinated in Saint Petersburg by members of the revolutionary movement Narodnaya Volya

March 1, 1887: Alexander Ulyanov and co-conspirators arrested for plotting to assassinate Alexander III

April 12, 1888: Ludvig Nobel dies; Emanuel succeeds his father as head of the family business

October 20–21, 1888: Alexander III and his entourage visit Baku for two days, and subsequently he offers Russian citizenship to Emanuel Nobel

November 1, 1894: Alexander III dies of kidney disease, which begins the reign of his son Nicholas II, the last tsar

December 1899: Stalin (Jughashvili) arrested for the first time by the secret police in Tiflis; the police photograph him and open a file

December 10, 1901: The first Nobel Prizes are awarded

February 8, 1904: Russo-Japanese War begins, lasting nineteen months to September 1905

January 22, 1905: Bloody Sunday

November 1, 1905: Rasputin meets Nicholas II and Alexandra for the first time

July 30, 1914: Russia announces a general mobilization in support of Serbia; within weeks the major powers of Germany, Austria-Hungary, France and Great Britain are at at war. The Ottoman Empire joins the war in October

August 23, 1915: Nicholas II takes command of the Imperial Russian Army and leaves Petrograd in the hands of Alexandra and Rasputin

December 30, 1916: Felix Yusupov and collaborators assassinate Rasputin

March 8, 1917: February Revolution begins, concluding a week later

March 15, 1917: Nicholas II abdicates

November 7, 1917: October Revolution begins and concludes the same day

March 3, 1918: Treaty of Brest-Litovsk formally removes Russia from the Great War

March 8, 1918: Lenin changes the name of the Bolshevik Party to the All-Russian Communist Party

July 17, 1918: Bolshevik/Communist guards assassinate Nicholas II and his family

August 30, 1918: The first attempted assassination of Lenin; he is shot twice and severely wounded

December 6, 1918: Sweden breaks off diplomatic relations with Soviet Russia; Emanuel Nobel completes his escape from the Caucasus to Stockholm; Gösta and Emil Nobel determine to flee Petrograd

May 31, 1920: Leonid Krasin meets with British prime minister Lloyd George to discuss Russian petroleum

July 30, 1920: Standard Oil of New Jersey signs an agreement with representatives of the Nobel family to purchase fifty percent of the Russian assets of Nobel Brothers Petroleum Company

October 25, 1922: The Red Army takes Vladivostok, extinguishing the last vestige of the White Army, and puts an end to the Russian Civil War

January 21, 1924: Lenin dies, age fifty-three, after suffering a series of strokes; five days later the government renames Petrograd Leningrad to reinforce the cult of Lenin

May 31, 1932: Emanuel Nobel dies in Stockholm, Sweden, at age seventy-two

1932–1933: Stalin engineers the forced starvation of the Ukrainian peasantry, resulting in the deaths of seven to ten million people

1936–1938: Stalin's Great Purge murders between 750,000 and 1,250,000 "political enemies"

August 20, 1940: Stalin's NKVD assassin drives a mountaineering ice pick into Trotsky's skull in Mexico City; he dies the next day

1945: Joseph Stalin nominated for the Nobel Peace Prize

1948: Joseph Stalin again nominated for the Nobel Peace Prize

APPENDIX

PRIVATE OWNERSHIP OF PRODUCTIVE PROPERTY AS TREATED BY IDEOLOGY

Anarchism: Yes, private ownership is permitted. The means of production should be held in common by the citizens without any state control, but rather through free association of the people.

Communism: No, private ownership is forbidden. The state owns all productive assets, and a government-led central authority operates the economic system to ensure equitable distribution of wealth among the citizens.

Socialism: Yes, private ownership is permitted. A highly interventionist government system ensures equitable distribution of wealth among the citizens.

Fascism: Yes, private ownership is permitted, though the state will also own certain critical industrial assets. The government supports capitalism; however, the government is also characterized by a high degree of hierarchy, authoritarianism, nationalism, and economic interventionism.

NOTES

PROLOGUE

1 *"half of Petrograd"*: Bengt Jangfeldt, *The Nobel Family: Swedish Geniuses in Tsarist Russia*, trans. Harry D. Watson (London: Bloomsbury Academic, 2023), 309.

CHAPTER 1: PRISON OR RUSSIA

7 *The cramped room*: An earlier bankruptcy petition that Immanuel filed in 1833 described the family's rented apartment and the extremely modest contents. Ragnar Sohlman and Henrik Schuck, *The Life of Alfred Nobel*, trans. W. H. von der Mülbe and Brian and Beatrix Lunn (London: William Heinemann, 1929), 6.

8 *sent to sea in 1815*: Ragnar Sohlman and Henrik Schuck, *Nobel: Dynamite and Peace*, trans. Brian and Beatrix Lunn (New York: Cosmopolitan Book, 1929), 27.

9 *started a rubber factory*: Jangfeldt, *The Nobel Family*, 19.

12 *"The small amount of"*: Jangfeldt, *The Nobel Family*, 42.

13 *General Schilder discussed*: Documents describing the conversation are in the Regional Archives in Lund, Sweden, and also mentioned in Robert W. Tolf, *The Russian Rockefellers: The Saga of the Nobel Family and the Russian Oil Industry* (Stanford, CA: Hoover Institution Press, 1976), 8–10.

14 *To the amazement of all*: Tolf, *The Russian Rockefellers*, 8–10, and also Jangfeldt, *The Nobel Family*, 31.

16 *ruling over peoples*: Stephen Kotkin, *Stalin* (New York: Penguin, 2014), 56.

16 *"Her power is"*: Peter Hopkirk, *The Great Game: The Struggle for Empire in Central Asia* (New York: Kodansha USA Publishing, 1992), 162.

17 *"We never cease"*: Jangfeldt, *The Nobel Family*, 41.

17 *"That which Providence"*: Sohlman and Schuck, *Nobel: Dynamite and Peace*, 88–89.

18 *Immanuel also designed*: Tolf, *The Russian Rockefellers*, 14.

19 *A lead-glass tube*: Tolf, *The Russian Rockefellers*, 18.

20 *In the summer of 1854*: Tolf, *The Russian Rockefellers*, 20.

20 *The mines were a successful*: Tolf, *The Russian Rockefellers*, 20.

21 *Napier considered*: Tolf, *The Russian Rockefellers*, 19.

21 *"any attack on"*: Tolf, *The Russian Rockefellers*, 19.
21 *he drafted a treatise*: Sohlman and Schuck, *The Life of Alfred Nobel*, 23.
23 *"In Europe the ruler"*: Edvard Radzinsky, *Alexander II: The Last Great Tsar*, trans. Antonina W. Bouis (New York: Free Press, 2005), 37.
24 *"A whipped soldier"*: Radzinsky, *Alexander II: The Last Great Tsar*, 150–51.

CHAPTER 2: REFORM, REPRESS, REPEAT

29 *Family letters suggest*: Jangfeldt, *The Nobel Family*, 54.
29 *Anna Lindal's husband*: Jangfeldt, *The Nobel Family*, 228.
30 *He took the lead role*: Nobel Brothers, Centre for Business History, Stockholm, Sweden, www.branobelhistory.com.
31 *Robert told her*: Jangfeldt, *The Nobel Family*, 62.
32 *"I shall never again"*: Jangfeldt, *The Nobel Family*, 64.
32 *"The worst of all"*: Jangfeldt, *The Nobel Family*, 76.
34 *firm was incorporated*: Tolf, *The Russian Rockefellers*, 24.
34 *"I have a great deal"*: Jangfeldt, *The Nobel Family*, 99–100.
34 *Ludvig also published*: Jangfeldt, *The Nobel Family*, 97.
35 *These painted signs*: Sir Robert Bruce Lockhart, *The Diaries of Sir Robert Bruce Lockhart: 1915–1938*, ed. Kenneth Young (London: Macmillan, 1973), 14.
41 *was sucking the blood*: Ana Siljak, *Angel of Vengeance: The "Girl Assassin," the Governor of St. Petersburg, and Russia's Revolutionary World* (New York: St. Martin's Press, 2008), 79.
42 *"They shot at the tsar!"*: Radzinsky, *Alexander II: The Last Great Tsar*, 180.

CHAPTER 3: "EVERYONE RUSHED FOR EVERYTHING AT ONCE"

43 *"Today is our fifth anniversary"*: Nobel Foundation Archive, letter, 1863.
44 *His circle of friends*: Jangfeldt, *The Nobel Family*, 106.
44 *"He was fortunate"*: Gunnar Hedin, *The Swedish Oil Kings*, trans. Paul Britten Austin (Stockholm: Ekerlids Forlag, 1994), 33.
46 *"Here a major"*: Nobel Files, letter in Regional Archives in Lund, Sweden.
46 *"When the wind"*: Gustaf Törnudd, *The Land of Oil and Winds: Letters from Baku*, trans. Eleanor Antell Virgil (New York: Vantage Press, 1975), 9.
47 *priests of the Magi*: Tolf, *The Russian Rockefellers*, 40, 44.
48 *Ivan Mirzoev drilled*: Tolf, *The Russian Rockefellers*, 44.
49 *The two settled*: Nobel Brothers, Centre for Business History, Stockholm, Sweden, www.branobelhistory.com.
51 *"The society is truly American!"*: Nobel Files, letter in Regional Archives in Lund, Sweden.
52 *first three hundred*: Tolf, *The Russian Rockefellers*, 47.
52 *"The required capital"*: Nobel Files, letter in Regional Archives in Lund, Sweden.
53 *They read and discussed*: Jangfeldt, *The Nobel Family*, 144.
53 *Ludvig and Emanuel stood*: Nobel Brothers, Centre for Business History, Stockholm, Sweden, www.branobelhistory.com.
54 *"In America"*: Letter in Alfred Nobel Archive.

54 *they submitted an*: Hedin, *The Swedish Oil Kings*, 50.
55 *The city renumbered*: Ingrid Carlberg, *Nobel: The Enigmatic Alfred and His Prizes*, trans. Ian Giles (Stockholm: The Swedish Academy, 2023), image caption, 368.
56 *"It was impossible"*: Carlberg, *Nobel: The Enigmatic Alfred*, 319.
56 *"Happiness is not to be found"*: Carlberg, *Nobel: The Enigmatic Alfred*, 319.
56 *"not to strengthen her"*: Carlberg, *Nobel: The Enigmatic Alfred*, 319.
59 *Ludvig began the*: Tolf, *The Russian Rockefellers*, 65.
60 *He abandoned wood*: Tolf, *The Russian Rockefellers*, 55.
60 *tankers with names*: Nobel Brothers, Centre for Business History, Stockholm, Sweden, www.branobelhistory.com.
60 *Globally, as of 2023*: John Frittelli, *The Global Oil Tanker Market: An Overview as It Relates to Sanctions*, Congressional Research Service, March 18, 2024, https://www.congress.gov/crs_external_products/R/PDF/R47962/R47962.1.pdf.
60 *Ludvig also designed*: Hedin, *The Swedish Oil Kings*, 53.
62 *He shipped in rich soil*: Sohlman and Schuck, *Nobel: Dynamite and Peace*, 81–82.
63 *"the brothers Nobel have"*: Sohlman and Schuck, *Nobel: Dynamite and Peace*, 65.
63 *numerous substantial gifts*: Jangfeldt, *The Nobel Family*, 105.
64 *"If I had your knowledge"*: Sohlman and Schuck, *Nobel: Dynamite and Peace*, 58.
64 *"Independent Natures"*: Letter in Alfred Nobel Archive.
64 *According to a different account*: Tolf, *The Russian Rockefellers*, 74.
64 *Robert's numerous*: Jangfeldt, *The Nobel Family*, 113.
65 *"Today I am asking you"*: Hedin, *The Swedish Oil Kings*, 55.
65 *"The fact is"*: Hedin, *The Swedish Oil Kings*, 53.
66 *"is brought to the idea"*: Radzinsky, *Alexander II: The Last Great Tsar*, 341.
67 *As Marx had preached*: Radzinsky, *Alexander II: The Last Great Tsar*, 208.
67 *throngs of cheering crowds*: Radzinsky, *Alexander II: The Last Great Tsar*, 261.
67 *"she would sooner"*: Radzinsky, *Alexander II: The Last Great Tsar*, 268–69.
69 *"He gave us freedom"*: Radzinsky, *Alexander II: The Last Great Tsar*, 297.

CHAPTER 4: FROM WELL TO WICK

72 *"I see that day"*: Letter in Alfred Nobel Archive.
73 *He built similar*: Tolf, *The Russian Rockefellers*, 63.
74 *Ludvig filed for*: Tolf, *The Russian Rockefellers*, 66–67.
74 *"When I first came"*: Törnudd, *The Land of Oil and Winds*, 70.
75 *"What do you think"*: Jangfeldt, *The Nobel Family*, 172.
75 *Once capped*: Tolf, *The Russian Rockefellers*, 98.
78 *"I owe my entire career"*: Radzinsky, *Alexander II: The Last Great Tsar*, 400.
78 *the Russian State Bank*: Tolf, *The Russian Rockefellers*, 82, 240.
80 *a group of these nobles*: Kotkin, *Stalin*, 14.
80 *A short, skinny, weak child*: Nigel Cawthorne, *Stalin: The Murderous Career of the Red Tsar* (London: Arcturus Publishing, 2012), 51.

80 *The boy fared no better*: Simon Sebag Montefiore, *Young Stalin* (New York: Alfred A. Knopf, 2007), 30.

CHAPTER 5: THE FIRST OIL WAR

81 *"Mr. Ludvig Nobel's young son"*: Törnudd, *The Land of Oil and Winds*, 47.
83 *When Palashkovsky approached Nobel*: Tolf, *The Russian Rockefellers*, 87.
85 *known as "Mr. Oil"*: *The Oil Interests of the Rothschild of Paris. Between World Competition and the Russian Government (1883–1912)*, European Business History Association, https://ebha.org/ebha2007/pdf/Jaloustre.pdf.
86 *the negotiation having failed*: Nobel Brothers, Centre for Business History, Stockholm, Sweden, www.branobelhistory.com.
86 *"wretchedly inadequate"*: Tolf, *The Russian Rockefellers*, 91.
88 *He dredged the harbor*: Tolf, *The Russian Rockefellers*, 87.
88 *The Tsar favored his precocious third son*: Michael N. Kalantar, *Russia Under Three Tsars* (Gerrardstown, WV: Irene Vartanoff, 2015), 31.
89 *Ulyanov's mother begged*: Kalantar, *Russia Under Three Tsars*, 26–27.
90 *Soso's left elbow*: Kotkin, *Stalin*, 20.
91 *"Several times"*: Essad Bey, *Blood and Oil in the Orient*, second ed., trans. Elsa Talmey (Freiberg, Germany: Bridges Publishing, 2008), 14.
91 *"For the journey"*: Bey, *Blood and Oil in the Orient*, 14.
91 *Initially the Rothschilds*: Bey, *Blood and Oil in the Orient*, 51.
91 *the second tier of oil magnates*: Bey, *Blood and Oil in the Orient*, 30.
92 *One owner built*: Tolf, *The Russian Rockefellers*, 102.
92 *"Our business is fully built"*: Nobel Files, letter in Regional Archives in Lund, Sweden.

CHAPTER 6: EMANUEL LEADS A RUSSIAN DELUGE

95 *"the entire expulsion of American petroleum"*: No. 600, Mr. Lothrop to Mr. Bayard, and all subsequent references to the report, Office of the Historian: https://history.state.gov/historicaldocuments/frus1887/d600.
96 *For perspective*: Proven Royalty Revenue Streams, Ranger: Land and Minerals, www.rangerminerals.com.
97 *"A man who"*: Carlberg, *Nobel: The Enigmatic Alfred*, 396.
98 *"I will miss in him"*: Letter in Alfred Nobel Archive.
98 *"his prominent position"*: Jangfeldt, *The Nobel Family*, 206.
98 *The French newspapers*: Carlberg, *Nobel: The Enigmatic Alfred*, 669.
99 *"Capital in pure money form"*: Letter in Alfred Nobel Archive.
101 *"into a man"*: Tolf, *The Russian Rockefellers*, 113.
101 *"Bravo nephew!!!"*: Letter in Alfred Nobel Archive.
101 *"medieval perception"*: Jangfeldt, *The Nobel Family*, 220.
104 *which cost the firm*: Nobel Brothers, Centre for Business History, Stockholm, Sweden, www.branobelhistory.com.
105 *the "trust shown to the company"*: Carlberg, *Nobel: The Enigmatic Alfred*, 442.
105 *the tactics of Standard Oil*: Tolf, *The Russian Rockefellers*, 94.

CHAPTER 7: CHANGING OF THE GUARDS

108 *Talks between Nobel and the Rothschilds*: Nobel Brothers, Centre for Business History, Stockholm, Sweden, www.branobelhistory.com, and also Tolf, *The Russian Rockefellers*, 113.
108 *"sweet alto singing voice"*: Kotkin, *Stalin*, 21.
108 *"there was hardly a day"*: Cawthorne, *Stalin: The Murderous Career of the Red Tsar*, 59.
108 *a game in the streets*: Kotkin, *Stalin*, 21.
109 *decided to give Lavrov a taste*: Montefiore, *Young Stalin*, 44–45.
110 *"get a better insight"*: Jangfeldt, *The Nobel Family*, 234.
111 *the "hateful Jew" Rothschild*: Letter in Alfred Nobel Archive.
112 *"In the environs"*: Jangfeldt, *The Nobel Family*, 234.
113 *"a scheme for parceling out"*: Tolf, *The Russian Rockefellers*, 116.
115 *To complicate matters*: Carlberg, *Nobel: The Enigmatic Alfred*, 542.
116 *On January 2, 1897*: Carlberg, *Nobel: The Enigmatic Alfred*, 562.
117 *"Your uncle was influenced"*: Carlberg, *Nobel: The Enigmatic Alfred*, 598.
117 *"the young ones"*: Jangfeldt, *The Nobel Family*, 247–8.
118 *"to see to the good reputation"*: Carlberg, *Nobel: The Enigmatic Alfred*, 596.
119 *He walked freely*: Kalantar, *Russia Under Three Tsars*, 73.
119 *In the 1990s*: Carlberg, *Nobel: The Enigmatic Alfred*, 299.
119 *draft of a play*: Carlberg, *Nobel: The Enigmatic Alfred*, 571.
120 *encrusted with gems*: Robert K. Massie, *Nicholas and Alexandra: An Intimate Account of the Last of the Romanovs and the Fall of Imperial Russia* (New York: Atheneum, 1967), 52.
120 *The crown featured*: Massie, *Nicholas and Alexandra*, 53.
121 *the latch of*: Kalantar, *Russia Under Three Tsars*, 81–82.

CHAPTER 8: ALL ROADS LEAD TO BAKU

123 *He smuggled in banned books*: Montefiore, *Young Stalin*, 63.
124 *Stalin later claimed*: Montefiore, *Young Stalin*, 66–73.
126 *Marta earned her degree*: Jangfeldt, *The Nobel Family*, 275–78.
128 *Standard Oil by itself*: *The Oil Interests of the Rothschild of Paris. Between World Competition and the Russian Government (1883–1912)*, European Business History Association, https://ebha.org/ebha2007/pdf/Jaloustre.pdf.
128 *James MacDonald represented*: Tolf, *The Russian Rockefellers*, 131–33.
130 *such that a Diesel-powered*: Douglas Brunt, *The Mysterious Case of Rudolf Diesel* (New York: Atria Books, 2023), 3.
130 *"a considerate and noble-minded man"*: Tolf, *The Russian Rockefellers*, 169.
131 *first Diesel installations*: Nobel Brothers, Centre for Business History, Stockholm, Sweden, www.branobelhistory.com.
131 *Russia was the most "Dieselized" country*: Brunt, *The Mysterious Case of Rudolf Diesel*, 120.
131 *Emanuel also owned*: Tolf, *The Russian Rockefellers*, 177.
132 *"Guess why I"*: Montefiore, *Young Stalin*, 90.
132 *"Hitler wants the oil"*: Montefiore, *Young Stalin*, 189.

133 *Stalin managed to bring*: Montefiore, *Young Stalin*, 92.
133 *Lenin and the Social Democrats ordered*: Kotkin, *Stalin*, 50.
134 *"Back to work or Siberia"*: Montefiore, *Young Stalin*, 94.
134 *"You'll never be a revolutionary"*: Montefiore, *Young Stalin*, 94.
134 *"Let's free our comrades!"*: Montefiore, *Young Stalin*, 94.
135 *"Today we advanced"*: Montefiore, *Young Stalin*, 95.
135 *"It stirred the whole country"*: Montefiore, *Young Stalin*, 96.
135 *"We're going to overthrow"*: Montefiore, *Young Stalin*, 96.

PART II: A WAR WOULD BE A VERY USEFUL THING

137 *"A war between Russia and Austria"*: Bertram D. Wolfe, *Three Who Made a Revolution* (New York: Stein and Day, 1984), 146.

CHAPTER 9: THE DANGER IS FROM WITHIN

139 *In the pre-boom era of 1850*: Peter Kropotkin for *Britannica*.
139 *"it was said there were only"*: Montefiore, *Young Stalin*, 189.
140 *"At what point then"*: Lincoln's Lyceum Address, January 1838, https://www.abrahamlincolnonline.org/lincoln/speeches/lyceum.htm.
140 *"deliberate incitement to disorder"*: Kotkin, *Stalin*, 52.
140 *"The exile system was a sieve"*: Montefiore, *Young Stalin*, 114.
143 *In December 1903*: Montefiore, *Young Stalin*, 116.
145 *"Workers of the Caucasus!"*: Montefiore, *Young Stalin*, 127.
145 *"stirring feuds by all sorts"*: Isaac Deutscher, *Stalin: A Political Biography*, second ed. (New York: Oxford University Press, 1967), 68.
147 *"Only on the bones"*: Deutscher, *Stalin: A Political Biography*, 76.
147 *became a member of*: Nobel Brothers, Centre for Business History, Stockholm, Sweden, www.branobelhistory.com.

CHAPTER 10: THE SECOND BAPTISM OF FIRE

150 *From 1904 to 1907*: European Business History Association, *The Oil Interests of the Rothschild of Paris. Between World Competition and the Russian Government (1883–1912)*, https://ebha.org/ebha2007/pdf/Jaloustre.pdf, 10.
152 *"thoroughly overpowered his audience"*: Montefiore, *Young Stalin*, 147.
154 *back on the Rothschild*: Cawthorne, *Stalin: The Murderous Career of the Red Tsar*, 118.
155 *"These are our last Mohicans"*: Deutscher, *Stalin: A Political Biography*, 100.
155 *"would be my second"*: Deutscher, *Stalin: A Political Biography*, 98.
156 *Emanuel developed a fifty-nine-thousand*: Nobel Brothers, Centre for Business History, Stockholm, Sweden, www.branobelhistory.com.
156 *Under constant threat*: Kotkin, *Stalin*, 114.
158 *"concentrated on collecting donations"*: Montefiore, *Young Stalin*, 197.
158 *On March 25, 1908*: Cawthorne, *Stalin: The Murderous Career of the Red Tsar*, 123.

CHAPTER 11: RASPUTIN

162 *Lenin himself later declared*: Louis Fischer, *The Life of Lenin* (New York: Harper & Row, 1964), 149.

162 *Like nearly all Siberian peasants*: Douglas Smith, *Rasputin: Faith, Power, and the Twilight of the Romanovs* (New York: Picador, 2017), 15.
162 *He married at*: Smith, *Rasputin*, 18.
163 *Rasputin quickly gained friends*: Smith, *Rasputin*, 33.
163 *When Nicholas II met*: Massie, *Nicholas and Alexandra*, 187.

CHAPTER 12: THE BEST CUSTOMER OF FABERGÉ

167 *the most valuable listing*: Jangfeldt, *The Nobel Family*, 290.
167 *From 1910 to 1912*: Brunt, *The Mysterious Case of Rudolf Diesel*, 120.
168 *He launched the world's first*: Tolf, *The Russian Rockefellers*, 175.
168 *the world consumed the equivalent of*: Jean-Marie Martin-Amouroux, "World Energy Consumption 1800–2000: The Results," Encyclopédie de l'énergie, March 14, 2022, https://www.encyclopedie-energie.org/en/world-energy-consumption-1800-2000-results/.
169 *"Russian subjects of non-Jewish faith"*: Nobel Brothers, Centre for Business History, Stockholm, Sweden, www.branobelhistory.com.
170 *"a fleet of ten"*: Tolf, *The Russian Rockefellers*, 189.
171 *In 1912 he sold*: Jangfeldt, *The Nobel Family*, 256.
172 *the business owners of Russia*: Nobel Brothers, Centre for Business History, Stockholm, Sweden, www.branobelhistory.com.
172 *"For Dr. Nobel"*: Will Lowes and Christel Ludewig McCanless, *Fabergé Eggs: A Retrospective Encyclopedia* (Lanham, MD: Scarecrow Press, 2001), 171.
173 *"was so generous in his presents"*: Franz Birbaum, *Memoirs*, in Géza von Habsburg's exhibition catalogue *Fabergé: Imperial Jeweler* (Saint Petersburg: State Hermitage Museum, 1993), 454.
173 *Emanuel had the exclusive rights*: Dorothy McFerrin, *From a Snowflake to an Iceberg: The McFerrin Collection* (College Station, TX: McFerrin Foundation, 2013), 264.
174 *"For Christmas and Easter"*: McFerrin, *From a Snowflake to an Iceberg*, 267.
174 *Much like his friend*: Brunt, *The Mysterious Case of Rudolf Diesel*, 205.
174 "Nationalism *is a pretty word"*: Tolf, *The Russian Rockefellers*, 229.
175 *"there is no end of the poverty"*: Jangfeldt, *The Nobel Family*, 273.
175 *The murder of a person*: Jangfeldt, *The Nobel Family*, 295.
175 *"so widespread that"*: Kotkin, *Stalin*, 104.
176 *"This is exactly the kind"*: Kotkin, *Stalin*, 123.
177 *"We have a marvelous Georgian"*: Kotkin, *Stalin*, 133.
177 *"The mistake we have been making"*: Kotkin, *Stalin*, 118–19.
178 *"For a Georgian from"*: Kotkin, *Stalin*, 137.

CHAPTER 13: WORLD ON FIRE

182 *on the Berlin stock exchange*: Tolf, *The Russian Rockefellers*, 190–91.
183 *He ultimately purchased*: Nobel Brothers, Center for Business History, Stockholm, Sweden, www.branobelhistory.com.
185 *Russian newspapers estimated*: Document in the Igor I. Sikorsky Historical Archives, FotoFile, Fairfield, Connecticut.

185 *In 1915, more than seventy percent*: Tolf, *The Russian Rockefellers*, 193.
186 *"new people altogether"*: Jangfeldt, *The Nobel Family*, 303.
186 *Emanuel converted the People's House*: Nobel Brothers, Centre for Business History, Stockholm, Sweden, www.branobelhostory.com.
187 *"Stories about the way"*: Jangfeldt, *The Nobel Family*, 301.
188 *When his niece Andriette*: McFerrin, *From a Snowflake to an Iceberg*, 269.
189 *"How am I?"*: Montefiore, *Young Stalin*, 291.

CHAPTER 14: THE TSAR CANNOT BE IN TWO PLACES AT ONCE

192 *"in its scale, in its slaughter"*: Nick Lloyd, *The Eastern Front: A History of the Great War, 1914–1918* (New York: W. W. Norton, 2025), flap copy.
192 *"My greatest pleasure"*: Montefiore, *Young Stalin*, 295.
194 *"trousers on unseen"*: Kotkin, *Stalin*, 159.
194 *"How can we repent"*: Kotkin, *Stalin*, 160.
194 *"I am obliged to report"*: Kotkin, *Stalin*, 161.
194 *"Come and I'll hang you"*: Document in the Igor I. Sikorsky Historical Archives, FotoFile, Fairfield, Connecticut.

CHAPTER 15: FEBRUARY

202 *German operatives funneled*: Antony C. Sutton, *Wall Street and the Bolshevik Revolution* (New York: Arlington House, 1974), 23.
202 *"I have two months"*: Lockhart, *The Diaries of Sir Robert Bruce Lockhart*, 26.
202 *peasants owned roughly*: Stephen Kotkin, *Stalin*, 189.
203 *The book value*: Nobel Brothers, Centre for Business History, Stockholm, Sweden, www.branobelhistory.com.
204 *"In view of the grave situation"*: Carolyn Harris, "The Abdication of Nicholas II Left Russia Without a Czar for the First Time in 300 Years," *Smithsonian Magazine*, March 13, 2017, https://www.smithsonianmag.com/history/abdication-nicholas-ii-left-russia-without-tsar-first-time-300-years-180962503/.
204 *"At this moment the only way"*: Harris, "The Abdication of Nicholas II."
204 *"there are no means"*: Harris, "The Abdication of Nicholas II."
205 *"At this moment"*: Harris, "The Abdication of Nicholas II."
205 *"The revolution appears"*: Louis de Robien, *The Diary of a Diplomat in Russia, 1917–1918* (New York: Praeger Publishers, 1970), 17.
205 *"Many [officers] were"*: De Robien, *The Diary of a Diplomat in Russia*, 24.
206 *"And it has all"*: De Robien, *The Diary of a Diplomat in Russia*, jacket blurb.
206 *"There is a constant stream"*: De Robien, *The Diary of a Diplomat in Russia*, 15.
206 *"All around is betrayal"*: Harris, "The Abdication of Nicholas II."
207 *"another country created through revolution"*: Harris, "The Abdication of Nicholas II."
208 *As bullets continued to zing*: Jangfeldt, *The Nobel Family*, 306.
209 *He took over as the*: Kotkin, *Stalin*, 177.
210 *when Lenin reached Finland Station*: Cawthorne, *Stalin: The Murderous Career of the Red Tsar*, 153.

210 *later testified to the Overman Committee*: Sutton, *Wall Street and the Bolshevik Revolution*, 23.
211 *"All power to the Soviet!"*: Ronald G. Suny, *The Baku Commune: 1917–1918* (Princeton, NJ: Princeton University Press, 1972), ix–x.
211 *"Fairy Godmother"*: Sutton, *Wall Street and the Bolshevik Revolution*, 25.
211 *"falling apart, like an old barge"*: Kotkin, *Stalin*, 183.
213 *"match the expectations"*: Jangfeldt, *The Nobel Family*, 308.

CHAPTER 16: OCTOBER

216 *"after many centuries of oppression"*: Tolf, *The Russian Rockefellers*, 203.
216 *"It is improbable that"*: Jonathan Schneer, *The Lockhart Plot: Love, Betrayal, Assassination and Counter-Revolution in Lenin's Russia* (Oxford: Oxford University Press, 2020), 14.
217 *"absence of a powerful counterrevolution"*: Kotkin, *Stalin*, 213.
217 *"complete triumph of the revolution"*: Kotkin, *Stalin*, 208.
218 *While on the Red Cross mission*: Sutton, *Wall Street and the Bolshevik Revolution*, 80–82.
219 *"could have its own press"*: Sutton, *Wall Street and the Bolshevik Revolution*, 82.
219 *"He [Trotsky] hated"*: Schneer, *The Lockhart Plot*, 43.
220 *"an oppressed class which"*: Wolfe, *Three Who Made a Revolution*, 371.
221 *"The Bolshevik stock phrase"*: DeWitt Clinton Poole, *An American Diplomat in Bolshevik Russia*, ed. Lorraine Lees and William Rodner (Madison: University of Wisconsin Press, 2014), 23.
221 *"It makes one's head spin"*: Montefiore, *Young Stalin*, 349.
221 *"Your second cable received"*: Sutton, *Wall Street and the Bolshevik Revolution*, 83.
222 *When Lenin later issued*: Sutton, *Wall Street and the Bolshevik Revolution*, 83.
223 *"It is with a feeling"*: Jangfeldt, *The Nobel Family*, 310.
223 *"I cannot deny that our friends"*: Jangfeldt, *The Nobel Family*, 310.

CHAPTER 17: CAMPAIGN PROMISE DELIVERED

225 *"it never occurred to"*: Kotkin, *Stalin*, 772.
226 *"was of a temporary nature"*: Kotkin, *Stalin*, 237.
226 *Louis de Robien observed*: De Robien, *The Diary of a Diplomat in Russia, 1917–1918*, 261.
226 *"Death solves all problems"*: Cawthorne, *Stalin: The Murderous Career of the Red Tsar*, 181.
226 *"If you look at what"*: Schneer, *The Lockhart Plot*, 111.
227 *"the Bolsheviks could only be regarded"*: John Silverlight, *The Victors' Dilemma: Allied Intervention in the Russian Civil War*, 1917–1920 (London: Barrie & Jenkins, 1970), 8.
228 *"no policy would be"*: Silverlight, *The Victors' Dilemma*, 8–9.
228 *"Your Lloyd George"*: Silverlight, *The Victors' Dilemma*, 9.
229 *On November 28, 1917, Wilson*: Sutton, *Wall Street and the Bolshevik Revolution*, 45.

229 *"It is considered inadvisable"*: Sutton, *Wall Street and the Bolshevik Revolution*, 46.
230 *"the greatest Jew"*: Lockhart, *The Diaries of Sir Robert Bruce Lockhart*, 33.
230 *"You will hear it said"*: Sutton, *Wall Street and the Bolshevik Revolution*, 96–97.
232 *In a single day, Lenin's men*: De Robien, *The Diary of a Diplomat in Russia*, 118.
232 *"It is a unique example"*: De Robien, *The Diary of a Diplomat in Russia*, 123.
233 *To expose the imperialist plans*: Poole, *An American Diplomat in Bolshevik Russia*, 25.
234 *"In the end the Allies"*: Kotkin, *Stalin*, 258.
235 *American media began to scrutinize*: Sutton, *Wall Street and the Bolshevik Revolution*, 18.
235 *explore clandestine Wall Street*: Sutton, *Wall Street and the Bolshevik Revolution*, 49–52.
235 *In fact, during the Great War*: Sutton, *Wall Street and the Bolshevik Revolution*, 64.
236 *"They are cold-bloodedly sacrificing"*: Sutton, *Wall Street and the Bolshevik Revolution*, 103.
236 *"we Russians make up a people"*: Sutton, *Wall Street and the Bolshevik Revolution*, 103.
237 *Lenin went a step further*: Anna Reid, *A Nasty Little War: The Western Intervention into the Russian Civil War* (New York: Basic Books, 2024), 26.
239 *"pressing issues concerning"*: Jangfeldt, *The Nobel Family*, 310.

CHAPTER 18: BURN DOWN THE MAST

241 *the first train in five months*: Jangfeldt, *The Nobel Family*, 313.
241 *"He is finished"*: Kotkin, *Stalin*, 271.
242 *A day after publicly*: Reid, *A Nasty Little War*, 46.
242 *with the stated purpose*: Lockhart, *The Diaries of Sir Robert Bruce Lockhart*, 35.
243 *a large Turkish force*: Suny, *The Baku Commune*, 287.
243 *Dunsterville had several thousand*: Suny, *The Baku Commune*, 273.
244 *"one fool can ask"*: Lockhart, *The Diaries of Sir Robert Bruce Lockhart*, 34.
245 *four primary responsibilities*: Vadim M. Rynkov, "Labor Market Regulation in Eastern Russia in 1918–1922: Institutional Factors, Mechanisms, and Outcomes," *Russian Journal of Economics* (July 9, 2021), www.rujec.org.
246 *"I had heard there were"*: Suny, *The Baku Commune*, 236.
246 *Commissars met three times*: Suny, *The Baku Commune*, 239.
246 *Upon Lenin's order of nationalization*: Suny, *The Baku Commune*, 248.
247 *On Stalin's first day*: Kotkin, *Stalin*, 301.
248 *"We have already printed"*: Jangfeldt, *The Nobel Family*, 313.
249 *"They're asking us to arrange"*: Tolf, *The Russian Rockefellers*, 205.
252 *"After all, you don't get"*: Poole, *An American Diplomat in Bolshevik Russia*, 172.
253 *The Soviets later nationalized*: Archive of the Republic of Dagestan: https://web.archive.org/web/20171006161817/http://www.cgard.ru/af/index.php?act=fund&fund=155.

254 *He penned a handwritten*: Kotkin, *Stalin*, 284.
255 *Of particular interest to Britain*: Silverlight, *The Victors' Dilemma*, 87.
255 *"By restoring order in"*: Lockhart, *The Diaries of Sir Robert Bruce Lockhart*, 51.
256 *"One of our greatest helpers"*: John D. Rockefeller, *Random Reminiscences of Men and Events* (New York: Doubleday, 1909), 48.
256 *"Through our agents"*: Major General Lionel Charles Dunsterville, *The Adventures of Dunsterforce* (London: Edward Arnold, 1920), 60.
256 *The day following the British departure*: Silverlight, *The Victors' Dilemma*, 99.
256 *"gigantic ethnographic museum"*: Silverlight, *The Victors' Dilemma*, 92.

CHAPTER 19: RUN FOR YOUR LIFE

260 *"listened politely"*: Reid, *A Nasty Little War*, 87.
260 *"the Armistice doesn't mean"*: Reid, *A Nasty Little War*, 89.
261 *"were taking a similar course"*: Silverlight, *The Victors' Dilemma*, 1.
263 *"with his knowledge, his experience"*: Jangfeldt, *The Nobel Family*, 316.
263 *"the well-known and top industrialist"*: Jangfeldt, *The Nobel Family*, 316.
266 *"The border itself"*: Jangfeldt, *The Nobel Family*, 317–18.
266 *"Not even the most intense imagination"*: Jangfeldt, *The Nobel Family*, 321.

CHAPTER 20: CIVIL IS THE WORST KIND OF WAR

267 *"[Mr. Nobel] had formed"*: Sir Robert Bruce Lockhart, *Memoirs of a British Agent* (London: Putnam, 1932), 215.
268 *"The Allies had floated to victory"*: *New York Times*, November 23, 1918.
268 *"as the [Peace] Mission"*: and subsequent references to the document: National Archives Kew, FO 608/230/27.
268 *By 1927, with the Caucasus*: Antony C. Sutton, *America's Secret Establishment* (Walterville, OR: TrineDay, 1983, additional materials 2009), 149.
268 *As of 2024*: https://www.statista.com.
270 *"cannot deny their energy"*: Silverlight, *The Victors' Dilemma*, 90.
270 *Lockhart proposed to his government*: Silverlight, *The Victors' Dilemma*, 90.
271 *In 1919, as American troops*: Sutton, *America's Secret Establishment*, 123.
271 *"might as well legalize sodomy"*: Reid, *A Nasty Little War*, 120.
273 *"been dependent upon mail"*: Poole, *An American Diplomat in Bolshevik Russia*, 43.
273 *Among the royals on the ship*: Paul Halpern, *The Mediterranean Fleet, 1919–1929* (Farnham, UK: Ashgate for the Navy Records Society, 2011), 32–33.
274 *"shrewd-looking"*: Lubov Krassin, *Leonid Krassin: His Life and Work* (London: Skeffington & Son, 1929), 32.
274 *Emanuel took his nephews*: Tolf, *The Russian Rockefellers*, 213.
276 *The family set up*: Tolf, *The Russian Rockefellers*, 213.
277 *"the Bolsheviks will be cleared"*: Daniel Yergin, *The Prize: The Epic Quest for Oil, Money & Power* (New York: Touchstone, 1991), 238.
277 *In early 1919 Standard*: Tolf, *The Russian Rockefellers*, 215.
278 *"a dream for an engineer"*: Jangfeldt, *The Nobel Family*, 331.

CHAPTER 21: WOE TO THE VANQUISHED

281 *"Curzon! Be a gentleman!"*: Yergin, *The Prize*, 239.

281 *"That swine Lloyd George"*: Yergin, *The Prize*, 239.

282 *For fifty percent*: Tolf, *The Russian Rockefellers*, 217.

285 *"ten innocent people"*: Cawthorne, *Stalin: The Murderous Career of the Red Tsar*, 259.

285 *"capitalist bloodsuckers"*: Tolf, *The Russian Rockefellers*, 209.

286 *In Document 65*: Richard Pipes, *The Unknown Lenin: From the Secret Archive* (New Haven, CT: Yale University Press, 1999), 122.

286 *"In informal conversations"*: The Ambassador in Italy (Child) to the Secretary of State, Office of the Historian, https://history.state.gov/historical documents/frus1922v02/pg_775.

290 *There has even been speculation*: Alan Boyle, "What Killed Lenin? Stress . . . and Maybe Poison," NBC News, May 4, 2012, https://www.nbcnews.com /id/wbna47296099.

290 *Stalin would name six more*: Cawthorne, *Stalin: The Murderous Career of the Red Tsar*, 190.

290 *The Ludvig Nobel Machine Factory*: C. Lyle Cummins Jr., *Diesel's Engine: Volume One, From Conception to 1918* (Wilsonville, OR: Carnot Press, 1993), 584.

290 *Below is a comparison*: Kotkin, *Stalin*, 333.

291 *The Petrograd location of*: Torbjörn Elensky, "Ericsson and the Russian Revolution," Ericsson, https://www.ericsson.com/en/about-us/history/company /an-emerging-global-company/ericsson-and-the-russian-revolution.

291 *Lessner Brothers became*: "Karl Marx Machine-Building Association (formerly Novy Lessner)," *Saint Petersburg Encyclopedia*, http://www.encspb.ru /object/2855694254?lc=en.

291 *"Every record has been destroyed or falsified"*: George Orwell, *Nineteen Eighty-Four* (London: Secker and Warburg, 1949; repr. London: Penguin Classics, 2021), 103.

291 *"Nobel Brothers was the leading"*: Jangfeldt, *The Nobel Family*, 341.

EPILOGUE: AT LAST

295 *"always gave great pleasure"*: Jangfeldt, *The Nobel Family*, 346.

295 *In 1920, Emanuel invested in*: Richard Byers, *Flying Man: Hugo Junkers and the Dream of Aviation* (College Station: Texas A&M University Press, 2016), 47.

296 *The celebration took*: Jangfeldt, *The Nobel Family*, 347.

296 *"a real devil of a"*: Jangfeldt, *The Nobel Family*, 353.

298 *"A communist state would be"*: Radzinsky, *Alexander II: The Last Great Tsar*, 210.

299 *"there are grounds for believing"*: Sutton, *Wall Street and the Bolshevik Revolution*, 115.

299 *"[Martens's] organization"*: Sutton, *Wall Street and the Bolshevik Revolution*, 116.

299 *to persuade American big business interests*: Sutton, *Wall Street and the Bolshevik Revolution,* 119.

299 *Julius Hammer was already*: Edward Jay Epstein, *Dossier: The Secret History of Armand Hammer* (New York: Random House, 1996), 120–21.

300 *In 1929, he ordered the arrest*: Cawthorne, *Stalin: The Murderous Career of the Red Tsar*, 200.

GLOSSARY OF TERMS

Bolsheviks: One of the most radical of the Russian social democrat factions. Led by Vladimir Lenin, the Bolsheviks sought to bring about a socialist government by means of a violent overthrow of the tsarist regime. The Bolsheviks ascended to power in autumn 1917, and on March 9, 1918, the Bolshevik Party formally changed its name to the All-Russian Communist Party.

Mensheviks: More moderate than their Bolshevik rivals, Mensheviks led by Julius Martov split from the Bolsheviks at the Second Party Congress in 1903. The Mensheviks aimed for a phased and negotiated approach to bring about a socialist form of government. Other differences through the years included the scope of party membership and Russia's continued involvement in World War I. Many switched loyalties between the two parties, including Bolshevik leader Leon Trotsky, who was initially a Menshevik.

Marxism: A political and economic philosophy created by Karl Marx and Friedrich Engels that posits that capitalism exploits the working class and that a legal system that allows for private property as a means of production should be replaced by a system of cooperative ownership. The first significant publication of Marxist principles was *The Communist Manifesto* in 1848.

Naphtha: Origins of the word in various languages translate to "crude oil," but by the nineteenth century, naphtha began to refer to a clear liquid, distilled from crude oil, used primarily as fuel for illumination, though it was also used in stoves and small combustion engines. A common current-day use is for the Zippo cigarette lighter. Colloquially, the word has become interchangeable with kerosene.

Paraffin: Also distilled from crude oil, paraffin liquid typically is more viscous than naphtha, though it can be used in similar ways. Paraffin wax is used for candles. The terms *kerosene*, *naphtha*, and *paraffin* (liquid) were often confused or used interchangeably by those not working in the oil business.

Red Army: The Workers' and Peasants' Red Army, established in January 1918 by Leon Trotsky and the Bolshevik Party.

White Army: A disorganized collection of factions that, in general, opposed the Bolsheviks and supported the prerevolutionary order of the monarchy or the Provisional Government.

The Great Game: A turn-of-the-century political conflict between Russia and Great Britain for influence in Central Asia. Rudyard Kipling popularized the phrase in his 1901 novel *Kim*.

LIST OF KEY LOCATIONS

Baku: A port city on the western shores of the Caspian Sea with settlements that date to the Bronze Age. With nearby pools of flammable petroleum bubbling to the surface and rock fissures leaking natural gas, Baku has been a spiritual and religious center since ancient times, including for the fire-worshipping Magi priests of Zoroastrianism. Baku is often referred to as the "City of Fire" and the "City of Wind," where the summers are hot and humid and the winters are cool and sometimes wet.

Batum: A port city on the eastern shores of the Black Sea built on an ancient Greek colony. From the 1500s the city was alternately controlled by the Ottoman Empire and the Kingdom of Georgia, then annexed by the Russian Empire in 1877 and kept under the control of Soviet Russia until 1991. Batum was a critical trade route for Baku's petroleum to travel from the Black Sea to the Mediterranean, then on to Asia or Western Europe.

Gori: The birthplace of Joseph Stalin, Gori is an ancient city in eastern Georgia with fortifications dating back to the time of Christ. The city is along the critical land pathway between the Caspian and Black Seas, fifty miles from the capital city of Tiflis.

Kislovodsk: A spa city in the northern Caucasus of southern Russia. The translation of the Russian-language name is "sour water" due to the locally abundant mineral water. Many Russian aristocrats and industrialists took refuge in this town during the Russian Civil

War, as the region was mainly controlled by the White Army still loyal to the tsarist regime.

Saint Petersburg:

1703: Peter the Great founded the city on the eastern shores of the Baltic Sea. He named the city for his patron saint.

1712: Peter the Great moved the government to Saint Petersburg from the ancient city of Moscow. Saint Petersburg was now the Russian capital.

1914: Nicholas II renamed the city Petrograd so that it sounded less German during the Great War.

1918: Lenin returned the government to Moscow, which remains the capital to this day.

1924: The Soviets renamed the city Leningrad five days after Lenin's death.

1991: By referendum, Russia restored the original name of the city to Saint Petersburg.

Tiflis: Renamed Tbilisi in 1936 by the Soviets to sound less Persian. The settlement has been continuously occupied since the Bronze Age, and Tiflis has been the capital of the unified Georgian state since 1122. After a period of Mongol and then Persian control of Georgia beginning in the thirteenth century, the Russian Empire annexed the Kingdom of Georgia in 1801. Georgia officially declared independence from the Soviet Union in April 1991.

COMMENTS REGARDING THE BIBLIOGRAPHY

The reason I came to know anything of the Russian Nobels is thanks to Rudolf Diesel. Peter Borland, my editor, and I have joked that one author's footnote can become another author's entire book. In this case it was a footnote in the Diesel story that led me to the Nobel story and to my own next book.

When building a historical narrative, the best place to begin is with first-person accounts. Capturing the perspective of those who lived and recorded the events is critical to bringing a faraway period back to life on the page. The letters and memoirs of Gustaf Törnudd, Robert Bruce Lockhart, Louis de Robien, DeWitt Clinton Poole, Pyotr Wrangel (a general of the White Army), and Lionel Dunsterville were especially helpful.

Regarding secondary materials, Isaac Deutscher wrote a sweeping biography of Stalin, first published in 1949 when Stalin was still alive and in control of Soviet archives. Deutscher updated this biography in 1966. More archival material about Stalin, particularly related to his early years, came to light after the collapse of the Soviet Union. This material has been ably picked up by Stephen Kotkin and Simon Sebag Montefiore.

As for the Nobels, in 1929 Ragnar Sohlman, who worked with Emanuel in connection with Alfred Nobel's will and was an executor of Alfred's estate, published the first information in book form about the Nobels in Russia. However, the information about the Russian Nobels was only a portion of the book, which was a biography of Alfred titled *The Life of Alfred Nobel*. (As an aside, the best and most comprehensive biography of Alfred Nobel, which also has fascinating family details that include Ludvig and Emanuel, is *Nobel: The Enigmatic Alfred and His Prizes*, published by Ingrid Carlberg in 2019.)

In 1976, Robert Tolf published a book fully dedicated to the Nobels in Russia titled *The Russian Rockefellers: The Saga of the Nobel Family and the Russian Oil Industry.* This terrific book laid the foundation for their story. When the Soviet Union collapsed in 1991, archives in Azerbaijan and Georgia that held valuable, lost pieces of the story became available. Access to these archives led to the Branobel History Project, which has collected and organized an enormous amount of information. Partners in this effort include the Nobel Family Society, the Baku Nobel Heritage Fund, the National Board of Archives of the Azerbaijan Republic, the National Archives of Georgia, and the Nobel Brothers Batumi Technological Museum. The project has delivered much of the newly gathered information to the public at www.branobelhistory.com, and this information is also reflected in Bengt Jangfeldt's 2023 book *The Nobel Family: Swedish Geniuses in Tsarist Russia*, which adds some of the new information to Tolf's foundation.

Lastly, if you can make it to Sweden, the archive at the Centre for Business History in Stockholm is a gold mine, and Vadim Azbel is an excellent guide.

BIBLIOGRAPHY

Arfa, Hassan. *Under Five Shahs.* New York: William Morrow, 1965.

Bey, Essad. *Blood and Oil in the Orient.* Translated by Elsa Talmey. Second Edition. Freiberg, Germany: Bridges Publishing, 2008.

Birbaum, Franz. *Memoirs*, in Géza von Habsburg, *Fabergé: Imperial Jeweler* (exhibition catalog). Saint Petersburg: State Hermitage Museum, 1993.

Bruce Lockhart, Sir Robert. *The Diaries of Sir Robert Bruce Lockhart: 1915–1938.* Edited by Kenneth Young. London: Macmillan, 1973.

———. *Memoirs of a British Agent.* London: Putnam, 1932.

Brunt, Douglas. *The Mysterious Case of Rudolf Diesel.* New York: Atria Books, 2023.

Byers, Richard. *Flying Man: Hugo Junkers and the Dream of Aviation.* College Station: Texas A&M University Press, 2016.

Carlberg, Ingrid. *Nobel: The Enigmatic Alfred and His Prizes.* Translated by Ian Giles. Stockholm: Swedish Academy, 2023.

Cawthorne, Nigel. *Stalin: The Murderous Career of the Red Tsar.* London: Arcturus Publishing, 2012.

Centre for Business History, Stockholm, Sweden. www.branobelhistory.com.

Cummins, C. Lyle, Jr. *Diesel's Engine: Volume One, From Conception to 1918.* Wilsonville, OR: Carnot Press, 1993.

de Robien, Louis. *The Diary of a Diplomat in Russia, 1917–1918.* New York: Praeger Publishers, 1970.

Deutscher, Isaac. *Stalin: A Political Biography.* Second edition. New York: Oxford University Press, 1967.

Dunsterville, Major General Lionel Charles. *The Adventures of Dunsterforce.* London: Edward Arnold, 1920.

Elensky, Torbjörn. "Ericsson and the Russian Revolution." Ericsson. https://www.ericsson.com/en/about-us/history/company/an-emerging-global-company/ericsson-and-the-russian-revolution.

Epstein, Edward Jay. *Dossier: The Secret History of Armand Hammer.* New York: Random House, 1996.

European Business History Association. *The Oil Interests of the Rothschild of Paris. Between World Competition and the Russian Government (1883–1912)*. https://ebha.org/ebha2007/pdf/Jaloustre.pdf.

Ferguson, Niall. *The House of Rothschild: The World's Banker, 1849–1999.* New York: Viking, 1999.

Fischer, Louis. *The Life of Lenin.* New York: Harper & Row, 1964.

Halpern, Paul. *The Mediterranean Fleet, 1919–1929.* Farnham, UK: Ashgate for the Navy Records Society, 2011.

Harris, Carolyn. "The Abdication of Nicholas II Left Russia Without a Czar for the First Time in 300 Years." *Smithsonian Magazine*, March 13, 2017. https://www.smithsonianmag.com/history/abdication-nicholas-ii-left-russia-without-tsar-first-time-300-years-180962503/.

Hedin, Gunnar. *The Swedish Oil Kings.* Translated by Paul Britten Austin. Stockholm: Ekerlids Forlag, 1994.

Hopkirk, Peter. *The Great Game: The Struggle for Empire in Central Asia.* New York: Kodansha USA Publishing, 1992.

Jangfeldt, Bengt. *The Nobel Family: Swedish Geniuses in Tsarist Russia.* Translated by Harry D. Watson. London: Bloomsbury Academic, 2023.

Kalantar, Michael N. *Russia Under Three Tsars.* Gerrardstown, WV: Irene Vartanoff, 2015.

Kotkin, Stephen. *Stalin.* New York: Penguin, 2014.

Krassin, Lubov. *Leonid Krassin: His Life and Work.* London: Skeffington & Son, 1929.

Lloyd, Nick. *The Eastern Front: A History of the Great War, 1914–1918.* New York: W. W. Norton, 2025.

Lowes, Will, and Christel Ludewig McCanless. *Fabergé Eggs: A Retrospective Encyclopedia*. Lanham, MD: Scarecrow Press, 2001.

Massie, Robert K. *Nicholas and Alexandra: An Intimate Account of the Last of the Romanovs and the Fall of Imperial Russia.* New York: Atheneum, 1967.

McDonald, Deborah, and Jeremy Dronfield. *A Very Dangerous Woman: The Lives, Loves and Lies of Russia's Most Seductive Spy.* London: Oneworld Publications, 2015.

McFerrin, Dorothy. *From a Snowflake to an Iceberg: The McFerrin Collection.* College Station, TX: McFerrin Foundation, 2013.

Montefiore, Simon Sebag. *Young Stalin.* New York: Alfred A. Knopf, 2007.

Pipes, Richard. *The Unknown Lenin: From the Secret Archive.* New Haven, CT: Yale University Press, 1999.

Poole, DeWitt Clinton. *An American Diplomat in Bolshevik Russia.* Edited by Lorraine Lees and William Rodner. Madison: University of Wisconsin Press, 2014.

Radzinsky, Edvard. *Alexander II: The Last Great Tsar.* Translated by Antonina W. Bouis. New York: Free Press, 2005.

Reid, Anna. *A Nasty Little War: The Western Intervention into the Russian Civil War.* New York: Basic Books, 2024.

Rockefeller, John D. *Random Reminiscences of Men and Events.* New York: Doubleday, 1909.

Rynkov, Vadim M. "Labor Market Regulation in Eastern Russia in 1918–1922: Institutional Factors, Mechanisms, and Outcomes." *Russian Journal of Economics* (July 9, 2021).

Schneer, Jonathan. *The Lockhart Plot: Love, Betrayal, Assassination and Counter-Revolution in Lenin's Russia.* Oxford: Oxford University Press, 2020.

Service, Robert. *Spies and Commissars: The Early Years of the Russian Revolution.* New York: PublicAffairs, 2012.

Siljak, Ana. *Angel of Vengeance: The "Girl Assassin," the Governor of St. Petersburg, and Russia's Revolutionary World.* New York: St. Martin's Press, 2008.

Silverlight, John. *The Victors' Dilemma: Allied Intervention in the Russian Civil War, 1917–1920.* London: Barrie & Jenkins, 1970.

Smith, Douglas. *Former People: The Final Days of the Russian Aristocracy.* New York: Picador, 2013.

———. *Rasputin: Faith, Power, and the Twilight of the Romanovs.* New York: Picador, 2017.

Sohlman, Ragnar, and Henrik Schuck. *The Life of Alfred Nobel.* Translated by W. H. von der Mülbe and Brian and Beatrix Lunn. London: William Heinemann, 1929.

———. *Nobel: Dynamite and Peace.* Translated by Brian and Beatrix Lunn. New York: Cosmopolitan Book, 1929.

Suny, Ronald G. *The Baku Commune: 1917–1918.* Princeton, NJ: Princeton University Press, 1972.

Sutton, Antony C. *America's Secret Establishment.* Walterville, OR: TrineDay, 1983, additional materials 2009.

———. *Wall Street and the Bolshevik Revolution.* New York: Arlington House, 1974.

Tolf, Robert W. *The Russian Rockefellers: The Saga of the Nobel Family and the Russian Oil Industry.* Stanford, CA: Hoover Institution Press, 1976.

Törnudd, Gustaf. *The Land of Oil and Winds: Letters from Baku.* Translated by Eleanor Antell Virgil. New York: Vantage Press, 1975.

Wolfe, Bertram D. *Three Who Made a Revolution.* New York: Stein and Day, 1984.

Yergin, Daniel. *The Prize: The Epic Quest for Oil, Money & Power.* New York: Touchstone, 1991.

ACKNOWLEDGMENTS

I was very lucky to meet many generous people around the world who freely gave of their time to help with this book. I'd like to mention in particular: Vadim Azbel, who showed me around the archives of the Centre for Business History in Stockholm; Géza von Habsburg and Ulla Tillander-Godenheim, who are stewards of the Fabergé legacy; Maria Wallin at the Swedish archives in Lund; Markus Künzel, Anna Krutsch, Irene Püttner, Matthias Röschner, Marlinde Schwarzenau, and Wolfgang Schinhan of the Deutsches Museum; Lisa Rebori of the Houston Museum of Natural History and the McFerrin family for their permission to access the collection; Charlotte Junkers and the Bernd Junkers Archive; Igor Sikorsky Jr., Jim Husvar, John Bulakowski, and Dan Libertino of the Sikorsky Archives in Connecticut.

Members of the Nobel family were also helpful, including Thomas Tydén, Robert Nobel, and Ingrid Wilbom.

Ingrid Carlberg, Swedish journalist and author of what is the definitive biography of Alfred Nobel, met with me for tea at the Grand Hotel, Stockholm. We shared our thoughts about the history of the Nobel family. Subsequently, she sent to me a key-word-searchable version of her book, which was beyond generous and very helpful to my work.

My thanks to Keith Urbahn and Matt Carlini at Javelin for their advice and unwavering support.

Peter Borland and Sean deLone are teammates as much as editors. They put in countless hours to make this book better and are just as emotionally involved with Nobel (and Diesel) as I am. Not only did they make the book better, but our work together has made me a better writer.

Also at Simon & Schuster, my thanks to Libby McGuire, Joanna Pinsker, and Dayna Johnson. A big thanks to Jon Karp for keeping the S&S mother ship on track. He has important responsibilities, so I'm relieved we didn't need to call on him for help with the book title yet again.

Finally, enormous thanks to my family. Megyn's advice and edits to multiple drafts of the book were always spot-on. Her ability to share complex information in a way that's easy to consume is world-class. Our three kids not only tolerated me droning on about events in the Caucasus from more than a hundred years ago, but they had questions and thoughts that kept the story alive in the house beyond the hours that I was crammed in my office. I'm lucky to be under a roof with such curious, intelligent, and awesome people.

IMAGE CREDITS

INSERT

1. Robert Nobel Archive
2. Robert Nobel Archive
3. Public domain
4. Centre for Business History, Stockholm, Sweden
5. Public domain
6. Robert Nobel Archive
7. Centre for Business History, Stockholm, Sweden
8. Centre for Business History, Stockholm, Sweden
9. Centre for Business History, Stockholm, Sweden
10. Centre for Business History, Stockholm, Sweden
11. Public domain
12. Centre for Business History, Stockholm, Sweden
13. Christie's Auction House
14. Centre for Business History, Stockholm, Sweden
15. Centre for Business History, Stockholm, Sweden
16. Tate Images
17. Russian State Library
18. Tate Images
19. Public domain
20. Public domain

INTERIOR

11: Centre for Business History, Stockholm, Sweden
26: Public domain
58: Public domain
61: Centre for Business History, Stockholm, Sweden
160: Public domain
198: Igor I. Sikorsky Historical Archives, Connecticut, USA

INDEX

NOTE: Page references in *italics* refer to photos.

O

P

R

S